The Emerging Church, Millennials, and Religion

The Emerging Church, Millennials, and Religion

Volume 2:
Curations and Durations

EDITED BY

Terry Shoemaker
Rachel C. Schneider
Xochitl Alvizo

Preface by Randall Reed

CASCADE *Books* • Eugene, Oregon

Cascade Books
An Imprint of Wipf and Stock Publishers
199 W. 8th Ave., Suite 3
Eugene, OR 97401

www.wipfandstock.com

PAPERBACK ISBN: 978-1-7252-7746-5
HARDCOVER ISBN: 978-1-7252-7745-8
EBOOK ISBN: 978-1-7252-7747-2

Cataloguing-in-Publication data:

Names: Shoemaker, Terry (editor). | Schneider, Rachel C. (editor). | Alvizo, Xochitl (editor).

Title: The emerging church, millennials, and religion : volume 2, curations and durations / edited by Terry Shoemaker, Rachel C. Schneider, and Xochitl Alvizo.

Description: Eugene, OR: Cascade Books, 2022. | Includes bibliographical references and index.

Identifiers: ISBN: 978-1-7252-7746-5 (paperback). | ISBN: 978-1-7252-7745-8 (hardcover). | ISBN: 978-1-7252-7747-2 (ebook).

Subjects: LSCH: Emerging church movement. | Christianity—21st century. | Church renewal—21st century.

Classification: BR121.3 E55 2022 (print). | BR121.3 E55 (ebook).

To our many interlocutors on this project

Contents

List of Illustrations

Contributors

Randall Reed is Professor of Religious Studies at Appalachian State University in Boone, North Carolina.

Xochitl Alvizo is Associate Professor at California State University, Northridge in Northridge, California.

Rachel C. Schneider is a Postdoctoral Fellow in the Religion and Public Life Program at Rice University in Houston, Texas.

Terry Shoemaker is a Lecturer at Arizona State University in Tempe, Arizona.

Stephanie Yuhas is an Instructor at Naropa University in Boulder, Colorado, and Lecturer at the University of Colorado, Denver.

Laine Walters Young is the Assistant Director of the Cal Turner Program for Moral Leadership at Vanderbilt University in Nashville, Tennessee.

Daniel Rober is an Assistant Professor in the Department of Catholic Studies and Assistant Director of the Thomas More Honors Program at Sacred Heart University in Fairfield, Connecticut.

Galen Watts is a Banting Postdoctoral Fellow at KU Leuven University in Belgium.

Annie Kyle is Director of Book Development at Find Your Voice.

Dustin Benac is a Louisville Institute Postdoctoral Fellow and Visiting Assistant Professor of Practical Theology at George W. Truett Seminary at Baylor University in Waco, Texas.

Preface

RANDALL REED

Towards a Theory of Religious Change

AT THE BEGINNING OF the twenty-first century, we are witness to an astonishing shift in many areas. As I write in the midst of a pandemic, the future looks cloudier than ever, but our dependence on technology and science has never been clearer. In the face of that, we stand at the precipice of a religious change equated by the late Phyllis Tickle to the great schism of the eleventh century when Orthodoxy separated from Catholicism, or the Reformation of the sixteenth century.[1]

Such language might seem to overreach, but Tickle's observations may have actually downplayed the depth of the change we are witnessing. The millennial generation, and subsequently Generation Z, has set the religious world aflame, bowing out of established institutional structures and setting their own paths. The task of the Emerging Church, Millennials and Religion Research Seminar established by the AAR in 2011 sought to document and understand this change. At the time we started our Seminar we thought that we were witnessing a significant change in Christianity. The Emerging Church was reaching its zenith. Rob Bell, Peter Rollins, Nadia Bolz-Weber, Doug Pagitt and Brian McLaren (to name only a few) seemed to represent a shift in liturgy, belief, and practice that threatened to revise the entirety of Christianity.

We in the seminar thought it was possible that we were witness to an important moment in history. We were not the first scholars to think about the Emerging Church, the path had been blazed by scholars like

---

1. Tickle, *The Great Emergence*.

James Beilo[2] and Tony Jones[3] and seemed to culminate in the definitive work of Gladys Ganiel and Gerardo Martí in 2014.[4] Our group assembled not just to explore the edges of the Emerging Church, but to try to understand it in an interdisciplinary venue where theologians, sociologists, historians, and practitioners would interact with each other, challenge each other and try to make sense of what was happening.

The fact was we were right, but in a way we did not expect. The Emerging Church was not destined to be a catalyst toward a new postmodern Christianity that sought to erase past mistakes, prejudices and barriers (though it did try) and would bring a new generation into the Christian fold. Instead, what happened as we watched over those five years is that new generation became more and more disconnected from the church.[5] The millennials were leaving church in ever increasing numbers, and as we watched those numbers climb each year, the Emerging Church looked more like the last gasp of a dying institution rather than a grand revitalization of the Christian Church.[6]

At this point the conclusion is still not clear. It is possible that the increase in the number of disaffiliated young people has plateaued[7] though the notion that more than one-third of young people would be unchurched is still a significant event. Even if the rate of growth of unaffiliated people that we have seen in previous years is not matched in the future years, we would expect a continual decline in what Robert P. Jones calls, "White Christian America" simply from the fact that the median age of unaffiliated people is much lower than those who are affiliated.[8] At the same time, those who have hoped for an "age effect" where millennials who grew older would return or discover church have also been disappointed.[9] Those who have left are gone, there seems to be no interest in returning.[10]

2. Bielo, *Emerging Evangelicals*.

3. Jones, *The Church Is Flat*.

4. Martí and Ganiel, *The Deconstructed Church*.

5. Pew Research Center, "'None' on the Rise" and "Millennials in Adulthood"; Jones, *The End of White Christian America*.

6. Cooper et al., "Exodus."

7. Shimron, "Is the Rise of the Nones Slowing?"

8. Jones, *The End of White Christian America*; Pew Research Center, "Age Distribution—Religion in America."

9. Cox and Thomson-DeVeaux, "Millennials Are Leaving Religion."

10. Cooper et al., "Exodus"

And so, what our seminar witnessed was a variety of religious experiments that were provocative, radical, and on a larger scale ultimately ineffective at redirecting what seems to be a generational shift with regard to institutional religion. What we did see was change. Not the kind of change that led to a restructuring of branches of the Christian church, but more of a decentralized change that affected some pockets of Christianity while the millennial generation and their younger siblings edged farther and farther from the Church's grasp. We were, in fact, witness to a massive shift in Christian religious culture, but one without the kinds of uniformity that comes to mind when we think of the 11th or the 16th centuries.

Religious Change in Classical Sociology

I will leave the historical analogies to the historians of Christianity. As a sociologist, I am more interested in the question of how we can theorize religious change. It is perhaps worthwhile to review some of the attempts to make sense of religious change in classical sociology. Beginning with the three pioneers of sociology—Marx, Weber, and Durkheim—it is interesting to note their differences on the issue of religious change. Durkheim was interested in the way that religion sustained itself over time. *Elementary Forms of Religion* takes a synchronic view in its understanding of religion.[11] Durkheim does not spend much time thinking about religious change.

On the other hand, Marx spends a lot of time talking about change, though his combination of Hegelian teleology in his early work, and reduction of religion to economics in later work, fails to provide a theory of religious change as well.[12] This is surprising in some ways given that Marx, as the communist manifesto makes clear, is very interested in change.[13] And yet by understanding religion as epiphenomenal to the economic base, he can only understand religious change as product rather than cause.

This is not to say that Marx was necessarily wrong, and even Engles tries to thread this needle when he talks about superstructural elements "exercis[ing] their influence" as a way in which phenomena like religion

11. Durkheim, *The Elementary Forms.*

12. Marx, "Marx's Critique of Hegel's Philosophy of Right, 1843-4."

13. Marx and Engels, *Manifesto of the Communist Party.*

may participate in social change without necessarily being just the expression of changes in the base.[14] Still, changes in the base certainly do affect the superstructure, and as we think about religious change, Marx's work urges us to consider economic changes as causal factors for religious change.

To that end, we can surely see economics as part of the environment that produced both the Emerging Church and the "nones." Both the millennials and the Emerging Church have embraced a political and economic progressivism as a part of their orientation. Moreover, the abandonment of institutional Christianity in the U.S. cannot be understood apart from the solidification of the relationship between strongly pro-capitalist policies/politics and conservative Christianity in both its evangelical and Catholic forms.

So while Marx lays the groundwork for explaining the change we see, it was Max Weber who self-consciously tried to create a theory of religious change. Consumed with the initial question of why capitalism rose in the west but not elsewhere, he returned to an understanding of the ideological power of religion. Weber's theory is complicated though not as well developed as it might be. Certainly, when one reads the *Protestant Ethic and the Spirit of Capitalism* one finds an interesting dance laid out. Religious developments affect economics and economics affect religion, though it seems in the *Protestant Ethic* the balance sides with religion as the first mover.[15]

It is later in his discussion of authority that Weber adds to the theory of religious change with his discussion of charisma.[16] Though Weber seems to focus on the charismatic prophet, it is not an inherent attribute of the speaker but really the speech interacting with the audience that is of most importance. That is, Weber, steeped in thinking about religion which focuses on individuals (Jesus, Martin Luther, and Calvin), puts an emphasis on the messenger that would not be universally necessary. But when Weber starts thinking about this within the context of authority, it seems necessary to have someone who exercised that authority.

And yet what Weber did not address is what happens when a message expires, when it no longer speaks to an audience. Perhaps Weber, in his understanding of history, could only envision competing religious

14. Engles, "Letters: Marx-Engels Correspondence 1890."

15. Weber, *The Protestant Ethic.*

16. Weber, *Economy and Society.*

principalities, rather than a withdrawal that was not limited to a few isolated individuals. Though when Weber gets to the end of the *Protestant Ethic* and he fast-forwards to his contemporary situation and the iron cage, he seems to be confronting exactly that kind of leaderless movement. Thus, what the *Protestant Ethic* recognizes is the power of ideas apart from the singular human prophets that began them. Calvinism, left to bloom in a thousand churches ultimately disconnected from Calvin in Geneva, changed an entire economic system.

In his discussion of religion, Weber recognizes this implicitly in his language of "carrier."[17] Ideas, like viruses, might be carried and distributed across time and space. Here, then, there is a much less personal understanding of the spread of religion. An idea may be carried by groups (Weber talks about warriors and bureaucrats as different kinds of carriers) not necessarily focused around a prophet, but rather around a kind of religious conception or ideology.

Theorizing Religious Change among Millennials and the Emerging Church

So while Weber provides a theory of religious change that seems more modeled on a "Great Man" theory, in reality he provides pieces of a theory of religious change that can essentially dispense with a charismatic leader as its pivot. This is important both in understanding the Emerging Church and the religious disaffiliation of the nones. While the Emerging Church has individuals who are revered (some who are merely referred to by their first name since they are so well known like "Nadia"), no one can claim the mantle of prophet for the group. And the dialogue between those leaders sounds more like the intellectual jousting of a salon rather than a hierarchical system of organization.

This is even more true for those disaffiliating. There is no Moses leading the millennials and Gen-Z out of the Egypt of the Church. Instead, a seemingly spontaneous occurrence gained steam only indicated by the checking of a box on a survey. The subtlety of the move was such that religion scholars, even those without religious affiliations themselves, dismissed it as a misreading or over interpretation of the data.[18] Had

---

17. Weber, *The Sociology of Religion.*

18. Ramey and Miller, "Meaningless Surveys"; Ramey, "What Happens When We Name the Nones."

there been a charismatic leader, someone who had gathered followers or had a message of withdrawal that could have been tracked and analyzed, in essence someone following the Weberian model, religion scholars may have been more likely to see what was happening. But the very fact that it seemed like thousands of individuals just leaned in the same direction without being told to was mystifying.

And yet, it is precisely this phenomenon that Weber may have prepared us for in the end. Modern scholars of religion focus on the messenger, probably because so many come out of monotheistic traditions where there is a founder with their legends of drawing followers that has colored expectations of how change works. Moreover, so much of religious studies was invented in Protestant strongholds, where the names of Luther and Calvin often competed with Jesus and Paul, that our models seem self-evident. Certainly, this influenced Weber when he wrote his sociology of religion.

But what we see with the Emerging Church is instead a notion of a charismatic message without a messenger, both in the Emerging Church movement and among disaffiliating millennials. We see carriers who spread the notion of a reinvented church or churchlessness. In the Emerging Church, small communities popped up in bars and coffee shops, rethinking what it meant to be Christian—to do Christianity. Because of this decentralization, when Gerardo Martí and Gladys Ganiel tried to define it, they could do so only in terms of an "orientation" rather than in the more traditional terms of doctrine or practice.[19]

Likewise, the question of "why now?" also pertains to the nones. Early on, there were attempts by the Pew Research Center to explain the movement of Christians into the "none" category as the result of a redesignation of nominal Christians.[20] Those more culturally Christian than practicing essentially gave up on self-designating as Christians. But such a conclusion may beg the question of why that was currently acceptable when a decade earlier it was not.

What may have actually been the case is that being a "none" was a self-perpetuating movement. Pew may well have been right that there was a shift of those who were previously nominally Christian into the "none" category, but they did so because there was suddenly a lot of publicity around the "none" category. Whereas since 1972 the category

---

19. Martí and Ganiel, *The Deconstructed Church.*
20. Pew Research Center, "'None' on the Rise."

"none" existed in the religious designation options on surveys, it was largely a negative category, short for "none of the above." But with publicity around nones, it may be that "none" became not something that symbolized what I was not (not Christian, not Muslim, not Hindu, etc.) but rather something that I *am*. Exactly what that *is* may not be clearly defined, but it becomes a positive space, not a negative one. So young people who I talk to regularly will volunteer that they are a "none" as though that is a competing religious identity.

We see evidence of this in PRRI's study of why people disaffiliate.[21] "Wasn't that religious to begin with" is certainly one of the categories and accounts for a percentage of why people disaffiliate. But the largest category is "No longer believed the teachings of the church." That is not simply a change in moniker, that is an intentional disaffiliation based on a decision to reject the church's teaching. It is one of the reasons I am not optimistic for the return of the millennials to church. How does one return to something one intentionally rejected?

But regardless of the future, the change we are seeing is one of a messengerless message being spread by carriers. Publicity may have had a role, as did a shift in socioeconomics and cultural dynamics (not to leave Marx behind) with the relative popularity of "socialism" and defection of much of evangelicalism to Trumpism. Still, for both the Emerging Church and for the religious disaffiliation of the nones what we see is a significant religious change that is not predicated on organized movements or charismatic leadership, but one which requires a much different model than what scholars of religion have often relied on, but which Weber may point us towards.

Thus, the Emerging Church and the religious disaffiliation of the nones points us towards a theory of religious change which is more decentralized. The issue that raises, and we can see this with both the Emerging Church and studies of nones, is that there ceases to be uniformity between practitioners. The clarity and bright lines that we scholars are so often comfortable with now dissolves into more vague "trends" and "orientations." Yet, given the breadth of the remarkable change in the religious space that these two movements portend, we must take this opportunity to rethink our theoretical apparatus.

21. Cooper et al., "Exodus"

Bibliography

Bielo, James S. *Emerging Evangelicals: Faith, Modernity, and the Desire for Authenticity.* New York: New York University Press, 2011.

Cooper, Besty, Daniel Cox, Rachel Lienesch, and Robert P. Jones. "Exodus: Why Americans Are Leaving Religion—and Why They're Unlikely to Come Back." Public Religion Research Institute, 2016. http://www.prri.org/research/prri-rns-2016-religiously-unaffiliated-americans/.

Cox, Daniel, and Amelia Thomson-DeVeaux. "Millennials Are Leaving Religion and Not Coming Back." FiveThirtyEight, December 12, 2019. https://fivethirtyeight.com/features/millennials-are-leaving-religion-and-not-coming-back/.

Durkheim, Émile. *The Elementary Forms of the Religious Life.* Translated by Joseph Ward Swain. Mineola, NY: Dover, 2008.

Engles, Friedrich. "Letters: Marx-Engels Correspondence 1890—Engels to J. Bloch in Königsberg." Marxist Archive, 1972. https://www.marxists.org/archive/marx/works/1890/letters/90_09_21.htm.

Jones, Robert P. *The End of White Christian America.* New York: Simon & Schuster, 2016.

Jones, Tony. *The Church Is Flat: The Relational Ecclesiology of the Emerging Church Movement.* Minneapolis: JoPa Group, 2011.

Martí, Gerardo, and Gladys Ganiel. *The Deconstructed Church: Understanding Emerging Christianity.* Oxford: Oxford University Press, 2014.

Marx, Karl. "Marx's Critique of Hegel's Philosophy of Right, 1843-4." Marxist Archive, 1979. https://www.marxists.org/archive/marx/works/1843/critique-hpr/.

Marx, Karl, and Friedrich Engels. *Manifesto of the Communist Party.* New York: Cosimo, 2009.

Pew Research Center. "Age Distribution—Religion in America: U.S. Religious Data, Demographics and Statistics." Pew Research Center's Religion and Public Life Project, 2015. https://www.pewforum.org/religious-landscape-study/age-distribution/.

———. "Millennials in Adulthood: Detached from Institutions, Networked with Friends." Pew Research Center, 2014. http://www.pewsocialtrends.org/files/2014/03/2014-03-07_generations-report-version-for-web.pdf.

———. "'None' on the Rise: One-in-Five Adults Have No Religious Affiliation." Pew Research Center, Pew Forum on Religion and Public Life, 2012. http://www.pewforum.org/files/2012/10/NonesOnTheRise-full.pdf.

Ramey, Steven. "What Happens When We Name the Nones." *Huffington Post*, February 21, 2013. https://www.huffpost.com/entry/what-happens-when-we-name-the-nones_b_2725169.

Ramey, Steven, and Monica R. Miller. "Meaningless Surveys: The Faulty 'Mathematics' of the 'Nones.'" *Huffington Post*, November 7, 2013. https://www.huffpost.com/entry/meaningless-surveys-the-f_b_4225306.

Shimron, Yonat. "'Is the Rise of the Nones Slowing? Scholars Say Maybe.'" *Religion News Service*, Feb. 11, 2020. https://religionnews.com/2020/02/11/is-the-decline-in-religious-affiliation-slowing-some-scholars-say-maybe/.

Tickle, Phyllis. *The Great Emergence: How Christianity Is Changing and Why.* Grand Rapids: Baker, 2012.

Weber, Max. *Economy and Society: An Outline of Interpretive Sociology*. Translated by Ephraim Fischoff. Berkeley: University of California Press, 1978.

———. *The Protestant Ethic and the Spirit of Capitalism: The Complete Text - Inclusive of Notes*. Translated by Talcott Parsons. Middletown, DE: Pantianos Classics, 2020.

———. *The Sociology of Religion*. Translated by Ephraim Fischoff. 2nd ed. Boston: Beacon, 1993.

Introduction

Xochitl Alvizo, Rachel C. Schneider, and Terry Shoemaker

IN 2018, A TEAM of scholars published a first volume of material resulting from three years of exploring religion in relation to the millennial generation and a progressive Christian movement referred to as the Emerging Church, which began to gain traction in the early 2000s. During this period, both millennials as well as those affiliated with the Emerging Church Movement (ECM) seemed to be challenging traditional religious categories as well as the role of Christianity in the United States through disaffiliation and critique. The first volume, published under the title *The Emerging Church, Millennials, and Religion: Prospects and Problems* analyzed both of these developments in light of the changing demographics of religion in America, and it examined how the ECM might be meeting the religious needs and spiritual desires of a maturing millennial generation.[1] The contributions to that volume also wrestled with issues of nomenclature and categorization due to the fact that many millennials and those who might be seen as part of the ECM resisted labels. This second volume continues this work and revisits questions regarding religious change, reform, and innovation since the publication of the first volume. What this second volume of material brings to the surface are the tensions associated with religious change and how innovation continues, despite stressors and external constraints.

The work of both volumes is rooted in a five-year research seminar at the American Academy of Religion, which brought together scholars from multiple disciplines to dissect changes at the forefront of American

---

1. Reed and Zbaraschuk. *The Emerging Church, Millennials, and Religion.*

religion. Here, panelists debated (often very vigorously) the supposed millennial renouncement of religion often referred to as "the rise of the nones" alongside the significance and implication of progressive trends within Christianity. Coupling these two themes drew a wide range of audience members from social scientific and theological backgrounds, creating unique conversations and vantage points. Further, the seminar format offered a rich, generative space for collaborative ideation. As we reflected together on emerging forms of religious life and the future of Western Christianity, the energy in our meeting rooms was palpable, even ecstatic. We hope some of this energy is captured in both volumes.

During our seminars, we also observed that there tended to be two types of responses to discussions of the ECM, generational trends, and religion. The first strain of unfolding responses often came from religious practitioners and leaders, though not exclusively. In short, some of the attendees found the religious innovations discussed and the quantitative decline of traditional religious affiliations threatening. Many within the audience often cited fears that a loss of shared narrative, a diminishing importance of Christianity in the West, and new innovations were unsustainable, and possibly disastrous, for future Christians and, more broadly, Americans. These attendees posed concerns regarding the influence of technology, contemporary re-stylizations of church models, and the fact that some contemporary forms of religious commitments do not mirror previous generations' commitments. For instance, using technology that builds opportunities for asynchronous spaces is quite different from weekly scheduled in person gatherings. Likewise, some progressive forms of Christianity maintain more fluid versions of participation, rejecting membership requirements. And many millennials simply refuse to accept religious labels—a signal of change making some uncomfortable. The audience members who held these fears held a sincere belief that something essential was going extinct before their very eyes.

These fears, based on the assumption that religion is a necessary social cement, are not ungrounded and echo scholars like Robert Bellah and Charles Taylor.[2] Often the response of these attendees was to redirect conversations to thinking about what steps could be implemented to ameliorate the vaporization of cultural institutions that have provided guidance and authority for many generations of Americans. In other words, a portion of our yearly audience struggled to imagine the world

2. Bellah, et al. *Habits of the Heart*; Taylor, *A Secular Age*.

without religious institutions and authority understood as absolutely vital for society.

Equally represented in the seminar audience were others, some social scientists, eager to better understand the changing demographics and practices related to religiosity and spirituality. The current trends highlight a disaffiliation from traditional forms of religion while also indicating renewed interest in spirituality. From this vantage point, the social conditions, generational redirections, and underpinnings of current trends are all part of an ecology of change within the United States and other Western countries. Changes to religion, then, can be correlated with other shifts occurring within societies. For instance, shifting power dynamics and relations within religious communities might correspond with moves to reconsider authority more broadly. The re-imaginings within and outside of religious institutions might offer new ways of being that are liberating and provide more equitable structures.

Both of these responses to the question of change—fear and liberation—were significant themes in the first volume of *The Emerging Church, Millennials and Religion: Prospects and Problems* and continue to play a significant part of this second volume. Whereas the first volume focuses on these trends as problems and prospects, this second volume shifts its focus to understanding how millennial and progressive Christian exploration, innovation, and resistance are intentionally curated and how it continues to endure, despite external pressures and internal tensions. This volume focuses more on the inherent tensions and curatorial practices emerging within progressive Christianity and millennial moves in religion and spirituality, especially as they respond to social issues and concerns.

Efforts to form progressive Christian communities take place in an often uncooperative social context. In the United States, like other Western countries, there is a general trend of younger people to disaffiliate with traditional forms of religion, particularly Christianity.[3] Some "Religious Nones," as they are called by scholars, simply refuse to join with any religious community. Others, such as the "Religious Dones" are skeptical or suspicious of religious institutions, even if they still identify with a religious tradition in some way, forming another complicated aspect of endurance.[4] Furthermore, more traditional Christian

3. Drescher. *Choosing Our Religion.*
4. Packard and Ferguson, "Being Done."

communities can sometimes perceive progressive Christian communities as either a market threat or worse, as heresy. Progressive Christian leadership along with participants must learn to endure criticism from other Christian communities while also assessing religious demands in unfavorable market trends. Finally, progressive Christian communities tend toward internal reflection regarding issues of gender, sexuality, and race. Thus, combined with external criticism is internal grappling with how to improve equity in leadership, church polity, and authority within the embodied ecclesiology.

The new forms of religiosity and spirituality are not homogeneous either. Differences often emerge during the curation and enduring efforts. Although this is certainly true as well in older denominational churches, denominations have the benefit of utilizing historical precedents and resources to ameliorate certain disagreements. This is not to say that denominations are immune to disagreements and schisms, but there are numerous issues that have been previously settled in older denominations. For many progressive Christian communities, previously settled theological topics (i.e., the divinity of Christ) and ecclesiological issues (i.e., ordination and tithing) are actively contested. Coupled with these issues are questions about social relevancy and innovations, which also create some internal tensions. Endurance then requires a continuous effort to mitigate old and new topics. Adding to these stressors, finances are a recurring issue in many progressive Christians communities. Typically divorced from denominational resources, many of these communities grapple with economic sustainability.

Nevertheless, despite these external critical pressures and internal debates, millennials and progressive Christians continue to experiment, and even curate, their sense of spirituality, conducted in church gatherings and non-traditional forms of religious/spiritual gatherings. Within these gatherings, there is a level of self-stylization, at both the individual and collective level, which vary greatly in different contexts. In this regard, the spirit of Emerging or progressive Christianity and millennial spirituality remains very active, offering continued insight into a variety of theoretical questions.

In Volume 1 of *The Emerging Church, Millennials and Religion*, editors Randall Reed and G. Michael Zbaraschuk reflect that, while there had been some academic study of the Emerging Church movement done by sociologists, anthropologists, and theologians, what was missing was "a larger interdisciplinary examination" of the topic that would bring humanistic and social scientific approaches to the study of religion into dialogue.[5] Part of the aim, then, of the first volume and our current volume is to create a space for this type of larger interdisciplinary dialogue.

From the start, ethnography has been a significant tool that scholars have used to try to capture the complexities and defining features of Emerging Christian communities,[6] and indeed several contributors to this volume draw on ethnography and other modes of qualitative research (Benac; Reed; Shoemaker; Alvizo, Schneider, and Shoemaker). These approaches are useful in capturing the nuance and complexity of individual and collective life as well as the creative ways in which millennials and Emerging Christians are responding to internal and external tensions. But we would also suggest that an interdisciplinary examination of the Emerging Church Movement as well as the spiritual and religious lives of millennials contributes to ongoing discussions within the sociology and anthropology of religion. In recent decades, anthropologists of Christianity have urged scholars to pay attention to the internal debates and tensions with Christianity as it is lived out in specific localities and communities to allow for both comparative work and thick description.[7] In many ways, the Emerging Church and its afterlives provides a prime site for understanding fissures within contemporary evangelical and Protestant Christianity more broadly. At the same time, the empirical attention given by volume contributors to processes of religious boundary making and unmaking reveals how questions of who or what is religious, generally, and who or what is Christian specifically, are not simply being posed by scholars. Rather, they are continually being asked and answered by everyday people on the ground. Similarly, sociologists and scholars of religion have argued over the past decades for the need to attend to "lived religion"—focusing on the experiential and practiced dimensions of religion, rather than simply on doctrines or text.[8] Millennials, in particular, have been characterized as a demographic who particularly value

5. Reed and Zbaraschuk, *The Emerging Church, Millennials, and Religion*, xi.

6. See for example, Bielo, *Emerging Evangelicals*; Markofski, *New Monasticism and the Transformation of American Evangelicalism*; Martí and Ganiel, *The Deconstructed Church*; Packard, *The Emerging Church*; Alvizo, "A Feminist Analysis of the Emerging Church"; Schneider, "The Ethics of Whiteness."

7. Bialecki, Haynes, and Robbins, "The Anthropology of Christianity"; Robbins, "What Is a Christian?"; Robbins, "The Anthropology of Christianity."

8. Ammerman, *Everyday Religion*; Ammerman, "Finding Religion in Everyday Life"; Hall, *Lived Religion in America*; McGuire, *Lived Religion*.

the experiential, and the types of religious or spiritual experiences they are seeking (or not seeking) are explored by several volume contributors (Reed; Rober; Kyle; Yuhas; Watts). In particular, Galen Watt's chapter explores these contours and the ethical and social worlds in which millennials dwell. But more broadly, the study of Emerging Christianity reveals how religion and spirituality is being actively curated in relation to the lived experience of individuals and groups amidst changing social conditions.

The chapters within this second volume also explore the shapes that religion and spirituality in North America, specifically, are taking. For instance, chapters by Randall Reed and Stephani Yuhas spotlight curated gatherings in the United States that are imbued with creativity and ingenuity in newer forms of religiosity and spirituality. These outdoor gatherings, some explicitly designed as spiritual or religious while others are not, create annual opportunities to physically meet, often building upon virtual relationships already formed. These types of gatherings are not necessarily new; instead, they harken back to previous religious explorations, like the Great Awakenings, while adding progressive and technologically embedded hues to the venues. Likewise, Dustin Benac's contribution pushes scholarship to recognize social structures beyond traditional denominational forms within religion.

These new shapes and forms do not dispel the idea that there is an embedded contextual responsiveness built into the religious and spiritual moves found within this volume. Terry Shoemaker's chapter highlights regional differences in North America, and how normativity creates countering moves. Similarly, Daniel Rober's chapter analyzes generational responses to the many unfolding Catholic abuse cases in North America. These contributions illustrate the discursive activities taking place with religiosity as participants seek to address issues, reclaim positive tenets, and fashion responses. In addition, these chapters suggest ways of remaining as critical loyalists within existing religious parameters that fuel reformations, but also accept specific aspects of religious inheritance.

Taken together, then, the essays in this volume provocatively suggest or push towards new questions and areas for future sociological and anthropological study such as the relationship between lived religion and identity evolution, the formation of sacred sites and spaces, and the relationship of modern technology to religiosity and spirituality. Such questions will hopefully spur further empirical research to how everyday people on the ground are seeking to individually and collectively transform themselves using a range of tools, sites, and practices that blur the boundaries between secular and religious.

Given that the larger global religious trend is towards a rise in evangelical, Pentecostal, and Catholic Christians, it may seem paradoxical to focus attention on a small Anglo-American movement that in many ways has sought to break from—or at the very least reimagine—its relationship to evangelical and Protestant forms of Christianity. However, the dynamics of deconstruction and deconversion paired with this volume's emphasis on dynamics of reconstruction and innovation offer insight into dynamics of social and religious change that impact both normative Christian traditions and emerging forms of Christianity. It is our view that these dynamics are central to the future of Christianity in the United States as well as the future of religion more broadly. Not only does the study of the spiritual aspirations and critiques of Emerging Christians and millennials, in particular, reveal the challenges to authority and structure facing traditional Christian institutions within an increasingly plural, diverse, and unchurched American society, it also raises the theoretical question of whether millennials, ex- and post-evangelicals are truly on a linear trajectory towards being "done" with religion or simply in the process of constructing spiritual alternatives suited to the demands of contemporary social life, and what, if any, impact these experiments might have to more traditional forms of religion.

The changing landscape of religion as it concerns millennials, progressive Christians, and those identified as spiritual but not religious reveals challenges and opportunities to theology proper as well. Against the polarized political and religious background of the United States in particular, the ECM is a self-conscious embrace of context, fluidity, and experimentation challenging prescribed modes of religious institutionalization, be they by theological decree or inherited tradition. In itself, this change in religious approach is long in the making, and the ECM is just one embodiment. But for the Christian theologian today, it is significant to recognize it as a constructive theological response emerging from the ground up that contains within a theological voice worth noting. Initially, a major segment of the ECM was born of denominational efforts to reach beyond the walls of its church buildings, connect to the "outside" world, and not lose the next generation. It sought to reach the margins and find ways to keep the margins connected to the center. The margins, however, can have a life and purpose of their own that refuse to be brought "in" or "back." To call on the words of bell hooks, feminist theorist and cultural

critic, the margins are a space of radical openness that calls willing participants to "the formation of counter-hegemonic cultural practice," which,
in the case of counter-hegemonic religious practice, brings worthwhile
theological implications not rooted or oriented toward the center.[9]

As the ECM addresses new social realities and political engagements, each of the stories and studies shared in this volume reflect
instances of communities that face and wrestle with live theological
questions together. Instead of assuming a fixed theological starting point,
Emerging Christian communities choose to participate in the "process
of revision" that is made possible in the openness of the margins.[10] In
that space, the ECM moves and transgresses theologically as it seeks to
give flesh and form, structure and ritual, that is liberating and pertinent
for the community brought together in its particular context. It engages
its Christian tradition with a posture of openness as it explores both the
expanse and constraints of its marginal boundaries. Theological certainty
is not the value and, as a result, this radical openness can and does at
times lead beyond explicitly religious forms and commitments, which
we see illustrated in the last chapter titled "The Emerging Church Movement: Possible Futures and Trajectories." By design, the ECM reflects a
constructive, practical theological method of practicing and theorizing
Christianity that seeks to maintain open its possibilities.

What this collective study contributes to theology, with the varied
manifestations of the ECM it includes, is a case study of communal (congregational) embodiments of Christianity attending to the theological
polarization of its day without necessarily "taking sides." It instead stays
in the space of openness, sometimes radical openness, delighting in "the
pleasure and power of knowing" and moves in a space and place in which
transformation is and feels more possible.[11] With the ECM, certainty, including theological certainty, is suspect, and what this volume provides is
a case study of the religious embrace of nuance and experience and a willing critique of its religious inheritance. As it seeks to address the critiques
it raises, the ECM willingly changes its embodiment. As scholars study
and witness aspects of the ECM taking shape and reshape over time, we
see a dimension of Christianity that attends not to the preservation of the
institution or its theological inheritance—not even or necessarily to the

---

9. hooks, "Choosing the Margin," 15.

10. hooks, "Choosing the Margin," 15.

11. hooks, "Choosing the Margin," 15.

perpetuation of the tradition itself as that is arguably not a priority—but to the gaps, the margins, the aspects of the lived religion that are deemed incongruent and in discord with the liberative message that is the very thing keeping Emerging Christians with one foot "in" even while seeing and moving beyond. In this, it exemplifies the living aspects of this religious tradition and of a liberative and embodied theological approach to it. Put differently, the ECM is the white church of the United States choosing to live in the open, uncertain, space of the margins—the space and location long inhabited by feminist and other liberationist Christians and theologians—and this may be the precise theological place the whole of U.S. Christianity is being invited into, where the most promising invitation to new life lies.

In contrast to the white dominant Christianity of the United States, which during the twentieth century likely got used to experiencing itself as the religious "mainland" (as opposed to the margin)—given recognition at even the national political stage—the Emerging Church Movement enters the Christian conversation on different terms. It distances itself from the ways it experiences Christianity as co-opted by strict doctrinal, moral, rhetorical, or ritual dogmatism. Entering from the margins, at the places of tension, incongruency, and disaffection, the ECM attends to the gaps that dogmatism, certainty, and cultural hegemony cover over without providing a comprehensive theological "whole." As with the tradition of feminist, liberationist, and decolonial theologians, Emerging Christians push the envelope and give practical theological voice to a Christianity that committedly embraces the radical space of the margins. It reflects a methodology that pays attention to the gaps, willing to critically reflect on its own (even hard) claimed truth to raise questions of it, to revise, resist, and experiment theologically, liturgically, organizationally, and to do it all over again, as and within community. And while it is not apparent that the ECM makes any explicit recognition of the liberationist Christians and theologians that have long done this work in relation to the margins inhabited by minoritized populations due to sexual, gender, racial, and colonial hierarchies, it nonetheless inhabits the margins of the white Christian church as a "site of radical possibility, [and as] a space of resistance,"[12] which is needed for its own transformation.[13]

12. hooks, "Choosing the Margin," 20.

13. For more on this feminist critique of the Emerging Church Movement, see Alvizo and Martí, "Emerging Out of Patriarchy?"; and Alvizo, "A Feminist Analysis of the Emerging Church."

The theological invitation represented by these chapters and extended to the invested reader is one of transgression, possibility, and creativity. It is the invitation to enter the openness of the margins as the space of good news (i.e., gospel) that the inhabitants of this space have long associated with Christianity. It is an invitation to be willing to see social, material, and economic realities very much alive for those already at the margins and to be grounded in an emancipatory approach to Christian theology and practice that affords an opportunity to evaluate Christian theological frameworks and practices for the ways they perpetuate and/ or contraindicate elements of heterosexism, racism, and colonialism embedded within and to revise and be renewed as a result. Whether it is toward a nonbinary theology that "validates the spirituality of young adults outside the institutional church," as with Anne Kyle's chapter, "Young Adults and the Church: Incarnation, Theosis, and a Non-binary Future for the Body of Christ," or a deep appreciation of the social and material conditions that have necessarily shaped millennials' embrace of "improvisation as an ethical style and process," as with Laine Walters Young's chapter, "Gender, Anxiety, and Millennial Romantic Lives: Embracing Agency through Intentional Improvisation," the studies in this volume reveal the logic and embodiment of an emerging, albeit predominantly white, Christianity that refuses to be boxed in. As Kyle states in her chapter, there is an implicit invitation to envision an ecclesiology that "commits itself to recognizing the Divinity of the outsider . . . breaks down the secular/sacred divide . . . [and] risks orthodoxy for the sake of loving humanity into its fullest self." For the theologian, this is a case study of a Christianity of today that, as bell hooks invites, "chooses the margin as a space of radical openness" and affirms the fidelity of the practice.

The moves and stylizations of millennials and the ECM highlight many of the changes occurring in the religious, spiritual, and theological landscapes of North America. Like previous generations before them, these participants respond to the technologies available to them, current political issues, and economic conditions. The observations and analyses contained within this second volume speak to the enduring and curating practices of progressive Christians and millennials while also illuminating the continued endurance of religion and spirituality. The malleable nature of religion and spirituality, and those continuing to mold religion and spiritual practices and institutions, are highlighted throughout the following pages. Religion and spirituality have yet to lose their usefulness for many people in the modern world despite existing stressors and pressures. And while Randall Reed, at the end of the preface, points out that our subject of study does not provide the "clarity and bright lines that we scholars" might prefer, inviting us to "rethink our theoretical apparatus," we likewise invite the reader to consider the political, economic, sociological, and theological implications that the religious changes taking shape in emerging progressive Christianity might have for the whole of the tradition in a time of flux but also creativity.

Bibliography

Alvizo, Xochitl. "A Feminist Analysis of the Emerging Church: Toward Radical Participation in the Organic, Relational, and Inclusive Body of Christ." Ph.D. Diss., Boston University, 2015.

Alvizo, Xochitl, and Gerardo Martí, "Emerging Out of Patriarchy?" In *The Emerging Church, Millennials, and Religion,* edited by Randall Reed and Michael Zbaraschuk, 236–59. Eugene, OR: Cascade, 2018.

Ammerman, Nancy T. *Everyday Religion: Observing Modern Religious Lives.* Oxford University Press, 2006.

———. "Finding Religion in Everyday Life." *Sociology of Religion* 75 (2014) 189–207.

Bellah, Robert N. *Habits of the Heart: Individualism and Commitment in American Life.* Berkeley: University of California Press, 1985.

Bialecki, Jon, Naomi Haynes, and Joel Robbins. "The Anthropology of Christianity." *Religion Compass* 2.6 (2008) 1139–58.

Bielo, James S. *Emerging Evangelicals: Faith, Modernity, and the Desire for Authenticity.* New York: New York University Press, 2011.

Drescher, Elizabeth. *Choosing Our Religion: The Spiritual Lives of America's Nones.* Oxford: Oxford University Press, 2016.

Hall, David D., ed. *Lived Religion in America: Toward A History of Practice.* Princeton: Princeton University Press, 1997.

hooks, bell. "Choosing the Margins as a Space of Radical Openness." *Framework: The Journal of Cinema and Media* 36 (1989) 15–23.

Markofski, Wes. *New Monasticism and the Transformation of American Evangelicalism.* New York: Oxford University Press, 2015.

Martí, Gerardo, and Gladys Ganiel. *The Deconstructed Church: Understanding Emerging Christianity.* Oxford: Oxford University Press, 2014.

McGuire, Meredith B. *Lived Religion: Faith and Practice in Everyday Life.* Oxford University Press, 2008.

Packard, Josh. *The Emerging Church: Religion at the Margins.* Boulder: First Forum, 2012.

Packard, Josh, and Todd W. Ferguson. "Being Done: Why People Leave the Church, But Not Their Faith." *Sociological Perspectives* 62 (2019) 499–517.

Reed, Randall W., and Michael G. Zbaraschuk. *The Emerging Church, Millennials, and Religion: Volume 1: Prospects and Problems.* Eugene, OR: Cascade, 2018.

Robbins, Joel. "The Anthropology of Christianity: Unity, Diversity, New Directions: An Introduction to Supplement 10." *Current Anthropology* 55.10 (2014) 157–71.

————. "What Is a Christian? Notes toward an Anthropology of Christianity." *Religion* 33 (2003) 191–99.

Schneider, Rachel C. "The Ethics of Whiteness: Race, Religion, and Social Transformation in South Africa." Ph.D. diss., Rice University, 2017.

Taylor, Charles. *A Secular Age*. Cambridge, MA: Belknap, 2007.

PART 1

Curating and Enduring at the Margins

1

Goosing the Emerging Church
The Wild Goose Festival

RANDALL REED

Abstract

Wild Goose Festival is an Emerging Church event held in the mountains of North Carolina every summer. From 2015 to 2017 my research assistants and I interviewed millennial attendees at Wild Goose. It appeared that the Emerging Church movement offered millennials a lot of what they want in religion. It is politically progressive, accepting of diversity, and committed to dialog. Our goal was to determine the issues important to and attitudes held by those millennials who attended a festival like Wild Goose both in regard to the traditional church and the Emerging Church. What we found was that while these millennials did have generally positive views of the Emerging Church as found at Wild Goose, they are not inclined to embrace it as the avenue to return to church.

Introduction[1]

Hot Springs is a small town nestled in the Appalachian Mountains in Western North Carolina. Located about an hour from the city

---

1. I wish to thank the many students who worked on my research team over the

of Asheville and three hours from the closest major airport of Charlotte, it is a tranquil place best known for its hot tubs and as a stopping point for hikers on the Appalachian Trail. Finding a room in one of the several inns around the area is not difficult and the town's most interesting historical aspect was it served as a prisoner of war (POW) camp during the second world war.[2]

But at the beginning of July things change dramatically as the Emerging Church festival "Wild Goose" comes to town. For five days, cars come streaming into town, every room in the town and surrounding environs is occupied, the scent of beer fills the air along with a hint of hymns and the smell of the unwashed. Wild Goose was started in 2011, fashioned as an American version of the British festival Greenbelt. It originally met at a farm outside of Raleigh, NC, but moved to the mountains of North Carolina in 2013.

The festival in 2011 included Emerging Church luminaries like Brian McLaren, Phyllis Tickle, Shane Claiborne, Tony Campolo, Diana Butler Bass, Frank Schaffer, Jay Bakker, Peter Rollins, Doug Pagitt, Tony Jones, Nadia Bolz-Weber, Kester Brewin, and many others. Today, Brian McLaren and Doug Pagitt remain on the board and many of that original cast still make occasional appearances.

The festival itself is part music, part community, part religion. Large tents with folding chairs and makeshift stages interspersed with food trucks line the thoroughfares within the campground leading to the main stage that has continuous music acts during the day and into the night with the occasional keynote speaker. Musicians are often religious though previous headliners have included the Indigo Girls and Dar Williams, who are more folk stars than noted for their religious music. The speakers in the tents vary from more religiously oriented themes to more activist and progressive politics mixed with religion. In 2017 the Rev. William Barber, known for his "Moral Monday" campaign of resistance against North Carolina's legislature, was one of the keynote speakers. Talks tend to focus on activism and/or self-help with titles like "Privilege, Power, Racism and Other Biases—Awareness & Action Steps," "A Faithful Response to Domestic Violence," "Smiling Heart Yoga," and "Peace, Justice, and Pentecostalism," to the more off-beat like "The Tantra of Jesus

---

three years that we conducted this research: Jenny Buchannan, David Colbert, Justin Davis, Alaina Doyle, Mattan Ervin, Sarah Hoover, Dustin Mailman, Katie Reynolds, and Tori Small.

2. "History of Hot Springs, NC—Hot Springs NC Travel & Visitor Information."

Christ," "My Altar is the Baseball Diamond," and "Christo-Shamanic Transfiguration Ceremony." But along with these speaker-oriented venues one finds tents where one can engage in art, in storytelling, a tattoo booth, and places to listen to poetry slams.

Pierre Bourdieu's groundbreaking essay, *The Genesis and Structure of the Religious Field*[3] suggests an economic model for understanding religion. Using the notion of "field," he argued that there is a relationship between religious producers of religious products, largely understood as churches and denominations, administered by the clergy, and religious consumers (laity). Bourdieu argues that within the religious field there is then the creation of religious capital. But Bourdieu also suggests that these religious producers function as a way of justifying and legitimating the status quo. As he notes, "theodicies are always sociodicies."[4]

The goal of religious producers, argues Bourdieu, is the creation of religious monopoly. Robert P. Jones, in his work *The End of White Christian America*, argues that essentially this is what has happened in the U.S., particularly in the latter half of the twentieth century.[5] Jones suggests that the combination of white mainline and evangelical Christianities constituted a homogenous block that naturalized a largely white Protestant Christian vision of society and culture in the United States. And while not eliding the differences between these two branches, the two share an ethos which, from Bourdieu's perspective, might well constitute a religious monopoly.

Into this religious marketplace, Bourdieu, envisions the emergence of the "prophet" who he calls a "petty independent entrepreneur of salvation."[6] Bourdieu, following Weber, focuses on the prophet as an individual. And yet, as we look at the Emerging Church as well as the rise of the nones and increasing religious disaffiliation among millennials and Gen-Z, the necessity of a singular leader seems an artifact of previous experience (modeled on the Protestant Reformation). However, even by extracting the individual leader from Bourdieu's model this analysis still seems quite explanatory in the example such as Wild Goose where a prophetic movement seeks:

3. Bourdieu, "The Structure and Genesis of the Religious Field."
4. Bourdieu, "The Structure and Genesis of the Religious Field," 16.
5. Jones, *The End of White Christian America*.
6. Bourdieu, "The Structure and Genesis of the Religious Field," 24.

> to produce and distribute the goods of salvation of a type that is new and fit to devalue the old ones . . . and . . . mobilize the virtually heretical religious interests of determinate groups or classes of laypersons through the effect of consecration. This consecration performs the feat of symbolization and explanation and contributes to the subversion of the established symbolic (i.e., priestly) order and to the symbolic putting to rights of the subversion of that order--that is, the desacralization of the sacred (i.e. of 'naturalized' arbitrariness) and the sacralization of sacrilege (i.e. of revolutionary transgression).[7]

What Bourdieu describes here is the breakdown of a religious social order (monopoly). Bourdieu envisions this monopoly being replaced by an alternative religious producer, and certainly when I began this study, I thought it was possible that the Emerging Church Movement might, in fact, function as that religious entrepreneurial movement that would break up the monopoly of the mainline-evangelical synthesis. The Emerging Church consists of not *a* prophet but the rejection of the prophetic office in favor of a more general adoption of prophecy. While there are leaders in the Emerging Church movement, most spend their time not actually leading any particular group or church. And yet the process of mobilizing "heretical religious interests" and "desacralization of the sacred" seems apparent in this movement.

I thus sought to explore the parameters of this movement particularly for the "determinate group" of millennials. From 2015 to 2017, I and my research assistants conducted semi-structured interviews and focus groups with millennial attendees at Wild Goose. It appeared that the Emerging Church Movement offered millennials a lot of what they want in religion. It is politically progressive, accepting of diversity, and committed to dialog and discourse.[8] The subversion of the mainline and evangelical religious order seemed a top priority for the Emerging Church. Thus, our goal was to determine the issues important to and attitudes held by those millennials who attended a festival like Wild Goose regarding both the traditional church and the Emerging Church. What I will show in this chapter is that, even though the majority of millennials were still in some way connected to the church, they saw significant problems with the institutional church. Additionally, while sympathetic to the ideas and approach of the Emerging Church movement, even

---

7. Bourdieu, "The Structure and Genesis of the Religious Field," 24.

8. Martí and Ganiel, *The Deconstructed Church.*

there they saw problems that indicated that they did not see the answer in that movement. Thus, while these millennials did have generally positive views of the Emerging Church as found at Wild Goose, they are not inclined to embrace it as the avenue to return to church.

Methodology

Over the course of three years, I and my team conducted semi-structured interviews and focus groups of about sixty millennials in groups or individually. Each of these interviewees also did a pre-interview survey. About an additional 20 millennials completed the survey without being interviewed.

The interview questions were largely the same from year to year, though we did make some changes based on the results from previous years. For instance, in the first year, we had a question about authenticity, but the category seemed to ring false for many of the interviewees, so we removed that question. In the second and third years, we added a question about the Bible as that issue came up regularly even without participants being directly asked about it. And in light of the election in the third year, we added a question about evangelical support of Trump and millennial political activism. The interviews and focus groups were then transcribed and coded.

Survey Data

During the festival, we asked all the millennials that interacted with us to complete a pre-interview survey. The survey consisted of ten questions most of which were directed at getting a sense of the respondents' theological and political perspectives. Several people did the survey but were not interviewed. In the end, there were eighty-three respondents to the survey. While this is certainly not a nationally representative sample, it does tell us something about the perspective of the millennials I interviewed in a comparable form.

Consistent with other studies of the Emerging Church movement,[9] the majority of respondents self-identified as Protestant (68 percent). Unchurched (meaning those who identified either as none/no affiliation or atheist/agnostic) constituted 12 percent. In terms of denominational

9. Martí and Ganiel, *The Deconstructed Church.*

affiliation, Methodist and Baptist predominated though there was a large swath of identifications.

The majority of respondents (64 percent) indicated they were not "born again," while a little more than a third self-identified this way.[10] This shows two things: First, while the Emerging Church is often seen as "emerging" from evangelicalism (as many of its early leaders came out of that tradition)[11] this is not necessarily where the Emerging Church has taken hold. It has taken root in more mainline traditions. Secondly, this number reflects a phenomenon that I have commented upon elsewhere[12] where what we see is that for the first time in the Southern U.S., millennial non-evangelicals (Christian and non-Christian) outnumber evangelicals. In terms of Wild Goose respondents that number is fairly lopsided, with non-evangelicals almost double the number of evangelicals.

Among millennial respondents at Wild Goose what we found in terms of self-reported religious-service attendance was that the majority (58 percent) said they attended weekly or more. Here it should be noted that this question was broadly phrased so that it did not just represent attending conventional church but could include religious gatherings in unconventional spaces (i.e., "pub churches"). Even still, 42 percent say they attend religious services only occasionally or less. Thus, while the division was slightly in favor of religious service attendance, the divide was not lopsided.

This then relates to another question asked regarding the respondent's satisfaction with the church as an institution. Asked to rate this on 5-point Likert scale, those who were Very Dissatisfied/Dissatisfied vastly outnumbered the Satisfied/Very Satisfied: 54 percent to 14 percent. A little less than one-third indicated they were neutral (32 percent). Still, it is interesting that religious service attendance did not seem to impact this. Of those who were regular service attenders, 52 percent were either Dissatisfied or Very Dissatisfied, while for non-regular attendees that number is 54 percent. Thus, regardless of religious service attendance, a majority of millennial respondents were dissatisfied with the institutional church.

10. For the purposes of this discussion, I will equate "born again" with "evangelical," though I acknowledge this is not always a clear equation. See Smith, *Christian America?*

11. Bielo, *Emerging Evangelicals.*

12. Reed, "Southern Strategy."

Again, this is probably not surprising overall. As I have argued else-where[13] millennials are skeptical of institutions and particularly skeptical of the church. Nevertheless, where one might have expected to see a difference is with those who regularly attended religious services and yet that was not the case for this (admittedly small) sample.

The survey then asked a series of theological questions that indicated a broadly liberal perspective among the respondents. Asked whether the bible was "literally true" 71 percent disagreed with that statement. Thus, clearly biblical literalism is not an issue for these respondents.

Not surprisingly, then, when asked whether people of the same gender should be allowed to marry, a paltry 2 percent disagreed while 94 percent agreed with the largest percentage being saying they "strongly agreed: (85 percent). Perhaps some dissent was registered in the 6 percent that "neither agreed nor disagreed." Some have suggested that while people may believe that people of the same gender should be allowed to marry, they morally still object to homosexuality. This, however, was not reflected with this set of respondents where again only 4 percent disagreed with the statement, "sex between two adults of the same gender is morally acceptable," whereas 86 percent agreed with that statement. It was really on the question of sex within marriage where we see some vestige of traditional values. However, even here the majority (56 percent) disagreed that sex should be reserved for marriage while about one-fifth agreed.

Thus, it is clear that even among these millennials of whom a majority attend religious services, the overwhelming majority feel strongly about LGBTQ+ rights and have rejected the evangelical tenant that homosexuality is a sin. Likewise, the majority of them are much more permissive about sex in general.

Drilling down further, things look slightly different among those respondents who self-identify as "Born Again" who constitute a little more than one-third of the respondents (36 percent). While it still true that the majority of these millennials likewise support the right for people of the same gender to marry (85 percent) and agree that homosexual behavior is morally acceptable (87 percent), they are more divided about sex outside of marriage. There the plurality holds the traditional view that sex should be reserved for marriage (44 percent) while 37 percent disagreed with 18 percent remaining neutral on the question.

13. Reed, "The Problem of Anti-Institutionalism."

Another theological question we measured was regarding whether there are many paths to heaven. Brian McLaren and Rob Bell[14] have both in different ways called into question the exclusivist claims of Christianity. This question asked whether this perspective had penetrated the consciousness of millennials at Wild Goose. In general, it appears it has. A majority (63 percent) agreed that there are many paths to heaven, only 12 percent disagreed. Among self-identified Born-Again respondents, a plurality (48 percent) agreed with the statement, whereas only 26 percent disagreed. Thus, even among evangelical millennials, this position seems the stronger one over the traditional view.

Finally, we asked whether Christians have a "biblical obligation to work to change the world to make it more socially/economically equal." Here once again a resounding majority (88 percent) agreed with this statement including 74 percent who strongly agreed. Only 2 percent disagreed. We intentionally included the economic aspect to see whether the connection of the bible with income equality was something that these millennials would agree with. I might note that some of these respondents were answering before the Bernie Sanders candidacy made income inequality a prominent issue in the 2016 election.

Thus, what we glean from this survey is that among the respondents, while there is still participation in religion, there is skepticism of the institutional church. That skepticism may be fueled by the church's traditionalist stance against same-sex marriage and condemnation of homosexual behavior and a more restrictive view of sexuality in general. It may also be connected to a failure of the institutional church, particularly the evangelical branch, to be strong advocates against social and economic inequality. Additionally, traditional evangelical theological perspectives that include exclusivist claims of the church and literalist readings of the Bible seem imperiled by these millennials.[15] In fact, what we will see looking at the qualitative work below is that the millennials' critique of the Church often runs along these lines.

14. McLaren, *Why Did Jesus?*; Bell, *Love Wins*.

15. In a more recent study of the various kinds of nones, the Public Religion Research Institute (PRRI) the number one reason was given for leaving the church was "you stopped believing in the religion's teachings." Cooper et al., "Exodus," 7. If this is also the case for millennials who are still active in the church, the distance between "nones" and "somes" may not be very great.

Qualitative Analysis

Semi-structured interviews and focus groups were conducted over the course of three years. These were transcribed and then coded. Additionally, each response from a subject was also individually fed to IBM Watson Discovery. Discovery allows one to ask natural language questions of the data and then reports not just the passages that address that question, but also provides an analysis of that data in a variety of ways. Most importantly Discovery gives a sentiment analysis of each answer. Is the participant's answer positive, negative or neutral? Additionally, it also scores the language of each answer in terms of its emotional freight along five axes: Joy, Sadness, Fear, Anger, and Disgust. The analysis I will provide here then uses a combination of the results from a traditional QDACS (Qualitative Data Analysis Computer System) in conjunction with Discovery.

Wild Goose Millennials and the Church

The first question we asked millennial participants was why millennials were leaving the church. No one ever questioned the factual basis of the question. Millennials at Wild Goose understood that there was an exodus from the churches by their cohort. In analyzing the answers given by interviewees the top three were that the church was judgmental, that it did not leave room for questions, and that it rejected certain groups. Typical responses were:

> When I got into the church I was swept up into [a] very fundamentalist evangelical[ism] and . . . what I experienced was the judgment, lack of creativity and [an attempt to] just get you to follow the rules and I really didn't like it.

> I just didn't like anything about it because they would shove ideas down your throat and try to make you conform to their ideas which I didn't necessarily agree with, and they're very judgmental.

But "judgment" manifests in two different ways for these millennials. First, respondents felt judged when they engaged in critical questioning of doctrine. Respondents reported asking questions in church, often in churches in which they had grown up, only to be attacked and rebuked.

I was engaging [the] Bible, intellectually, academically, spiritually, and there wasn't, for whatever reason, a home for questioning in my conservative church.

There's a general close-mindedness within the church. As you're
growing up, when you ask tough questions, they often don't like
to answer tough questions. And knowledge is so cheap now that
that's not something that the church can afford really. Because
you can go look up all the different angles and then you're sifting
through them on your own. And oftentimes, in that context, you
may not find the church's angle most persuasive.

I just think that questions were shut down before they could
even be voiced, in my experience, I was afraid to ask the questions which may be judged instead of trying to figure it out. I
just totally abandoned [church] at one point.

On the other hand, the issue of rejection of the church of particular
groups, most often LGBTQ+ folks, but other groups as well, such as the
poor or mentally ill, were most often not an experience the respondent
had themselves (though that was reported sometimes) but more often
talked about as an alienation that happened second hand.

I never really felt like I was a part of the church because I felt
like it was not inclusive of everyone. When I think of God or
spirituality [it's under the] heading of love and forgiveness and
acceptance and not other humans telling people what they are
not allowed to do based off of the scripture in the Bible.

I left one church because it wasn't open to homosexuals and
even though I am not [homosexual], I have friends who are
so as [other respondent] said I couldn't hold Jesus' love for all
people with that sort of exclusion of a certain group of people.

There is a sense of unity among millennials and I think a big
problem for many people in our generation is a frustration with
seeing that there is not, in many cases, an equal opportunity or
value placed on all persons.

These millennials are turned off by the church because of its perceived
judgmental attitude. For Wild Goose participants this judgment has most
often been directed towards them in terms of a stifling of theological
questioning, but they are likewise alienated from the church because they
see the way it treats groups that the millennial respondent is most often
not a part of, particularly LGBTQ+ groups. And yet, as we might expect

from the survey data it is the attack on LGBTQ+ people that is unacceptable to these millennials who support same-sex marriage and do not see homosexual practices as morally problematic. For these millennials, then, the judgment of the church against them and others becomes the major thoroughfare by which they leave or at least stokes dissatisfaction.

Two other reasons seem connected. The first is a complaint that the church is not meeting their needs spiritually. Millennial respondents complain that they were not getting much out of church services, particularly traditional sermons.

> I think that sitting in the pews on Sunday morning is associated with this kind of traditional structure that I think that people our age don't like anymore. It's too rigid. It's too like "stand, kneel, pray" . . . kind of the same old Sunday morning routine and I think that people our age are like, it's old, it's jaded, it's kind of like we don't see the point.

But this ties into a larger problem hinted at towards the end of the quote. Not that traditional congregational style of worship is not speaking to them, but the entirety of the church institution seems irrelevant. The respondents at Wild Goose often articulate this critique.

> I would say from my observations that people are not finding the church, millennials are not finding the church, to be relevant to their identity and their way of life.

> I just think it happens to be really bad theology and the emphasis that [the churches] work with are not relevant to the pain and the needs of the world and I think that as more millennials have become aware of pain and need in the world they're seeing a great disconnect between the church's message.

> I feel like, for us, church has lost its sense of relevance for us and our culture. And our society is raising a lot of questions that the church isn't doing a very good job of grappling with or answering in a way that we feel is relevant. Mainly it seems like . . . our society is raising a lot of moral questions and the church isn't doing a very good job of grappling with or giving answers for that.

This issue of relevance is not restricted to respondents at Wild Goose, though they express it often, it also is a phenomenon that is appearing in polling on millennial attitudes. Pew's Religious Landscape Study shows that the majority of those ages eighteen to twenty-nine said that religion was either "not at all important" or "not too important" (64 percent). Thus, millennials, in general, seem to feel that religion's relevance and thereby its importance has significantly waned.[16]

The IBM Watson Discovery analysis sheds further light on these millennials' attitudes. Discovery indicates that when talking about leaving the church these millennials have a much more positive sentiment than negative. Largely then, when talking about leaving the Church, these respondents see it as a positive thing.

FIGURE 1.1

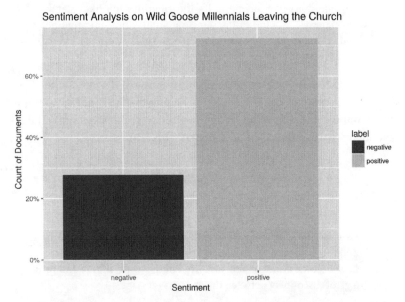

Perhaps more interesting, when doing an emotional analysis of the answers given by respondents one sees a preponderance of sadness followed closely by joy. What is likewise striking is the low level of anger shown. Joy and sadness score at more than twice the level of fear or anger. This combination of positive sentiment populated by feelings of both sadness and joy indicate how complex the relationship of these millennials is (or was) to the church.

16. Pew Research Center, "Religious Landscape Study."

FIGURE 1.2

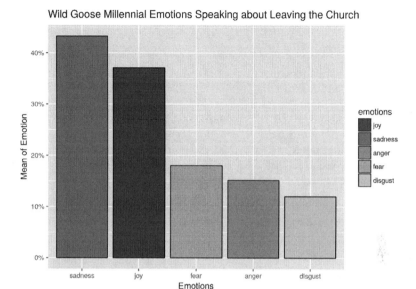

Wild Goose Millennial Emotions Speaking about Leaving the Church

I might suggest then that while these millennials believe millennial abandonment of the church is ultimately a good thing, they do so with a feeling of sadness in the face of it, but also with an almost equivalent amount of joy. To return to Bourdieu, the products of salvation produced by the church and the monopoly it has held has been, at least in part, because of its claim that not being a part of the institution would have dire eternal consequences. However, we can see from this analysis that such a strategy is not working with these millennials. But likewise, we can also see that these respondents do not leave in anger, which may be the most hopeful thing those committed to the church might take from this.

On the other hand, when asked what prompted millennials to stay in the church those interviewed listed "community" as the number one reason. Interestingly, these respondents sometimes talked about this as being a reason to stay in spite of the church, almost as an unintended consequence of the church. For example:

> . . . for some reason that baffles me, a lot of [millennials] find great things and structure in community.

> I derive value from church because of the community and from the forced introspection.

> I think that we feel alone and it's important to be called by our names and to be hugged. I stay because I need routine in my

life and the greatest gift that I get is that God makes order out
of chaos and I'm just too scattered to not have some kind of
consistent reminder of some basic things: that I'm loved and
remembered and held.

Still, others talk about the importance of family and the need for church
as a primary way of connecting with family. Alternatively, at least one respondent spoke quite tellingly about the social cost of leaving the church.

When you feel rejected, when the church rejects you, especially
for those of us who grew up in this church, you lose everything.
You lose an identity, you lose a way of life, you lose boundaries
and parameters that you grew up knowing and are comfortable
with and so it can be and is very lonely.

My big thing is rediscovering what community means because
I didn't really realize that I was leaving it. So that's my impression for a lot of [millennials] it's just there. That's their family,
and that's their community and the box works for them still, for
most of them at least, on the surface.

More positively, however, several respondents talked about the need
and desire to be agents of change within traditional church structures.
Some might attribute this to the enthusiasm of youth, but some of these
millennials were (or knew those who were) unwilling to abandon the
church and vowed to fight to reclaim it.

So I remember reading a Pew Research statistic about how a
majority of millennials feel that they . . . that it is possible to
create change in the world and that a chunk of those . . . that a
majority also believe they can be instrumental in that change.
So I feel that a lot of millennials stick around within the church
because they want to be instrumental in creating change, to
make a better world and to take ownership of the church and
reclaim concepts like evangelism [and] redefine a lot of things
[that] have become stigmatized.

I also think that there is however a segment of millennials that
have stayed in the church and that are much braver than I am
because they understand the need to transform the church from
within.

If we want people to realize . . . what it means to be Christian, we
have to have people who are willing to stay in and stand up and
say what they're doing is not what every Christian does and not
what we see is what Jesus taught, and so I stay to try to change

that narrative even though I'm still working through how to do that and how comfortable I am with it. I think it's important to have people who are willing to do that.

This certainly was not the largest category talked about by respondents when discussing millennials who stay in church, though among those who did talk about it, they did so with a passion that was often missing in some other, more clinical analyses that the respondents engaged in. Perhaps this should not be surprising at a venue like Wild Goose which certainly has a reformist aspect to it as it tries to creatively reinvent both doctrine and practice. Yet when we look at the emotional response from Discovery for this, we see that sadness has diminished compared to the previous graph and joy becomes clearly dominant. What we may be seeing is the result of hope for the church in light of millennial enthusiasm for change.

FIGURE 1.3

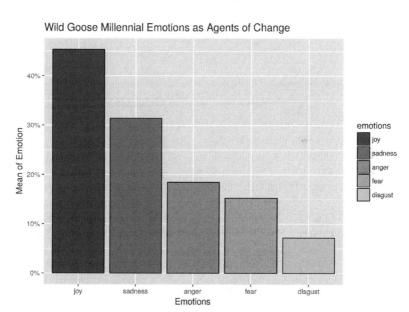

One of the hallmarks of the Emerging Church is its challenge to traditional theological concepts.[17] Certainly, as the aforementioned session titles indicate, Wild Goose is not immune to this sort of theological

17. McLaren, *A New Kind of Christian*; Rollins, *Insurrection*; Moody, *Radical Theology*; Zbaraschuk, "Playing Offense or Defense."

exploration. In fact, many of the millennial respondents could name Emerging Church theologians, and several of these thinkers made appearances at festivals where my team was doing interviews. To that end, one of the questions we asked millennial respondents was about Emerging Church theological innovations, what was their opinion of these changes?

Participants were reminded of an entire list of theological innovations from Brian McLaren's rethinking of Christianity's relationship with other religions[18] and alternative view of the authority of the Bible[19] to Peter Rollins's death of God theology.[20] Overall the respondents who mentioned these thinkers by name did so in order to endorse them rather than to denounce them or argue with them. In fact, using a sentiment analysis, more than 60 percent of the time thinkers like Nadia Bolz-Weber, Peter Rollins, Brian McLaren, and Rob Bell were mentioned (and they were mentioned in about a third of interviews), they were mentioned positively.

FIGURE 1.4

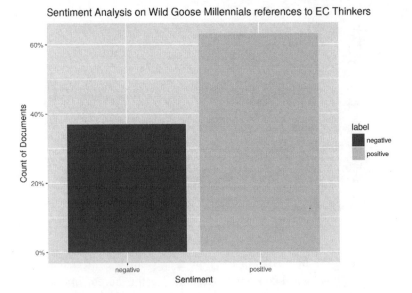

Sentiment Analysis on Wild Goose Millennials references to EC Thinkers

18. McLaren, *Why Did Jesus?*
19. McLaren, *Brian McLaren: Q2 The Authority Question*
20. Rollins, *Insurrection.*

And yet, unsurprisingly given the survey data we examined earlier, the number one theological issue that these millennials felt the Emerging Church is engaged in that would be attractive to millennials, in general, is its openness on the issue of LGBTQ+ relationships. This issue came up in the vast number of interviews (65 times in all) and in large part theological moves towards greater tolerance were perceived positively.

> Nadia, Bakker, and anybody who is advocating for the acceptance of homosexuality, add them to the [good] list, you know it's a call towards greater humanity . . .

> Queer people are just as sacred as other people and that the tools that have been used against those people need to be thrown out which include things like hell and traditional notions of sin so . . . I think queerness and homosexuality are becoming the no brainer where it's like if you don't have that, you're not there yet, you know like that's baseline . . .

> I mean obviously, I love this stuff about queerness . . .

The last participant's comment that it is "obvious" that millennials are in favor of the advocacy that Emerging Church thinkers have engaged in for LGBTQ+ issues is telling. For it is this issue, far more than any other, which was continually brought up. The death of God theology, a Lacanian reading of sin, a rethinking of hell, or a reevaluation of biblical authority all pale in comparison to this issue for the millennials interviewed.

Wild Goose Millennials and Politics

But another related issue that the participants were asked about was the relationship between church and politics. Should the church be involved in politics and to what extent? Generally, there was unanimity on the issue of candidate endorsement. The respondents agreed that churches should not tell their members who to vote for. But beyond that, these millennials believed the church has a requirement to be politically involved in standing against oppression.

> I think the theological is also personal and also political, and so I think the church has a responsibility to support the people of God which is all people and if that means taking on political forces and taking political stands I think that that's a requirement.

> Christians are not supposed to be apolitical. I mean Christians
> are supposed to be like a revolutionary challenge to empire. That
> is . . . that is the nature of Christianity. It's like you take . . . you
> take the challenge to systems or oppressions out of Christianity
> and you get a fish without fins. You're just floating there and it
> doesn't have much point.

> I believe that we are called to stand up and against oppression.

These quotes represent a common idea among the millennials interviewed that the church, whether done well or poorly, has a political witness. For these millennials, the church is rightfully called by Jesus and the
scriptures to challenge any system that facilitates oppression. For many of
these millennials, the homophobia of the evangelical tradition represents
a failure of the church in the face of this calling. But that calling extends
beyond that into areas of economic justice as well.

One paradigmatic quote from the interviews was, "I believe in the
separation of Church and State, but I also believe in the separation of
Church and Hate." This quote indicates that at the same time that there
is a reluctance to have the church engaged in politics, largely recognizing
the church as having been on the wrong side of the culture wars, there is a
simultaneous demand for different sort of church that seems to exemplify
these millennials' perspective on politics and a new call to political activism in the church.

What seems clear throughout our interviews is that the millennials
we talked to purposefully reject the conservative values that have been
historically associated with the church, particularly evangelical and conservative Catholic traditions. The hot button issues of the culture wars of
gay marriage, abortion, and prayer in school came up in discussions, but
they were often examples of what the church had typically done wrong
when it came to exercising its authority in the political realm.

> I mean I don't think [the church's role in politics] has anything to
> do with prayer in school. It has nothing to do with abortion and
> gay marriage but everything to do with loving your neighbor.

> The church needs to maybe sit down and just stop trying to take
> its place on certain issues. I don't think it's the church's job to,
> like for example, in the topic of homosexuality, in my mind,
> the church doesn't really get a say on gay marriage, you know
> what I mean? Nationally I just think that the church as a whole
> shouldn't take it upon itself there.

These millennials then steadfastly reject the conservative cultural values that the church is often known for. But this does embroil them in what has been called "the paradox of tolerance." How can they be intolerant of the intolerant? Ideally, a progressive Christianity invokes a transcendent standard of Jesus to break this paradox.[21] However, in the few times this issue was raised, millennials did not take that option and instead tended towards a kind of befuddlement in the face of it.

> Where I get tripped up as I feel really comfortable about [tolerance] when it's in alignment with my beliefs and my interpretation of scripture and church, and I get really angry and upset when other people actually do that [as well] but have values that I don't agree with.

> I think we should absolutely be in there because people are being hurt and it's our job to stand up for people who are being hurt and help them to [be] care[d] for. I think that makes the line really murky about where do you stop. And it's interesting before you finished the question I was thinking well now [the church] shouldn't be involved in questions concerning education and legalizing guns and issues like that because that's all that stuff of the people on the right care about. But of course, we should be in it for like gay marriage and things that I care about. So that made me stop and think well what would be that line because there's two sides to every issue right? Now my comfortableness with uncertainty is coming, I don't know what I think.

This also ties into more current events. In 2017, after the election of Donald Trump, we included another question noting the overwhelming support of white evangelicals for Trump[22] and whether millennials expected this to energize or depress millennial political involvement. What we saw was not anger but sorrow.

21. Claiborne and Haw, *Jesus for President*.

22. In 2016 white voters who responded yes to either that they were born-again or Evangelical voted 80 percent for Donald Trump. These voters constituted 26 percent of the electorate. "2016 Election Results: Exit Polls." Among Millennials only 37 percent voted for Donald Trump, the lowest percentage of any age cohort.

FIGURE 1.5

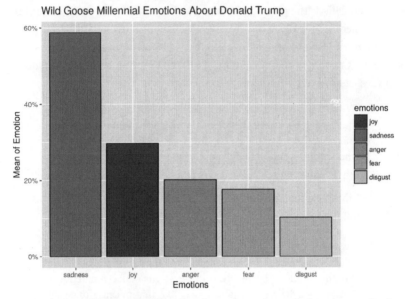

Particularly with regard to the fact that 80 percent of white evangelicals voted for Trump these millennials responded:

> You know what the first feeling was that came up and I think might come up for other folks is just grief, it's just how f**king sad is that.

> I think it's made me sad about the ways that we have perceived who Jesus is.

> That still we are not hearing the message in the church of . . . of kingdom love, of redemption, of costly radical love, that makes me sad.

> I think folks who vote that way based on their faith, I would imagine have a faith that doesn't love them very much or has a faith that requires fear, that must be really difficult to live with.

So the question that follows is: will Trump energize millennials, will they become the foot soldiers of the resistance? The answers were alternatively hopeful, tentative, and fearful.

> For a lot of people that I know, it was more of a wake-up call of, like, people need to be more involved in . . . the political sphere, like, people need to have a firmer hand in it to not get to this point.

Burn out. Burn out. A faith burn out. Political burn out. A sense of despondency and despair, a further justification for why the church doesn't feel like home to many people. I mean it's sanctioning, it's sanctioning ignorance as our lord. Thank you [millennials]. Beautiful.

I think it seems like more [political activism may occur]. Possibly. I think there is a sense of millennial apathy in some ways, I think, to the political process or it seems that way to me. But I honestly think that for a lot of people, that Trump kind of scared the sh*t out of them and now it's like "oh my god we have to do, like, something so this can't happen again." I think there will be more participation. But still, I think the kind of sense of apathy that a lot of people have will carry through. But I think Trump in some ways is a wake-up call . . .

Clearly, one can hear the tentativeness in these responses. The desire for millennials to step up and lead, but the fear that they will not. They worry that instead that apathy will win the battle of hearts and minds and that the wake-up call that the election of Donald Trump should be will not actually happen.

FIGURE 1.6

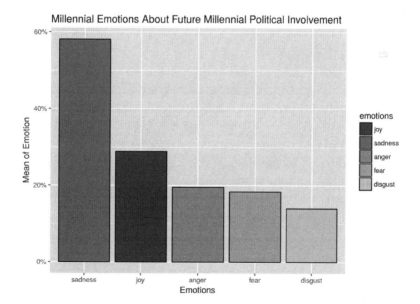

Millennial Emotions About Future Millennial Political Involvement

On this issue there is far less confidence than above that millennials will be agents of change in their world. The 2016 election was a blow to the confidence of these millennials. In their generation and its current experience of the hard work of political resistance, as the above chart shows, not much joy is generated and instead there is the predominance of sadness.

There was certainly no support of Donald Trump in evidence at Wild Goose. However, what we did see is the awareness of race, particularly of whiteness. References to "whiteness" increased significantly in 2016 and 2017 over 2015. And 2017 showed some increase over 2016. Some of that may be connected to the fact that the question in 2017 specifically asked about white evangelical voting patterns, but this was not the case in 2016. Thus, it seems fairly clear that the results of the Trump candidacy and the Trump presidency served to problematize race for these millennials in a way that was not on the radar in 2015.

In the end, then, what seems clear is that the church that will attract the millennials who attended Wild Goose will be a political church, a "woke" church. A church that is not mired down in the conservative political culture wars agenda of the conservative evangelical and Catholic churches, but one which has an aggressive progressive political agenda that fights for the poor, the oppressed, the marginalized, and anyone disadvantaged by the system. As one respondent said, the church should be fighting for "the people of God which is all people." While mainline churches have the right theology, too often for these millennials they have hidden their light under a bushel. A panel I attended at Wild Goose in 2017 made this point as two pastors of liberal mainline churches talked about how they were admonished by their elder boards about being "too political" for preaching about climate change. For these millennials, the church needs to be a political entity, and they believe it is charged with righting social and economic injustice. A modest middle-class church with a liberal theology but afraid of politics will not appeal to them. The church that has any hope of attracting the Wild Goose millennials is the politically active and engaged church.

Wild Goose Millennials on Wild Goose

Finally, the last question we asked was an open question on what our respondents thought about Wild Goose. Some background is important here. One of the realities of the rural and lovely wilderness setting of Wild Goose is that cell phone reception is horrendous. Voice calls and text messages are sketchy at best and often completely unworkable depending on the mobile provider. But no one, regardless of cell phone provider, has internet access. What this means is that millennials cannot tweet, check their Facebook, update their Snapchat story, post their Instagram pictures or any of the other myriad of social media options that they have at home. The downside is that parents, partners, and friends do not get the regular check-ins they have come to expect. Meetings that are often ambiguously planned happen only by luck and often are missed altogether, and while millennials dutifully charge their phones (and the festival provides an entire tent of chargers to facilitate this) they often stare blankly in despair at their phones that have become oversized watches.

But what this means, on the other hand, is that often for the first time in a long time, the ever-demanding screen has gone dark. They are suddenly free. They experience living in the moment, being where they are, because they have no other choice. The response is positive.

> I think it is so hard to escape the constant chatter of the internet and 24-hour news cycle and bosses that can call you on your cell phone at 3 o'clock in the morning and all of these things that keep us tethered to the non-spiritual to do the things that distract us from God that when we come to a place like this where there is no cell phone service . . . [it] becomes where you make space for God.

> Like if you start to feel really uncomfortable in a talk or something you can't pull out your phone and like start browsing Facebook you kind of have to sit in it with whatever you're sitting in.

> I love, I absolutely love, being unplugged. I turn my phone on one time every night, and other than that I have not touched it and it's amazing. It's like I could do that at home right? But I couldn't. So that's been really freeing being out here and away from everything else and it's forcing me to interact with people. I'm a huge introvert and honestly, if I had cell service I would never come to talk to you guys because I could play on my phone. I can't do that so let's go talk to people right? And it's been a push for me but it's been really cool.

Beyond the experience of freedom from technology, Wild Goose also exemplifies much of what these millennials say they are looking for in religion. This is not just a result of selection bias, several participants reported that it was their first time at Wild Goose, and yet they report positive experiences.

> This is . . .my first year, and I love it. I love being able to walk around and just see so many people just being themselves.

> This is one of the very few gatherings of Christians that I would actually come to because the conversations here are very different and the people that I meet here are very different, and they're much more accepting of who I am in the fullness of who I am and connected to the issues that I believe about very strongly.

> I think Wild Goose really captures one of the biggest truths that I sort of want to express to the existing church about millennials and about the future of the church, which is: not to worry about what's going to happen with the millennials and the church, not to live out of fear. And not to expect it to look the same as it's always looked. It's gonna look different. It may not involve budgets, it may not involve buildings, it may not involve all these structures it's always involved for so many decades, centuries really, but why should that mean that it doesn't, the church, the body of Christ, does not live on in the same powerful way, if not more powerful, more prevalent, more embedded, more in the world than it ever has, because of those changes, and because of how millennials are treating faith in the church. Wild Goose kind of illustrates that in such a beautiful way.

The last statement entails the notion that Wild Goose acts as a kind of replacement for church. This is a theme that was sometimes expressed by millennials respondents. Wild Goose acted as a model for how an authentic type of religiosity could be achieved with which these millennials could connect. Comments often involved affirmations that Wild Goose had a strong community, put a primacy on acceptance, embraced and affirmed creativity, and all within an environment that these respondents thought was rejuvenating intellectually and spiritually.

But this does not mean that there was not some criticism of Wild Goose from these millennials as well. Generally, the criticism of Wild Goose ranged around the issue that a majority of the participants were white, older, and generally well-off folks. There was a concern that Wild Goose created its own sort of progressive silo mentality. Some respondents were concerned that that might also lead to a kind of liberal dogmatism. But probably the most telling critique of Wild Goose was exemplified by a Black respondent:

To be quite honest with you I find, I find the deconstruction of spirituality to be a privilege. Most of my Black brothers and sisters who have their faith are so caught up in the life struggle that this type of deconstruction that happens here isn't something that they can afford time or consciousness . . .conscious effort to fulfill. So I love it. I'm here, I'm soaking in the privilege, I am privileged in the space but I think that this event and millennials need to get off of their high f**king spiritual . . . you know, their high horse, and get off the purely superficial contemplative path and put some reality into the mix, right? That this is not a self-serving endeavor . . . Like I am walking around here thinking about how . . . how this is going to fuel my activism, right? And I wonder for myself how many people are doing that versus just trying to deconstruct their faith so that they can love themselves a little bit more in the privileged life that they already have.

This trenchant quote gets at the crux of critiques that we heard of Wild Goose. While millennials reveled in the affirmation, the intellectual stimulation, the expressions of creativity and joy, what they often failed to connect with was a political activist agenda. Too often they worried that "the Goose " was a flight from the world, rather than a brief respite before returning to the fray or, perhaps even more helpfully, a place to strategize new ways of engaging in the fight.

Conclusion

The Wild Goose festival represents a kind of perfect microcosm within the Emerging Church movement. It is theologically progressive, liturgically experimental, and politically progressive. It embraces all people from a variety of backgrounds and welcomes all to come as they are without requirements of doctrinal assent or institutional membership. It provides a venue that is set apart in a place of beauty where participants can enjoy each other and look for God. In some ways, it should be exactly what was ordered for millennials. It checks all the boxes.

For many of the millennials we talked with it is just that. It is the ultimate expression of a kind of religiosity some never knew was possible. As one millennial said:

Before I came here, I kept trying to ask people, you know, "What is the Wild Goose?" You know, "What's it like?" And no one could affirmingly tell me what it is, so actually getting to come

> here and seeing the different stuff, SO much stuff, it's super cool.
> There definitely needs to be more stuff like this everywhere in
> the world.

Expressions of love and joy about the festival were common. No millennial that we talked to said that they were unhappy about being there even when they complained about the effect of camping on their hair or hygiene. Instead, they often said, a community that practiced acceptance in the face of bad hair and dicey hygiene made it a memorable experience. In Bourdieu's terms, then, Wild Goose does represent a kind of charismatic movement that offers to desacralize much of what the traditional mainline and evangelical churches designate as sacred.

And yet we noticed, particularly in the last year (2017), that we heard more critical reflections, most often reflected in a variation of the phrase, "I just want to know, then what?" or "It's awful white, isn't it?" Among some millennials, there was a sense that a festival that cost $300 to attend, which was settled at a spa in the remote mountains of North Carolina was not going to attract the most diverse crowd. And even though many people of color were on the stage from Rev. William Barber to a gospel choir from Chicago, the audience looked like what you might see in the congregation of any suburban Presbyterian Church.

In light of the Trump election, we wondered if we would see a difference at the festival. Would we see a decline in millennial participation, or would a progressive Christianity see an increase as millennials sought a new foundation from which to fight the Trumpian backlash? The evidence is unclear, unofficial totals indicate that, while total attendance increased, the rate of increase had declined from previous years. Our experience was that we found fewer millennials to interview in 2017 than we had in 2016 and 2015 respectively but the decrease was not significant (as we would expect with the low numbers of people we interviewed).

But what did become apparent is that the millennials we did interview were particularly adamant about the necessity for the church to take a political stand for justice, tolerance, and minority communities. The criticism of Wild Goose was directed at points where that seems either lacking or at least not the focus. And here it is perhaps important to contrast the Emerging Church (as shown at Wild Goose) with the other charismatic movement that seems to be a competitor to the Emerging Church and far more successful: pious religious disaffiliation.[23] By this

---

23. The name I have chosen here is merely a space saving moniker, there may be

term, I want to indicate a movement of millennial religious disaffiliation often coupled with more popular conceptions of notions of tolerance, intersectionality, and progressive politics. This would in Bourdieu categories constitute another "petty independent entrepreneur" movement which for a determinate group mobilizes heretical virtues and challenges the religious social order. What we saw repeatedly was that it was the pious disaffiliation movement, which likewise desacralizes the traditional sacred and sacralizes a new set of "heretical" priorities, that seemed a constant pull on our respondents, even for those who were still in the evangelical or mainline camps.

Thus, what seems clear is that millennials, particularly in the age of Trump, are not interested in the deconstruction of faith in lieu of activism. Particularly when pious disaffiliation will allow them to deconstruct faith and engage in activism free of the baggage of mainline and evangelical churches. Wild Goose perhaps offered the purest expression of the promise of the Emerging Church, and yet its ability to be a real alternative to pious disaffiliation was not clear. It may be that ultimately some of the contradictions of pious disaffiliation (particularly regarding the paradox of tolerance) will drive millennials and the next generation to seek an alternative like the Emerging Church. Yet, for now, this remains only a possibility not an actuality.

Bibliography

"2016 Election Results: Exit Polls." CNN. http://2016.elections.cnn.com/election/2016/results/exit-polls.

Bell, Rob. *Love Wins: A Book about Heaven, Hell, and the Fate of Every Person Who Ever Lived.* San Francisco: HarperCollins, 2011.

Bielo, James S. *Emerging Evangelicals: Faith, Modernity, and the Desire for Authenticity.* New York: New York University Press, 2011.

Bourdieu, Pierre. "The Structure and Genesis of the Religious Field." *Comparative Social Research* 13 (1991) 1–44.

Claiborne, Shane, and Chris Haw. *Jesus for President: Politics for Ordinary Radicals.* Fourth Impression. Grand Rapids: Zondervan, 2008.

Cooper, Betsy, Daniel Cox, Rachel Lienesch, and Robert P. Jones. "Exodus: Why Americans Are Leaving Religion—and Why They're Unlikely to Come Back."

---

better descriptors for it. But my hope is that it signifies the combination of both disaffiliation and a cultural ethos among millennials. Likewise, the term recognizes that this is not simply a form of secularism (since a majority of millennials still believe in God), but a new morally grounded set of principles that while often not explicitly articulated seems to underlie many of the responses we heard.

Public Religion Research Institute, September 22, 2016. http://www.prri.org/research/prri-rns-2016-religiously-unaffiliated-americans/.

"History of Hot Springs, NC." *Hot Springs Tourism Information*. https://www.hotspringsnc.org/about/history/.

Jones, Robert P. *The End of White Christian America*. New York: Simon & Schuster, 2016.

Martí, Gerardo, and Gladys Ganiel. *The Deconstructed Church: Understanding Emerging Christianity*. Oxford: Oxford University Press, 2014.

McLaren, Brian. *Brian McLaren: Q2 The Authority Question*. theOOZE.tv. YouTube Video, 2010. https://www.youtube.com/watch?v=puBolEen9yQ.

————. *A New Kind of Christian: A Tale of Two Friends on a Spiritual Journey*. San Francisco: Jossey-Bass, 2008.

————. *Why Did Jesus, Moses, the Buddha, and Mohammed Cross the Road?: Christian Identity in a Multi-Faith World*. New York: Jericho, 2012.

Moody, Katharine Sarah. *Radical Theology and Emerging Christianity*. Intensities: Contemporary Continental Philosophy of Religion. New York: Routledge, 2017.

Pew Research Center. "Religious Landscape Study." Pew Research Center's Religion & Public Life Project: Religious Landscape Study, May 11, 2015. http://www.pewforum.org/religious-landscape-study/.

Reed, Randall. "The Problem of Anti-Institutionalism in Millennials." In *The Emerging Church, Millennials and Religion*. Volume 1: *Problems and Prospects*, edited by Randall Reed and Michael Zbaraschuk, 166–87. Eugene, OR: Cascade Books, 2018.

————. "The Southern Strategy." In *The Emerging Church, Millennials and Religion*. Volume 1: *Problems and Prospects*, edited by Randall Reed and Michael Zbaraschuk, 15–30. Eugene, OR: Cascade Books, 2018.

Rollins, Peter. *Insurrection: To Believe Is Human To Doubt, Divine*. New York: Howard, 2011.

Smith, Christian. *Christian America?: What Evangelicals Really Want*. Berkeley: University of California Press, 2002.

Zbaraschuk, Michael. "Playing Offense or Defense? The Theological Playbook of the Emergent/ing Church, with Some Armchair Quarterbacking." In *The Emerging Church, Millennials and Religion*. Volume 1: *Prospects and Problems*, edited by Randall Reed and G. Michael Zbaraschuk, 31–43. Eugene, OR: Cascade Books, 2017.

2

Crafting Subversive Church

The Ecclesiological Life
of Emerging Christians in the Upper South

Terry Shoemaker

Abstract

This chapter investigates the Emerging Church movement in the Upper South region of the United States (Kentucky, Tennessee, and North Carolina). Based on two years of ethnographic research, the overall argument is that Emerging Christian communities are in responsive engagement with the dominant form of Protestantism in the region *and* broader social norms. This creates conditions whereby participants in Emerging Christian communities must disidentify with the dominant strand of Protestantism that I refer to as culture war Christianity. Through disidentification, Emerging Christians interact with the dominant social structures that seek to regulate normativity. Overall, I argue that scholarship must consider social contexts when analyzing religious change in the United States.

Religious expressions exist in a constant mode of navigation and negotiation with multiple external and internal factors. Increased pluralism and demographic changes often affect how religious people and institutions understand their relationship with people of other religious traditions or with those who have no traditions, whether positively or negatively. Changes in legal codes and recognitions can modify practices and rituals. Forms of religious socializations are often transformed with increases in scientific knowledge. In short, religion and religious people do not operate within a space devoid of influences. The opposite is also accurate—religion and religious persons impact the broader community in which they operate. Thus, influential actions are multidirectional.

One recent case study that highlights these types of interactions includes what scholarship refers to as "Emerging Christianities."[1] In a recently published article, James Bielo argues that one approach to studying this evolution within Christianity is through analyzing the discourse of this movement in relation to forms of American Christianity, referring to this as cultural change.[2] By doing so, he is able to offer ways of thinking about new forms of manifesting religiosity that work both internally (inside the religious community), and externally (outside of the religious community). Using anthropological lenses, he posits that, internally, Emerging Christians attempt to create new religious forms that work for both "cultural durability and openness to transformation."[3] As an example from his ethnographic fieldwork, Bielo notes that his consultants utilize mainstream Christian resources as well as alternative resources from monastic and Eastern Orthodox traditions. By externally, Bielo posits that the internal moves inform and influence other Christian institutions. He asserts that the Emerging Christians' creativity of worship and programming influence the structures of other Christian institutions including various Christian denominations, (para)denominations and traditions.

This chapter seeks to build from Bielo's attention to cultural change by analyzing the ways in which Emerging Christians in the Upper South (Kentucky, Tennessee, and North Carolina) are in continual negotiation with a broader form of pervasive Protestantism existent within this context. Yet as stated in the opening paragraph, religion is also in constant navigation with sociocultural structures, institutions, and modifications. Thus, this research expands this notion of cultural change to include the

---

1. For more on "Emerging Christianities," see Bielo, "The Question of Cultural Change"; Moody and Reed, "Emerging Christianity and Religious Identity"; and Martí and Ganiel, *The Deconstructing Church*.

2. Bielo, "The Question of Cultural Change."

3. Bielo, "The Question of Cultural Change," 23.

broader sociopolitical discourses existent in this complex, regional cultural web. This chapter argues that these Emerging Christianities are not only in direct and indirect discourses with other Christianities but also with a broader regional structure that regulates life in the Upper South. Once the structures are illuminated, then the attempts at reconfiguring religious life—individually and collectively—can be understood as direct challenges to this regulative system encompassing all aspects of life. My ethnographic research reveals a manifesting dissatisfaction with the culture war metanarrative and the regional structures of the Upper South by some initially socialized into culture war Christianity. This dissatisfaction prompts many to disaffiliate with Christianity, but for others they remain in the Christian tradition hoping to reform from within. This positions two competing forms of Christianity within the milieu—a culture war Christianity and a newer, emerging form of Christianity.

Working from ethnographic data collected over eighteen months (2016 to 2018), this research posits that a rich, regional snapshot of Emerging Christianities in the Upper South manifests once religious identification, ritual and experimentation of these communities are examined in light of an over-determined context. In order to support these finding, this research argues, along with Bernadette Barton, that a Bible Belt panopticon monitors various aspects of individuation within this region.[4] This leads to the conclusion that Emerging Christians within this context seek to *disidentify* from the particular form of Christianity so dominant in the region *and* craft a new form of Christianity that dismantles the panoptive structures of the Bible Belt bringing into sharper relief the experimentations with religious forms.

The Bible Belt Panopticon and Disidentification

In the Bible Belt region, a particularly conservative form of Protestantism continues to dominate the landscape. The present-day form of this conservative Protestantism incorporates a religio-political metanarrative, referred to as a culture war, and maintains a generational prominence.[5] Although too broad to completely explicate here, the idea of a culture war is predicated on a "political and social hostility rooted in different systems of moral understanding. The end to which these hostilities tend

4. Barton, *Pray the Gay Away.*

5. Hunter, *Culture Wars*; Wuthnow, *The Restructuring of American Religion.*

is the domination of one cultural and moral ethos over all others."[6] The adoption and dissemination of this culture war metanarrative in the Bible Belt region creates strict symbolic boundaries between who is not accepted only as Christian, but truly American, and regionally who truly is Southern. By blurring the lines between national, regional and religious identity, the metanarrative engenders religio-political energy revolving around numerous crises of loss—losses of a Christian nation, a Christian majority, Christian principles, and Christian faith—caused by various identified enemies (homosexuals, domestic and international political actors, and minorities).

This culture war version of Christianity continues to captivate multiple strands of conservative Protestants across denominational and categorical lines like Evangelicals, Fundamentalists, Pentecostals, some Mainline churches, and even some Catholics in the Upper South. Because of the complications with taxonomies internal to conservative Protestant Christianity and due to the successful congealing of the religio-political metanarrative, it is useful to refer to this particular kind of Christianity hereto forth as "culture war Christianity."[7] Hence this chapter argues that, although there are differences in theologies and forms of worship in various denominations, the culture war metanarrative is ubiquitous across conservative Christianity in the Upper South. It is not that distinctions within religious groups are uninformative, but that culture war Christianity is determinative in many of the values and engagements of conservative Christian groups.

Culture war Christianity exemplifies the power and prowess of a religiosity that undergirds a broader cultural system in operation. Churches, Christian colleges, and parachurches, along with other Christian symbols, permeate the region. These symbols supply a form of external

6. Wuthnow, *The Restructuring of American Religion*, 42.

7. Because Protestantism is constituted with various forms that each seek to highlight particular distinctions, categorization are quite problematic. Denominational categories like Baptist, Method, Presbyterian, Lutheran and Assemblies of God note particular institutional differences of doctrine, structure, and leadership. Many of these denominations can be categorized under broader umbrellas of foundational theologians like Calvinism, Lutheranism and Anabaptists. Add to these categories the interdenominational categories like Evangelical, Mainline, Fundamentalist and Pentecostal and classification begins to become laborious and overlapping. To confuse the varieties of Protestantism further, non-mainstream movements like Jehovah's Witnesses, Amish, Mennonites, Latter Day Saints and current non-denominational trends seeking to disaffiliate with the denominational, theological, and interdenominational categories listed above muddy the waters of categorization even further.

pressure that monitors regional values and norms. And although numerous studies indicate the pervasiveness of these religious communities,[8] no one quite explicates the structural power of this conservative Protestantism like Bernadette Barton.[9] In her study of the South, Barton describes the physical dominance of this particular form of Christianity:

> Christian crosses, messages, paraphernalia, music, news, and attitudes saturate everyday settings. Bible Belt Christianity thus influences a wide range of local secular institutions like schools and workplaces, and Bible Belt Christians exert a powerful influence on city, county, and state political and cultural institutions.[10]

Thus, what is often overlooked are ways that the constructed power structures extend beyond strictly religious institutions and into the society. Because of the powerful influence of this style of Christianity, Barton calls this dominance the "Bible Belt panopticon." Using Foucault's notion of the modern world being surveilled by regimes of power to ensure the regulation of members, Barton argues that this rural panopticon, "manifests through tight social networks of family, neighbors, church, and community members, and plethora of Christian signs and symbols sprinkled through the region."[11] In her work, she specifically examines the ways that the panoptive mechanisms attempt to monitor and regulate sexuality, but my research finds that the panopticon works from both heteropatriarchal and systemically racist norms. In sum, culture war Christianity and Christian symbols are important parts of a broad structural regime that attempts to regulate politics, religion, familial life, social networks and economics.

Barton's notion of the Bible Belt panopticon is extremely useful in understanding the dominance of the panoptive structures in the Upper South.[12] Unless one has traveled or lived in the area, it is difficult to

---

8. Wilson, "Preachin', Prayin', and Singin'"; Najar, *Evangelizing the South*; Thompson, *The New Mind of the South*.

9. Barton, *Pray the Gay Away*; Barton, "1CROSS + 3NAILS = 4GVN."

10. Barton, *Pray the Gay Away*, 14.

11. Barton, *Pray the Gay Away*, 24.

12. Barton notes the powerful impact and the broad ways that Christianity operates in the Upper South. She prefers to call this form of religion "compulsory Christianity." I think that she is correct to note the unavoidable form of Christianity in the South. This research notes that even those who have not attended any church in the area are quite familiar with the religio-political metanarrative described herein. But

overestimate the extensive control the Bible Belt panopticon maintains through both visible and invisible means. One consultant on my project aptly describes the controlling power within the region: "You can't be yourself. You have to watch what you say. You can't be an individual. There's always someone watching and judging."

The panoptive mechanisms operate through the symbolic and physical structures that permeate the region but also through intense socialization for many who are acculturated through culture war Christianity. This socialization includes an alignment of political, religious and familial components all predicated on the notion of an ongoing culture war. The church becomes the primary institution for disseminating this culture war ideology.

The discursive ways in which these two forms of Christianity contend in the region are demonstrated through the project consultants attempt to religiously identify. The consultants spent the majority of their formative years in culture war churches and are currently in the process of formulating a different kind of Christianity in response to their upbringing. The responsive posturing creates the need to differentiate. As one consultant explains, "When I identify, I always start out with 'I'm Christian, but. . .'" or others simply identify as "progressive Christian." Still others struggle to explain their religious identity altogether. Nathan (thirties, Kentucky) acknowledges, "As much as it might make me uncomfortable at times based on other Christians' actions, I would identify as Christian, but I tell people that [my family and I] are a little different. I don't really have a name for it." Each of these rhetorical techniques highlights the shifting understanding of the category Christian by the project's consultants. Whether an Emerging Christian identifies as "Christian + Disclaimer" or attaches "progressive" or "liberal" to Christian as a label, the goal is the same—to claim a form of the identity "Christian" which succeeds in adequately describing who they are within the milieu. And this identity is based on differentiation. To identify as simply Christian makes one complicit with culture war Christianity and, therefore, all the inherent values and norms associated with it. Moreover, the nuances of identity also reveal a means of engaging with broader sociocultural structures. In this way, these Christians within the Upper South find it

---

this research finds that compulsory Christianity is quite generic in nature. It gives little information as to what it is obliging Christians and non-Christians to adhere to or to practice. Instead, culture war Christianity locates the specific nature of religio-political ideology.

necessary to both identify as the dominant religious category (Christian) and also attempt to redefine that same category. The term Christian in this sense is more than mere affiliation; rather, it is a struggle to define one's self, the religious tradition of Christianity, *and* the regional culture over and against a particularly repressive context.

This form of identification parallels what José Esteban Muñoz calls "disidentification."[13] Muñoz recognizes that disidentity is a way in which people must, "work with/resist the conditions of (im)possibility that dominant culture generates."[14] Disidentification supplies a more nuanced lens that recognizes the dominant identity formations and situates these identity formations in relation to structures of power. The regimented and monitored space of the panoptive structures creates the necessity for emerging Christians to engage with the dominant identification of "Christian" while reclaiming their variations on this identity. The working with/resistance to is constituted through laborious, ongoing processes— working, negotiating, reworking, renegotiating. In this way, disidentification becomes the norm for emerging Christians in the Upper South. Furthermore, disidentification engages beyond religious identification in working to dismantle and reconstruct the structures of the Bible Belt panopticon—political, ecclesiological and familial. This is exemplified in the praxis of the Emerging Church in the Upper South.

Social Results of Disidentification

Once one begins to disidentify from culture war Christianity and the broader milieu, social networks tend to fracture. Since religious community is the centralizing and mobilizing institution of culture war Christianity and the Upper South's panoptic structures, it might make sense that many disidentifiers would look outside of religious community as a means of rebuilding social networks. In fact, this is the case in several instances. Numerous consultants discuss yoga and art classes, sporting commitments, and hobby groups that they find allow them to reconstruct communal life.[15] But more often than not, church community

13. Muñoz, *Disidentifications*.

14. Muñoz, *Disidentifications*, 6.

15. More work should be conducted on this topic. To limit religious, spiritual, or sacred activities to institutions recognized by scholarship as religious creates a restrictive set of guidelines for constructing analyses. Works highlighting fandoms, popular culture, sporting commitments, etc. could provide keen insight into how many culture

continues to be the primary place to challenge existing social norms. As a means of detailing these challenges to the dominant social norms, this research utilizes the communion ritual and experimentation with church to demonstrate the interplay of religiosity with the panoptive structures.

The communion ritual in culture war Christianity is a means of acknowledging and granting full membership into the church community but also into the broader authority system. By participating in the communion ritual, it can be argued that Christians within the Upper South are indicating their allegiance to the Bible Belt panopticon.[16] Alternatively, the ritual of communion can serve also as a mechanism of exclusion within this milieu for those unwilling to fully acquiesce to the demands of the Bible Belt. Responsively, in all of the Emerging Christian communities of this research, an intense focus on broadening the inclusive borders of the communion ritual is evident. To understand these movements of inclusivity, one must understand the generative histories of those participating in Emerging Christian churches.

Kathy's (twenties, Kentucky) experiences accentuate the often-fragile family relationships that exist after one decides to disidentify from culture war Christianity. Speaking of the religious involvement of her youth, Kathy describes herself as "entrenched in the mentality" of culture war Christianity. Thus, when she made the decision to begin attending church with her husband who attends an Emerging Christian community, she explains that she was originally uncomfortable in the new church space. Two aspects of her husband's church disturbed her sensibilities. The first aspect dealt with people's attire at the Emerging Christian community. Her previous church experience included very specific, formal ways for women and men to dress. Women wore dresses and men wore shirt and tie. Although this initially perturbed her, she admits that she quickly adjusted to more informal attire.

The other, more troubling, element of the Emerging Christian community, according to Kathy, pertained to the communion ritual. Unlike her previous church that restricted communion to members only, the Emerging Christian community practices a weekly open communion

---

war Christians transition into other forms of "'religion."

16. This is a statement that certainly requires further elucidation and is part of a broader study of the culture from which Emerging Christianities manifest in the Upper South. But this statement might also apply to other regions of the United States where the church serves as the civil religious epicenter. To take communion is to demonstrate ritually one's commitment to the nation-state system.

table—anyone, visitor/member, Christian/non-Christian is permitted to participate in the ritual. Another interviewee proudly describes a time when a Sikh visited the church and took communion with everyone else in attendance. Even after a discussion with the lead minister, Kathy recounts that she still maintained her positions regarding the exclusivity of the Lord's Supper. But during our interview, she chronicles that a return visit to the church of her youth changed her position regarding communion. Kathy told me that her church holds a "homecoming service" each year to attract those who were a part of the church and have either transitioned to another church or have relocated away from the area. She was happy to attend with her parents and grandparents. Yet at the communion time of the service, the elders of the church prepared the ritual elements, which they began to distribute to the attendees. It is customary in many Southern Protestant churches to have the male leadership disseminate the bread and wine (grape juice) pew by pew. Kathy describes what happened: "I went back to visit [my previous church]. I had already removed my [church] membership. I was not offered communion. They skated right by me." Continuing Kathy explains, "I felt rejected, overlooked, looked down upon. I felt apart from the community." After reflecting on this experience, Kathy decided that the open practices of the Emerging Christian community resonated with her. "It meant a lot to be excluded. I don't like the hate."

Kathy's personal religious experience of exclusion altered her perspectives regarding the primary sacrament of her Christian faith. Kathy states, "It's one of the reasons that I have not been back [to the church of her youth]." Like Kathy, others in the study relay stories of religious exclusion that pushes them to be more welcoming of others.

Take for instance Miller (thirties, North Carolina) who details his story of excommunication. Born in North Carolina, he states, "I was raised in a religiously moderate home. You went to church because that was the right thing to do." After participation in some parachurch organizations like FCA (Fellowship of Christian Athletes) at his high school, Miller claims, "I became way more conservative in my faith than my parents were." When explaining why this was the case, he suggests that culture war Christianity, "offered me a certain kind of rigidness. This was an expression of faith that made sense to me for about ten years."

His participation within this church came to a close, however, when he and his wife chose to get a divorce. At this point, Miller recalls that formal proceedings were initiated to excommunicate him from his church and denomination. He had been an active member within the music program of the church even traveling the country representing the denomination. "It was sad, shameful, and hilarious at the same time. Church discipline withholds communion from those under discipline. They announce in every pulpit in the [denomination's conference], 'This person does not have salvation.'" Because of the withholding of communion and the ostracizing, Miller left his culture war church seeking another Christian community.

Like Kathy, Miller's personal experiences of exclusion from the church inform his more inclusionary values and practices today. Numerous other stories of personal exclusion manifest during the interview processes. Supplementing these stories are various stories detailing others' treatment that inform consultant's perspectives of the communion ritual.

Joan (forties, Kentucky) recounts that as a little girl, the members of her culture war church volunteered to physically erect a new church building. She remembers her stepdad, who was not a member of the church, laboring each evening after he completed his day job of being a carpenter to assist with the building. When she asked her stepdad why he was so adamant in assisting with the construction project, he simply responded, "It's the right thing to do." At the completion of the project, the church held a grand opening service. Her stepdad proudly attended since he had built strong relationships with the men of the church during construction. Yet her stepdad was prohibited from taking the communion even after he had contributed his labor and time. Joan says, "This experience stuck with me after all these years." To this day, Joan supports the attempts of her emerging Christian community to broaden the inclusionary parameters.

Relational experiences vis-à-vis the communion ritual profoundly transform and affect the viewpoints of many people within this study. To personally experience ostracization from one's religious community within a culture war Christian milieu can effectively motivate the ostracized to work toward alleviating such practices for themselves and others. Thus, the expansion of who is included and permitted to participate in the communion ritual signals a shift in the normative way of constructing this ritual in the Bible Belt region; however, it should be argued that this is also a means of challenging the strict boundaries inherent in the panoptive structure. Racial, religious, sexual and gender hierarchies are reconfigured within the church institution. By permitting non-Christians and Christian disidentifiers to fully integrate into the religiously communal activities, a subversive dismantling of the entire panoptive structures of clearly defined boundaries occurs. But these reconfigurations also signal a restructuring within Southern society.

As the panoptive mechanism reveals itself as exclusionary, new modes of disidentification manifest seeking to create a religious community that works both within the authority structure and challenges that same structure. The communion ritual is still central to the church gathering and often practiced in similar forms to other churches in the area, but boundaries are restructured. Like the communion ritual, other forms of church praxis are also considered malleable within Emerging Christian communities. This is one way in which an understanding of the experimental models of emerging Christians begins to manifest. Church gatherings become spaces for trying new forms of religious cultivation. Numerous consultants denote the exploratory modes of operating that is inherent within their religious communities:

> We teach people to experiment with alternative forms of Christian community. —Lucas (twenties, NC)

> We are in an unfolding tradition and story. So there are always new things to be said, new experiences to be had. —Jackson (thirties, KY)

> We are orthodox in that we are comfortably struggling with and within the Christian tradition. —Travis (fifties, NC)

> You can't understand freedom of worship until you've been a slave in worship. —Claire (sixties, KY)

> We are looking at some of these different elements of Christianity—the life of Jesus, God, heaven or the afterlife—we're looking at all of these more traditional elements and saying, 'yes and it's so much bigger than we ever realized.' Which is really exciting and fun for us. Which parts of the traditions that we carry so deeply within us are helpful as we continue on this journey. What pieces of that feel genuine and true that would be helpful and healthy to carry with us. —Abigail (thirties, TN)

The idea, however, that these churches are simply spaces for cultivating religious orientations constrains the purposes of the religious community. Instead, church for Emerging Christians extends beyond the institution and is holistically political, religious, personal, educational, and relational. Church is understood as a place to experiment with religious expression, but the institutional model of church is expanded to include domains outside of traditional forms to build relationships. Religious community then becomes a place for creatively and collectively (re)imagining what social community could be in direct contradistinction to the broader sociopolitical regimes of power.

At one of the church sites for this research, a leader within the church explains, "We want to have a space for people to gather and let people do what they do." The leader is identified with the title of *cultivator* not as minister, pastor, or reverend. This person's job is to create spaces for people to build relations around physical work. At first, this sounds like a charismatic form of church worship where minimal planning occurs to allow the "spirit to move." But the statement from this church leader references intentionality outside of the church worship service. Lucas (twenties, NC) describes some of the spaces as "cultivating the soil, beekeeping and raising chickens" with a purpose of "making connections." He went so far as to explain, "creating community is church." When asked if this is simply a marketing maneuver to increase membership, he responds, "Participants don't have to believe like us. It's not a backdoor 'come to our church.' That's not our plan. It's not our job to dictate belief."

This church emphasizes the usage of their space for the cultivation of relationships and religiosity in a mode corresponding with what Matthew Crawford calls *soulcraft*.[17] Critiquing modern marketplace theories, Crawford argues that the agency of human "interaction with his world through hands . . . highlight[s] the appeal of manual work in a way that is neither romantic nor nostalgic, but simply gives credit to the practice of building things, fixing things and routinely tending to things, as an element of human flourishing."[18] He continues to argue that the working with one's hands is what it means to be human. Church, in a soulcraft manner, becomes a workshop of sorts for interfacing with the milieu through hands-on techniques.

Like Crawford's notions, another experimental model of church that was discovered during these field operations provides insights into how church can be reconfigured beyond the normative, institutional scope. There is a small group of Emerging Christians who have started a microbrewery in the Upper South. The microbrewery is the earliest stages

17. Crawford, *Shop Class as Soulcraft*.
18. Crawford, *Shop Class as Soulcraft*, 64.

of operation; however, the unique aspects of this microbrewery are two-fold. The brewery includes a "common space" for community events and the entrepreneurs are theologically trained ministers with understandings that the brewery is church. Regarding the former, the facility itself is built with a large, open area that can house various types of events. Thus far, the microbrewery has housed wedding ceremonies, weekly open-mic nights for the local community arts program, community potluck meals, and organizing room for participating in political marches. Yet the space is also unique for what is not physically present. There are no Bibles, no crosses, no Bible studies, no attempt to convert anyone to a particular religion, and no label of church posted anywhere. The brewery is not an outreach of a church or denomination with the intentions of recruiting members. Building a space for community to emerge is central. And for the proprietors of the facility, their work is religious. One owner notes that cultivating the common good is church and that brewing the best beer possible is his Christian discipline. He further explains that he holds his Christianity loosely (as far as a label) and seeks to discover the "path of Jesus through the economics of the brewery, the relationships with the community, and through everyday theological conversations in a non-violent and non-forceful way."

Church, like other recent moves to value craftsmanship (farmers' markets, mechanics, artistry), can be understood as a space that highly respects and values the physical nature of life lived and creative explorations. Church in this way might be thought of as an active humanist venture where systemic theology becomes less relevant, but physical creativity to construct the sacred is prized. Due to this, the frameworks of denominations or doctrines collapse under the weight of these ventures; instead, analytical frameworks that include beauty, relevance, authenticity, relational components, and craftsmanship supply more appropriate ways of approaching these constructs. In other words, to craft an excellent beer might correspond to crafting a good church, which is understood as crafting quality relationships.

If the constructed world of the Upper South is understood as over-determined for numerous people, broadly speaking, but also including ecclesiological structures, then one can begin to see the correlations of artisanal projects and the valuing of handiwork and craftsmanship within these religious communities. This might be able to be understood as a new epistemology in the Heidegger sense where, "the nearest kind of association is not merely perceptual cognition, but, rather, a handling, using, and taking care of things which has its own kind of 'knowledge.'"[19] For the consultants of this project, knowing church is parallel to the praxis of crafting church. This form of ecclesiological epistemology works at religious life by coming at it indirectly.

More than religious marketplace demands, the Emerging Christian community can be understood as a posture of attentiveness to a project. Crawford suggests, "Getting it right demands that you be *attentive* in the way of conversation rather than *assertive* in the way of a demonstration."[20] The way for Emerging Christians to work in forming what church should be, then, is through the ongoing process of tinkering with the elements and introducing new components. Differing ecclesiological variations yield new results, both of failure and success.

Nevertheless, the crafting of church also participates in a broader discourse in direct relation to the Bible Belt panopticon. Here, church is the means of perpetuating the panoptic system. Individuals are monitored through a specific way of constructed church. There is certainly some room for differences within the Bible Belt, but in order to be acknowledged as church, certain formations and protocols must be maintained. The religious sites of this project confirm that certain forms are followed like the communion rituals. Yet there is more occurring within these cultivations of church that subversively undermine the dominance of the culture war metanarrative. Through the creation of new forms of ecclesiology that are typically unrecognized by the Bible Belt panopticon, fresh expressions of Christianity *can* emerge. A microbrewery and gardening are less understood as church, broadly speaking, within this milieu; consequently, these domains provide a space for new kinds of religious explorations to engage with cultural change.

The religious communities of Emerging Christians in the Upper South include both laborious fashioning and are heavily influenced by previous, exclusionary religious episodes. Many new experimental and experiential forms of church provide a venue for emerging Christians to build new relationships with people of various religious orientations seeking to discover what church and society can be. Nevertheless, these religious communities physically exist in a region regulated by an enormous network of churches, communities, and associations. Like the personal relationships that must be navigated with family and friends,

19. Heideggar, *Being and Time*, 63.
20. Crawford, *Shop Class as Soulcraft*, 82.

collective groups must also negotiate numerous interactions with other churches, other religious communities, and social organizations.

Several cases where adverse responses to these religious communities epitomize a backlash directed at the churches:

> Do we get pushback? The denominations at times don't know what to do with this ... What kind of metrics do you use for [our church]? Maybe our metric is the stories that we tell and how we know each other? —Lucas (twenties, NC)

> [Our church] is not very popular at all. There have been Facebook posts with pastors calling us heretics from traditional churches. It's difficult. I'm a traditional guy and grown up around here and all of a sudden people react differently to me. It's a serious thing. —Taylor (fifties, KY)

> When you challenge people's long held religious beliefs, they can really get upset. It's interesting how it works out. We've had a backlash from other churches when we invited certain speakers to our church. —Jackson (thirties, KY)

Like inviting certain speakers, some of the actions of the church receive particularly harsh reactions from community members. For example, one of the churches took a group from their congregation to a local Islamic center with a goal of breaking down any possible stereotypes of Muslims that congregants might maintain. After the event, one of the church staff members posted some pictures of the event with a caption of "Our Muslim brothers and sisters" on the church's social media page. This resulted in several threatening responses from other Christians and non-Christians in the area. Further instances include one church being picketed by the infamous Westboro Baptist Church once they announced that they were gay affirming. Moreover, the children of members of these churches are often the targets of bullying within the local school systems. Diana (forties, KY) recounts that her son has been the object of mocking at his school because he "doesn't go to a real church" or that his pastor is a "heretic." Another Emerging Christian community in Tennessee told me that other churches "gun for them"—a revealing metaphor. She claims that her daughter was also "bullied about her religion."

The institutional forms of Emerging Christian communities experience episodes where portions of the membership leave the church altogether due to specific stances adopted by the church. "With every broadening of the boundaries, you lose people. People that you love.

That's the downside," conveys Martha (forties, TN). As a female in leadership of her church, she explains, "I'm a target on all sides. I'm a target because I'm a woman, outspoken and strong, a woman with position and platform. It's complicated and empowering all at the same time." Many of the consultants of this project might agree with Martha's "complicated and empowering" description.

Through this research, numerous stories were told about how churches and Christians attempt to regulate the practices of the Emerging Churches in the Upper South. To add to this, the consultants also revealed stories describing how they lost jobs and financial opportunities due to their participation in an Emerging Church.

Conclusion and Discussion

Church experimentation is not only a portion of religious life, but of the sociopolitical lives of Emerging Christians in direct and indirect discourse with the dominant structures existent in the Bible Belt region. This extends Bielo's argument of discursive relations into thinking about how contextual social conditions inform church interactions. And this research highlights the fact that there is a craft to navigating this discourse. Focusing on building relationships with the religious and non-religious Other through religious rituals and constructions constitutes overstepping the panoptive parameters. Broadening the boundaries of who is included in the communion ritual is a way of dismantling an essential ritual within the milieu and challenging the religio-political meta-narrative of culture war Christianity. Furthermore, it is a tangible way of knowing what church is.

These communities also provide another value for Emerging Christians. Abigail (thirties, TN) explains why she continues to maintain the label Christian and participate in church as she transitions away from culture war Christianity in this revealing statement:

> [Leaving Christianity], that's the final frontier. You can still label yourself [as a Christian], but differ on beliefs. We can call ourselves Christians and disagree on whatever points of theology, but once you remove that label of Christian, then what? Then you're just floating out in the ether. So letting go of that last little thread, that's the thread that connects everything. And once you let go of that thread, then what? I'm still willing to call myself a Christian and that doesn't bother me at all. It's more a matter of

whether that's allowable to the rest of the world. I'll just let [my Christianity] evolve into whatever it may be. That's the nature of my Christianity.

Abigail indicates that a world outside of the Christian category results in floating untethered. She keeps asking, "then what?" For many who have been socialized in the Upper South, the idea of withdrawing completely from Christianity is unimaginable at this moment in their lives. "That's the thread that connects everything," astutely argues Abigail. Christianity is understood as the continuing means of social cohesion.

Furthermore, Abigail's response recognizes the importance of maintaining a Christian designation in her milieu. If her response is read through the social realities of Bible Belt panopticon, to completely disaffiliate with Christianity is to lose a strategic means of challenging the regulatory system. Within this region, the labels of Christian and church carry with them a social and political currency. To fully disaffiliate from *Christian* results in a diminished ability to further disidentify. As Muñoz clearly offers, "Disidentification is about recycling and rethinking encoded meaning. The process of disidentification scrambles and reconstructs that encoded message of a cultural text that both exposes the encoded message's universalizing and exclusionary machinations."[21] Thus the collective groups of Emerging Christian disidentifiers can both confront and cooperate with the panoptive system. This is strategically important because "The political, cultural, and linguistic territory of movements such as the Religious Right must be occupied, colonized, and relandscaped from internal and contrary points of view."[22] Any deviation that continues to claim the monikers Christian and church within the structures of the Bible Belt panopticon both conforms to particular norms while simultaneously disputing the norms.

The result of these religious communities is collective disidentification attempting to dismantle or subvert the Bible Belt norms. Structurally in order to achieve any level of success in cultural change, Christianity is the *lingua franca* to engage in a continuing dialogue, both with other Christians and non-Christians in the region. Thus, this emerging form of Christianity exists in relationship to other forms of Christianity to be sure; but, just as significantly, this emerging form of Christianity exists in relationship to the regulatory devices of the Bible Belt. This is exceedingly

21. Muñoz, *Disidentifications*, 31.
22. Harding, "Get Religion," 360.

important in understanding this movement. Although it might be too early to quantify any large-scale impacts of cultural change within the region, it is conclusive that the effort is being made to reconfigure regional social norms.

Bibliography

Barton, Bernadette. "1CROSS + 3NAILS = 4GVN: Compulsory Christianity and Homosexuality in the Bible Belt Panopticon." *Feminist Formations* 23 (2011) 70–93.

———. *Pray the Gay Away: The Extraordinary Lives of Bible Belt Gays*. New York: New York University Press, 2012.

Bielo, James. "The Question of Cultural Change in the Social Scientific Study of Religion: Notes from the Emerging Church." *Journal for the Scientific Study of Religion* 56 (2017) 19–25.

Crawford, Matthew. *Shop Class as Soulcraft: An Inquiry Into the Value of Work*. New York: Penguin, 2009.

Harding, Susan. "Get Religion." In *The Insecure American: How We Got Here & What WeShould Do About It*," edited by Hugh Gusteron and Catherine Besteman, 345–61. Berkeley: University of California Press, 2010.

Heidegger, Martin. *Being and Time*. Translated by Joan Stambaugh. New York: State University of New York Press, 1996.

Hunter, James Davison. *Culture Wars: The Struggle to Define America*. New York: Basic, 1991.

Martí, Gerardo, and Gladys Ganiel. *The Deconstructed Church: Understanding Emerging Christianity*. Oxford: Oxford University Press, 2014.

Moody, Sarah, and Randall Reed. "Emerging Christianity and Religious Identity." *Journal for the Scientific Study of Religion* 56 (2017) 33–40.

Muñoz, José. *Disidentifications: Queers of Color and the Performance of Politics*. Minneapolis: University of Minnesota Press, 1999.

Najar, Monica. *Evangelizing the South: A Social History of Church and State in Early America*. Oxford: Oxford University Press, 2008.

Thompson, Tracy. *The New Mind of the South*. New York: Simon & Schuster, 2013.

Wilson, Charles Reagan. "Preachin', Prayin', and Singin' on the Public Square." In *Religion andPublic Life in the South: In the Evangelical Mode* edited by Charles Reagan Wilson and Mark Silk, 9–26. New York: AltaMira, 2005.

Wuthnow, Robert. *The Restructuring of American Religion*. Princeton, New Jersey: Princeton University Press, 1988.

3

Festivals as Experiential Spiritual Ritual Space for Millennials and Gen Z

STEPHANIE YUHAS

Abstract

Rejecting institutionalized and organized religious gatherings, millennials and Gen Z participants explore sacred space and ritual in a variety of genres and formats. The festival circuit in the Western United States provides a snapshot into the activities and experiences that millennials and their younger counterparts identify with spiritual expression. This chapter will explore several popular festivals, discuss what attracts young people to these events, and how spirituality and ritual are embedded in them. A survey of some of the more popular festivals will highlight how music festivals are shifting to transformational happenings and provide a glimpse into the multi-faceted offerings that encourage an experiential spirituality.

Rejecting institutionalized and organized religious gatherings, millennials and Gen Z participants explore sacred space and ritual in a variety of genres and formats. The festival circuit in the Western United States provides a snapshot into the activities and experiences that millennials and their younger counterparts identify with spiritual expression. Although many festivals appear at first glance to be about music and performance, the underlying draw to these events is an eclectic menu of spiritual practices, speakers, yoga, and healing offerings, as well as the chance to encounter like-minded participants. This chapter will explore several popular festivals, discuss what attracts young people to these events, and how spirituality and ritual are embedded in them. A survey of some of the more popular festivals will highlight how music festivals are shifting to transformational happenings and provide a glimpse into the multi-faceted offerings that encourage an experiential spirituality. Analysis of the role played by ritual, liminality, and communitas from the theoretical perspectives of VanGennep, Turner, and Eliade among others attempts to shed light on the elusive spiritual experience that seems to be missing in the lives of modern Western culture. In closing, I will share some thoughts on the COVID-19 pandemic and how this may shift our cultural engagement with large gatherings and festivals, and the potential to use the time of physical distancing to strengthen our resolve to find our inner truth and find ways to live into a reframed social structure.

The Allure of Festival Culture
and Transformational Festivals

The Sixties hippie culture that launched the Woodstock music festival, the Human Be-In at San Francisco's People's Park, and spurred fascination with exotic spiritual culture—from the Beatles relationship with Indian guru Maharishi Mahesh Yogi who founded Transcendental Meditation to the acid-infused religious experience of a Grateful Dead concert—foreshadow the transformational festival scene of the early twenty-first century. The adage of "sex, drugs, and rock and roll" and the appeal to "turn on, tune in, and drop out" uttered by Timothy Leary mark the aspirations of boomer culture, which are now being revived and reinvented by millennials and Gen Z seekers longing for a glimpse of the transcendent.

Music has always been an access point for spirituality in numerous traditions from Indian kirtan to indigenous ceremonies and the singing of hymns in the Protestant church. In the Sixties, music became the root of the counter-cultural experience, and many people experienced spiritual epiphanies at concerts, whether aided by substances or not. Observing the large crowds attending festivals from Coachella to South by

Southwest, it is evident that music still feeds a primal urge in people to gather, commune, and shift out of ordinary experience.

Over the past decade new types of festivals or gatherings have gained popularity, expanding from concert venue to a place to seek transcendent experiences on many levels. These countercultural festivals place an emphasis on community, sustainability, and personal expression. Personal growth, social change, and healthy lifestyles are focal points of these gatherings.

The term transformational festival was coined by documentary filmmaker Jeet Kei Leung in a 2010 TEDx talk in Vancouver.[1] As journalist Kim Doucette in *Rolling Stone* describes in an article on Leung:

> These are destinations where anything goes, active participation is encouraged, the weird is wonderful and eye contact, ecstatic dance, long hugs, incense, sacred space and psychedelics permeate the scene. The events tend to take place in a natural setting over multiple days and, according to Leung, all share "the co-creation of an immersive, participant driven reality." "We may never be able to define a set of characteristics that could guarantee a festival to be transformational," says Leung. "There's no doubt that many participants are having life-altering experiences at festivals and an increasingly coherent culture is emerging that fosters and supports these experiences."[2]

Although it is difficult to categorize these festivals, as each one attempts to create a unique identity, there are enough commonalities among them to give a basic overview of a few major festivals that have existed for at least a decade.[3] While musicians remain a large draw, the multitude of additional offerings creates the atmosphere for inner development including spiritual seminars and classes, yoga and embodied practices, ritual and

---

1. Leung, TEDx Talks, *Transformational Festivals.*

2. Doucette, "7 Wildest Transformational Festivals."

3. As Doucette describes: "Transformational festivals exhibit features commonly found in cults and new religious movements. The events are characterized by heightened transpersonalism, collective ecstasies, utopian narratives, and community allegiance. They attract the atypical attendance of a social class characterized by expendable amounts of financial and temporal wealth. Their charismatic deployment of spiritual and entheogenic information emboldened by on-site ecstatic experience closely parallels religious revivals. Attendees may disengage conservative social norms and identify as an 'evolved culture'—a worldview influenced by millenarian archetypes of planetary transcendence, and the evolution of consciousness." Doucette, "7 Wildest Transformational Festivals."

ceremony, drum circles, visionary art, organic vegan food, tarot readings and alternative bodywork such as massage and acupuncture. Held outdoors, the festivals provide an earth-based ethos, often punctuated by the celebration of entheogenic substances.

American Festival Culture

While festival culture is a global phenomenon, this chapter will focus on the American experience. For those interested in researching international gatherings, Envision in Costa Rica, Boom in Portugal, and Shambhala in British Columbia, Canada are among the most recognized festivals. Before exploring some of the specific festival activities, it will be helpful to consider what attracts millennials and Gen Z participants to engage in these gatherings.

In 2019, I conducted an informal survey on SBNR (Spiritual But Not Religious) trends with students in a graduate-level Religious Studies class. I asked them to locate at least five people to respond to the survey instrument and had one student compile the results. Out of sixty-nine respondents, fifty fell into the age range of millennials, four identified as Gen Z and the rest were Gen X.[4] Geographically, of those respondents who indicated their place of residence, 18 percent were from the East Coast, 35 percent from the Midwest, 15 percent from the South, 12 percent from the Mountain time zone and 20 percent from the West Coast. Based on a four-part Likert scale, forty-five people agreed or strongly agreed with the statement, "I find spirituality at music festivals I attend." A majority of the respondents agreed that their spirituality is embodied, that they identified with the label Spiritual But Not Religious, and that nature played a large role in their spirituality. About half were looking for a community of like-minded individuals or already followed a spiritual teacher outside of mainstream religion and attended yoga classes or workshops. Surprisingly with all the recent emphasis on entheogens, only about 20 percent acknowledged that psychedelics played a role in

4. Gallup Inc., MSW Research, the Resolution Foundation use 1980–1996, PricewaterhouseCoopers has used 1981 to 1995, and Nielsen Media Research has defined millennials as adults between the ages of twenty-two and thirty-eight years old in 2019. In 2014, U.S PIRG described millennials as those born between 1983 and 2000.

Gen Z: Gen Z is the newest generation to be named and were born between 1995 and 2015. They are currently between four and twenty-four years old (nearly 74 million in U.S.) Jul 29, 2019.

their spirituality. All of these characteristics find representation in the new wave of spiritually infused festival culture.

Indeed, over the past twenty years, music festivals have been slowly expanding beyond the embodied dance scene into the realms of mind and spirit. While Coachella set the tone for large festivals featuring established and emerging musicians, its growth since the inaugural event in 1999 has led to massive crowds, and a corporate culture that rivals South by Southwest (which also morphed from a small stage incubator for up-and-coming bands to a major annual event in Austin, Texas). At the same time, California is well-known for an edgy progressive spiritual scene from Esalen in Big Sur to Spirit Rock in Woodacre, in counterculture towns from Ojai to Mount Shasta. Thus, it is no surprise that the festivals began to incorporate more spiritual elements.

While music remains a thematic element in this new form of festival, there are elements of rave culture and psychedelic trance music that are interwoven, so rather than a list of bands, sometimes there are DJs who might create a late-night dance environment. The vibe is more participatory and embodied, more akin to a dance club than a concert hall. However, there are additional elements that earn these gatherings the label transformational festival.

> At TF [transformational festival] events, participants discuss new age, and neo-spiritual ideologies while maintaining a shared experience of leisure and openness. They dance as a unified ecstatic mass. They buy, sell and ingest a multiplicity of psychedelic narcotics. . . . They attend several workshops on tantric sexual healing, mediation, raw-food dieting, or astrological channeling. Attendees claim to be positively changed by the experience—hence their transformational label. Many TFs also advertise themselves as forbearers of a new worldview, with many of their attendees claiming to be a part of a larger social movement paving the way for a new planetary culture.[5]

A good example of this evolution is the Bhakti Fest that began in 2008 in Joshua Tree, but has its roots in the Woodstock generation. Founder Sridhar Silberfein promised his guru Swami Satchidananda during the 1969 Woodstock gathering that he would develop a festival devoted to raising consciousness. As one participant described it, "The festival is essentially Coachella for the higher consciousness community, offering a four-day schedule populated by yogis, devotional musicians,

5. Johner, "Transformational Festivals," 58.

lecturers, astrologers, and artists with names like Windsong and Light Hawk."[6] Mind, body, and spirit wellness is an important component of the offerings that range from classes and lectures to experiential sessions of bodywork, movement and dance, and visionary art making. There is a commercial side to these festivals with vendors selling everything from crystals to tarot readings, from yoga mats to essential oils.

Another name for these festivals is wellness festivals. While they offer esoteric music line-ups, the draw for many is the yoga culture that began with Hindu gurus offering exotic spiritual paths and developed into a billion- dollar industry as postural yoga. As Andrea Jain reminds us, "Many of the attempts to define postural yoga as essentially religious— most often as Hindu—or as essentially nonreligious (or nonspiritual)— most often, as mere exercise or commodification—betray a tendency to ignore the more complex perspectives of many insider to postural yoga."[7] Millennials began to adopt yoga for fitness and body sculpting, but then some recognized the shallowness of their approach and incorporated yoga philosophy and spiritual practice.

Many local and regional festivals are incorporating yoga teachers and meditation sessions to appeal to this group who are seeking something meaningful beyond dancing and alcohol. An article in *The Guardian* noted:

> Elena Byers, the curator of Mesa, the wellbeing space at Meadows in the Mountains [a festival in Bulgaria], said there had been a rise in music festivals adding a wellness element. "Absolutely. I find as a teacher as well you've got more and more people who come to festivals now than ever before and they are much more curious and open-minded about things like wellbeing . . . They feel more inclined to try stuff that they haven't before." She said the diversity of what was on offer had also changed. "It used to be that there were just yoga classes but now you've got more interesting things, like you've got chanting circles and cacao ceremonies or breath work."

It comes as young people turn their backs on alcohol. Research, published in the journal *BMC Public Health*, found more than 25 percent of young people classed themselves as "non-drinkers." Those behind the study said abstaining from alcohol was becoming "more mainstream" among people aged 16 to 24 after the analysis showed a rise in the proportion of

6. Bain, "I Tried to Find Spiritual Enlightenment."

7. Jain, *Selling Yoga*, 169.

non-drinkers. "The sober movement is also a huge part of what is happening with festivals . . . It's becoming more socially acceptable not to drink so people at festivals don't have the same peer pressure,' said Holbrook [founder of spiritual wellbeing platform Otherness].[8]

At Bhakti Fest, the minority of attendees, just 9 percent, are under thirty with a hefty segment of millennials, 26 percent, between the ages of thirty and thirty-nine.[9] By comparison, the audience at Lightning in a Bottle is described as a mix of mature and affluent members of the Lifestyle of Health and Sustainability demographic mix (thirty-five to forty-four) and a younger (eighteen to thirty-five) trendsetting demographic who are estimated as 75 percent of attendees.[10]

As this blogger describes it, "Elements of Bhakti culture have seeped into the West Coast 'transformational festival' circuit–Lightning in a Bottle, Symbiosis, Lucidity–where it's possible to hear a lecture on awakening into divine love before getting blasted on nitrous and going to see Lee Burridge."[11] All of these festivals are held outdoors and include musical performances, but each has a different appeal and location. Lightning in a Bottle was conceived at a birthday party near Santa Barbara and moved to a more remote location in central California. In 2019, the festival moved to Buena Vista Lake near Bakersfield and featured yoga classes; visionary lectures; artistic creation zones; and multiple stages designed to resemble flowers, trees, and other natural edifices that add depth to an eclectic selection of world and electronic music. LIB is environmentally conscious with power generated from solar and biodiesel, no small feat when the annual attendance is close to 20,000. Beloved is another popular festival held annually in Tidewater, Oregon. Their website describes it succinctly.

> Held in a stunning coastal forest a few hours south of Portland, Beloved focuses on "presenting a highly curated combination of sacred music and a carefully chosen sequence of artists to tell a continuous story." All of the action takes place on one stage, so "when festival-goers want to jam out, they are all doing so in the same place at the same time, which creates a powerful, unifying force." Beloved's definition of sacred music represents a large swath of ancient, contemporary and futuristic sounds, joined by their ability to incite "deep joy and reverence." From

8. Marsh, "Boom in Wellness at Festivals."
9. Taylor, "Inside One of the Year's Biggest Trends."
10. Bloom Connections, "Lightning in a Bottle."
11. Bain, "I Tried to Find Spiritual Enlightenment."

Middle-Eastern chants and obscure instruments to thumping EDM (Electronic Dance Music), past lineups showcased artists as diverse as Krishna Daas and the Les Nubians with more traditional EDM DJs like Rob Garza and Cut Chemist. "Part spiritual awakening, part music festival, Beloved is a classic west coast transformational festival," says Chip Conley. "It's not Coachella. It's not superficial. You better be ready to eye-gaze with a few wide-eyed fellow attendees and if sacred ain't your thing, Beloved ain't your festival."[12]

Across the globe and in America, the face of festival culture is changing. As millennials begin to have children, they are looking for family friendly events sans alcohol and drugs. Young people, and by that I mean anyone under 40, are increasingly aware of their ecological footprint and respond positively to festivals that have a sustainability ethos. They are looking for festivals that are outdoors, are carbon neutral, and minimize plastic bottles. Young people are increasingly health conscious and are drawn to events that feature yoga, jogging, and even group exercise. They have a desire to form community and to participate in educational workshops that range from aromatherapy to sound healing. According to Theo Larn-Jones, co-founder of the Love Trails festival, "Basically, the crux of it is that it is tapping into the desire from, especially younger people—so those in their twenties and thirties—to live fuller and healthier lives and feel good."[13]

Why do young people opt out of traditional religions and convene in interspiritual activities found at festivals? According to Netanel Miles-Yepez, co-founder of the HeartFire festival in New York and Boulder, Colorado, "Festivals are radically fun multi-media experiences, while mainstream religions are identified with forms associated with parents and grandparents. Young people want a primal experience, an opportunity to engage with the exotic."[14] Miles-Yepez noted that millennials and particularly Gen Z individuals were feeling disconnected and socially isolated even before the COVID-19 pandemic created the need for "social distancing." A desire for community and authentic embodied spiritual teachings are at the top of the list for young people whose idealistic vision of transforming society resonates with the vision of the Aquarian Age promised in the Sixties. Although several large festivals are designed

12. Official website: www.belovedfestival.com
13. Marsh, "Boom in Wellness at Festivals."
14. Netanel Miles-Yepez, personal conversation, May 28. 2020.

around yoga, tai chi, and qigong, along with other embodied practices, there is a sense that the sincere intentions of some festivals may be perverted and subverted by commercialism and financial interests.

Although immediate gratification appears to be the demand of many young people, a growing number are looking for deeper meaning and challenges to bring transformative energy into their lives. Miles-Yepez, a millennial, is a student of Jewish Renewal founder, Rabbi Zalman Schachter-Shalomi. Together, they co-founded the Sufi-Hasidic, Inayati-Maimuni Order, fusing the Sufi and Hasidic principles of spirituality and practice espoused by Rabbi Avraham Maimuni in thirteenth century Egypt with the teachings of the Ba'al Shem Tov and Hazrat Inayat Khan. Miles-Yepez, who teaches Sufism at Naropa, collaborated with a recent graduate Yasha Wagner to put on the HeartFire festival in Boulder and New Lebanon, New York. His festivals feature highly regarded spiritual teachers, including Ven. Pannavati, (a former African American Christian pastor now ordained in the Buddhist Theravada and Mahayana traditions), Maestro Manuel Rufino (an indigenous elder in the Taino tradition), and Rabbi Tirzah Firestone (a highly regarded Jewish Renewal teacher). Spiritual teachings, art, local food, breathwork, astrology, bodywork, qigong, and sacred fire are among the offerings at these gatherings.

Of course, festivals can also be places of superficial spirituality, often associated with a culture of substance use to access transcendent experiences. MDMA, mushrooms, and ayahuasca are among the entheogens most often referenced at festivals, with an accompanying presence of people providing harm reduction. This chapter would be negligent if it did not mention the psychedelic culture frequently invoked by young people seeking a fast, immediate way to access spiritual experience. HeartFire co-founder, Yasha S. Wagner, recalls:

> I remember one massive festival, which included a large encampment of Indigenous elders and Native wisdom-keepers of various nations and tribes . . . They were keeping a large sacred fire for ceremony and prayer, and I'll never forget the look on their faces as drunk party-goers passed by, throwing cigarette butts in their ceremonial fire and swearing disruptively in that sacred space . . . I knew then that we needed a festival environment that could better hold and represent our sacred traditions.[15]

---

15. Yasha Wagner, personal correspondence.

Creating a culture of respect for traditions that spiritual seekers draw from is an important component that is often overlooked. While festivals are generally open to all forms of spiritual practice, few advocate the awareness that HeartFire cultivates. A key consideration for scholars is to view how today's youth borrow from other traditions to create their own hybrids of spirituality and how this practice might inform the reinvigoration of more established religions, while at the same time analyzing how the inter-spiritual nature of millennial and Gen Z spiritual exploration intersects with race, ethnicity, and cultural appropriation in ways that can be problematic.

White Utopias, a recent monograph by Amanda Lucia, notes that, "few scholarly works on transformational festivals focus on ethnicity. Among American scholars of religion, in many cases, it is an unacknowledged fact that practitioners of Mesmerism, Spiritualism, New Thought, meditation, and yoga were (and are) white."[16] Indeed, cultural appropriation runs rampant throughout festivals, the New Age movement, and the bricolage of SBNR practices. Offerings borrow from Native American ritual, Hindu fire ceremonies, and Tibetan ritual to name a few. Ironically, persons of color are often excluded from these festivals, not by design, but by the high cost of the events and the predominantly white culture that pervades them. In our current era, this seems to be a condition of white privilege, that allows certain groups the time and money to explore their own personal spiritual reality without engaging the diversity of humanity.

While this is a problematic aspect to be called out, I would also suggest that both African Americans and Native Americans, for example, have insisted that they must do their own healing work within their own groups, before they can join a more united effort.[17] White Americans also have work to do to recognize their contributions to oppression, and by feeling more secure in their own spirituality, they may generate more compassion and empathy in reaching out to marginalized groups rather than reacting in fear.[18]

16. Lucia, *White Utopias*, 16.

17. Further reading on this issue includes Alfred, *Peace, Power, Righteousness*; Weaver, *Trauma and Resilience*; and Deloria and Deloria, *The World We Used to Live In*.

18. Menakem, *My Grandmother's Hands*; Saad, *Me and White Supremacy*.

Burning Man—A Ritualized Festival of Transformation

A discussion of festival culture would be incomplete if it did not include the festival that set the tone for many of the current offerings. For all its flaws, Burning Man is the most referenced, analyzed, and innovative of all these transformative events. The Burning Man festival held annually in Black Rock City, Nevada, is considered the prototype of festivals since its original gathering in 1990. Burning Man's reputation as a place for inner transformative rituals has made it appealing to younger generations seeking sacred experiences. The average age of attendees from 2013 to 2019 is thirty-five.[19] The freedom of self-expression and self-transformation is touted by the festival goers as a primary reason for attending what many consider a pilgrimage to the desert. Attendees have a sense of creating alternate identities, challenging normative behaviors, and invoking ritual to re-create their purpose in the world. According to ethnographer Lee Gilmore, "Burning Man has become a ritualized space for those who seek spirituality but not religion and thus appropriates and ritualizes symbols from a variety of global cultures."[20] Although the news media and popular culture view the event as a hedonistic display of eclectic individualism populated by intoxicated participants seeking to escape the banality of their often lucrative professions, the festival is also a venue for self-renewal and self-discovery. Aligning festivals with transmodernism and transpersonal psychology, David Lane Bottorff explains, "in that little or no explicit guidance is offered and there are few formalized rites and rituals. Rather, the search for meaning and healing relies upon self-direction and peer support."[21] According to Irena Ateljevic, "Transmodernity can generally be characterized by optimism to provide hope for human race. Ghisi . . . describes transmodernity as a planetary vision in which humans are beginning to realize that we are all (including plants and animals) connected into one system, which makes us all interdependent, vulnerable and responsible for the Earth as an indivisible living community."[22] Even if it does not always reach its lofty goals, Burning Man provides a place for renewal and revisioning that allows participants opportunities to glimpse the sacred.

19. Black Rock City Census, "BRC Census Population Analysis, 2013–2019."
20. Gilmore, *Theater in a Crowded Fire*, 67.
21. Bottorff, "Emerging Influence."
22. Ateljevic, "Visions of Transmodernity," 203.

The Burning Man event and its affiliated communities are guided by ten principles that are meant to evoke the cultural ethos that has emerged from the event. They were originally written by founder Larry Harvey in 2004 as guidelines for regional organizing, and later became a universal criterion of the general culture of the multifaceted movement. They are radical inclusion, gifting, de-commodification, radical self-reliance, radical self-expression, communal effort, civic responsibility, leaving no trace, participation, and immediacy.[23] Although there is not space in this brief overview to consider each principle individually, suffice it to say, there is an ethical backdrop to the organization of the event and the community that has formed around it. For those who see the festival turning into a playground for the uber-rich tech billionaires, one must acknowledge that there is a dark side of non-participatory tourists and "burnerprenuers." References to "Earning Man" and "Grifting" as satirical plays on Burning Man and gifting were originally created by Dave Clooney in the BRC Weekly and the terms are discussed at length by Graham St. John in "Blazing Grace."[24] "Grifting" is a play on the idea of gifting, one of the core principles of the event. All participants pledge to spend the week without purchasing anything. Instead, they bring items to give away that others might need—everything from bottled water to chapstick, which they offer to others in need. Charles Eisenstein wrote about reclaiming the gift economy in *Sacred Economics*. He explains, "Whereas money today embodies the principle, 'More for me is less for you.'" In a gift economy, more for you is also more for me because those who have give to those who need. Gifts cement the mystical realization of participation in something greater than oneself which, yet is not separate from oneself."[25]

In chronicling the expansion of Burning Man from its simple beginnings as a bonfire on a beach to a massive festival with over 50,000 participants, Steven T. Jones explains the desire to create a new culture that pushes the boundaries of human community.

> Within a capitalist world, our personas and social standing are often derived from the job we hold or the career we have chosen (which itself is often limited by our class and family connections), our environments are usually regulated by corporate

23. Gilmore, *Theater in a Crowded Fire*, 38.
24. St John, "Blazing Grace."
25. Eisenstein, *Sacred Economics*, 9.

or government entities, and many of our daily interactions are actually economic transactions. We aren't exactly who we are, so most Burners refer to this as the Default World. The central tenets of Burning Man stand starkly opposed to such paradigms—indeed, deliberately challenging them. Participants are encouraged to build the city of their dreams with almost no regulations or limitations, most economic transactions are prohibited in favor of a gift economy, and the encouragement of "radical self-expression" to pick any persona they choose . . . while the twin ethos of self-reliance and participation create the expectation of a far more engaged citizenry than the real world asks of us.[26]

However, it is well documented that there is an exclusivism that persists in festival culture with a high price point of entry and a privileged group that seems oblivious to important social factors in creating the change that spirituality in its best form would advocate. Responding to Brian Duffy's article, "How Burning Man and Festival Culture Make Change Personal," David Nickles writes:

> Burning Man's principle of radical inclusion only applies to people who can buy-in to begin with; the claim that Burning Man "lets people attend regardless of their social status or ideological affiliation" is simply not true. Class is a social status. If you cannot afford Burning Man, you are excluded. If you cannot take off work because your family depends on you in a society that seems rabidly fixated on decimating the few social safety nets still in place, you are excluded. Burning Man, by its very nature, is exclusive on the grounds of social status.[27]

Each year evokes a theme around which the costumes, pageantry, construction and events of Burning Man revolve. The theme for 2017 was "Radical Ritual."[28] The Facebook post that announced the theme described it as follows:

---

26. Jones, *The Tribes of Burning Man*, 16.

27. Nickles, "Festivals, Politics, and Change."

28. The theme for 2018 was "I-Robot" and for 2019 Metamorphoses. Here is that description: The 2019 theme, Metamorphoses, was a celebration of change, and an exploration of uncertainty. As such it invites a consideration of time; not its circular nature, or its attendant ritual, but in this case the relentless flight of time's arrow, and an embrace of the elusive now. Memory is fickle, and the future is uncertain. None of us knows what they will become, but we can seek to understand where we are at this point in our transformative trajectory, this fleeting chord on the strings of existence.

Beyond the dogmas, creeds, and metaphysical ideas of religion, there is immediate experience. It is from this primal world that living faith arises. In 2017, we will invite participants to create interactive rites, ritual processions, elaborate images, shrines, icons, temples, and visions. Our theme will occupy the ambiguous ground that lies between reverence and ridicule, faith and belief, the absurd and the stunningly sublime. The human urge to make events, objects, actions, and personalities sacred is protean. It can fix on and inhabit anyone or anything. This year our art theme will release this spirit in the Black Rock Desert.[29]

One worldview that mirrors the experiential dimension of Burning Man is expressed in Mircea Eliade's *The Sacred and the Profane*. For Eliade, a departure from the everyday profane world creates the space for a potential hierophany and the shift into sacred time is essential for rites of passage, an event of transition that is sorely lacking in modernity. Eliade defined hierophany as an "appearance of the sacred/holy." Millennials seeking a mystical connection with the transcendent are drawn to events like Burning Man like a moth to a flame. They long for a glimmer of illumination, to find meaning in their mundane lives and to explore a purpose and destiny beyond the mechanistic and technological world they have inherited.

While Erik Davis has conceived of a quintuple categorization of cults present at the festival, he does not insinuate that Burners resemble doomsday cults like Heaven's Gate or the People's Temple. Instead, he frames the cults as those of experience, intoxicants, flicker, juxtapose and meaningless chaos. According to Davis, the experience manifests as physical sensation, seduction and stories "pointing back to the *mysterium tremendum* of consciousness itself."[30] Many Burners, the self-referential term attendees call themselves, view their annual journey to the Black Rock desert in Nevada as a pilgrimage akin to anthropologist Victor Turner's rites of passage. They shed their ordinary identities in the phase of separation, take on alternate personas in the liminal stage, and reflect on the transformational quality of their experience as they reintegrate into society a week later.[31]

29. Burning Man Project, "Burning Man 2017."

30. Davis, "Beyond Belief," 21.

31. An archive of all Burning Man events from 1986 to the present is available at https://burningman.org/culture/history/brc-history/event-archives/.

When Victor Turner discovered Arnold Van Gennep's authoritative encapsulation of the stages of an initiation or rites of passage ritual, he searched for an understanding of what happened in the liminal stage, that is betwixt and between.[32] Attempts to probe and understand the transformative experience of the liminal stage has intrigued many other authors including Bjorn Thomassen who defines it as "moments or periods of transition during which the normal limits to thought, self-understanding and behavior are relaxed, opening the way to novelty and imagination, construction and destruction."[33] Describing Van Gennep's contribution to anthropology, Thomassen notes that, "He clearly sensed that rites of passage, with their symbolic representation of death and re-birth, illustrate in a more general way the principles of the regenerative renewal required by any society and any human being."[34] Turner himself sought the understanding of what occurs in the space between crossing the threshold, or entering what we consider as sacred space and the re-incorporation phase of integrating one's learning for application in the wider world.

Turner went beyond Durkheim's theory that religion provided the function of social bonding. In the shared experience of liminality, Turner noticed a shared sense of solidarity that occurred within the heightened state of a ritual. This is a communal effervescence that happens outside of the mundane, everyday structured reality.

> Beyond the dogmas, creeds, and metaphysical ideas of religion, there is immediate experience. It is from this primal world that living faith arises. In 2017, we will invite participants to create interactive rites, ritual processions, elaborate images, shrines, icons, temples, and visions. Our theme will occupy the ambiguous ground that lies between reverence and ridicule, faith and belief, the absurd and the stunningly sublime. The human urge to make events, objects, actions, and personalities sacred is protean. It can fix on and inhabit anyone or anything. This year our art theme will release this spirit in the Black Rock Desert.[35]

The Zen formulation "all is one, one is none, none is all" well expresses the global, unstructured character earlier applied to communitas. The hippie emphasis on spontaneity, immediacy, and "existence" throws into relief

32. Turner, "Betwixt and Between."

33. Thomassen, *Liminality and the Modern*, 4.

34. Thomassen, *Liminality and the Modern*, 3.

35. Burning Man Project, "Burning Man 2017."

one of the senses in which communitas contrasts with structure. Communitas is of the now, structure is rooted in the past and extends into the future through language, law, and custom.[36] The sense of communitas is tangible in festival culture. Events like Burning Man cultivate this by demanding a severance from daily life. To attend, one must travel to an unfamiliar place, with few belongings and bring an attitude of willingness to encounter cognitive dissonance, to be surprised by new revelations.

At Burning Man, the forty-foot effigy, once a simple wooden construction and now perched on an elaborate temple, is the central focal point of the festival. The culminating event is literally a ritual burning of the "Man" and all it symbolizes. "Some participants toss an object into this central fire as a form of personal sacrifice, or as a way of symbolically releasing a burden or pain that they no longer wish to endure."[37]

With regards to relating to organized religion, Gilmore interviewed an evangelical Christian attendee from the Midwest, who expressed a desire for liberation from the constricting atmosphere of traditional services.

> I find it weird that the church world appears to have been made from a cookie cutter. While worshipping a God that values creativity, the church has managed to squash it at every turn . . . Particularly in America, we have homogenized worship to the point where our distinctive (gifts) given to us by God to be celebrated have dissolved into an evangelical unitarianism.[38]

The interplay of religious themes and the desire for unaffiliated spiritual freedom intertwine into a helix of spontaneous play and internal reflection in Burning Man devotees. And this sense of play and festivity is not something new, it has invigorated the human spirit for millennia.

Festival Cultural and Millennial Desire for Transformation

Although established religious traditions have no shortage of rituals from baptism and communion in Christianity to keeping Shabbat (the Sabbath) and kashrut (Jewish dietary laws) in Judaism, young people today are seeking a direct experience of the sacred in their lives rather than

36. Turner, *The Ritual Process*, 113.

37. Gilmore, "Fires of the Hearth," 47–48.

38. Gilmore, "Fires of the Hearth," 56.

relying on traditional rituals. In her book *Belief Without Borders*, Linda Mercadante interviewed numerous young people unaffiliated with a tradition that she termed "seekers" or "explorers." She explains, "For many interviewees, having a heightened spiritual experience—wherever they found it—was not only sought after for its own sake, but seen as a confirmation of any belief or group's validity . . . having a heightened spiritual experience justified mixing and matching, borrowing, or using whatever touched them."[39]

Millennials are frequently accused of shallow spirituality, cultural appropriation, commodification of religious symbols and lack of commitment to a particular path among other criticisms. However, it is important to imagine growing up with negative messages about climate change, nuclear threat, transhumanism, and unemployment among other scourges. Young people not only want to assert themselves with a sense of their independence and potential contributions to society; they seek a meaning of life beyond the bleak outlook they have inherited.

This worldview is called into question, however, in *White Utopias* through the interrogation of personal transformation as a higher goal than collective, societal transformation. Contrasting Burning Man with other kinds of spiritual festivals, Lucia writes:

> At both LIB [Lightning in a Bottle] and Burning Man, there are numerous practical and instructional workshops about how to build alternative economies and social networks, whereas at the more explicitly yogic festivals, there are few concrete initiatives aimed at revisioning society. Instead, in these environments, yogis come together to do their "inner work," and they are convinced that their personal transformation will change the world. Their goal is not to directly activate social change through pragmatic forms but rather to lead loving and conscious lives and to spread that vibration through personal connections, by spreading yoga and bhakti and by becoming living examples of more evolved ways of being—changing the world one person and one connection at a time.[40]

With racial injustice in the spotlight of the world following the senseless murder of George Floyd and many others, the thought of young white people navel gazing while violence erupts over social oppression seems too internal a lens for our time. The Irregular Labs survey,

39. Mercadante, *Belief without Borders*, 89.
40. Lucia, *White Utopias*, 13.

conducted "in 7 countries, including the United States, United Kingdom/ Germany, India, China, Brazil, and South Africa, among nationally representative samples of 300 girl and GSM [gender and sexual minority] Gen Zs in each country," found that 75 percent of respondents said being politically or socially engaged is very important to their identity."[41] Younger generations have begun protesting and finding their voice in the community even as many also seek heightened spiritual experience.[42]

Secularization, Disenchantment, and the Protestant Ethos

Even as we discuss the problematic aspects of festival culture catering to a relatively small percentage of the population, it is important to recall the historical roots that preceded this movement. Having characterized a majority of festival attendees as "white" which in general terms indicates their European ancestry, it is important to consider both the historical legacy of Christianity and the vestiges of pagan celebratory rituals. The religious establishment, and Protestant Christianity in particular, are concerned about a demographic shift, with young people leaving the church, membership dropping and a secular perspective pervading the developed world both in Europe and the Americas. Charles Taylor in his book, *A Secular Age*, traces the factors that have led to this demise of relation to religious tradition. He describes the "buffered self" that evolved with the domestication and civilization of barbarian peoples, including European pagans, and compares it to a more "porous self" that inhabited the festival culture of a more enchanted and sacred time. This corresponds with Max Weber's theory of disenchantment, in which modernity, rationality, science, and existentialism were valued over the infinite and ineffable.

Taylor describes the festival culture of the Middle Ages in which the ordinary order of things is disrupted, inverted, and "turned upside down." He notes, "the explanation was offered that people needed this as a safety valve. The weight of virtue and good order was so heavy, and so much steam built up under this suppression of instinct, that there had to be periodic blow-outs if the whole system were not to fly apart."[43] He then modifies aspects of Victor Turner's classic work *The Ritual Process* to

41. MacColl, "Statistics On Gen Z."
42. Parker and Igielnik, "On the Cusp of Adulthood."
43. Taylor, *A Secular Age*, 46.

describe the need for renewal and reinvigoration of society and suggests that the function of the carnival and other festivals was to return order to its original meaning by suspending it temporarily, creating an egalitarian space for creative debauchery and then restoring a sense of structure for the society through this transgression. In Lucia's *White Utopias,* she acknowledges this same importance of festivals as a way of managing the oppression of a structured society that needs relief from the mundane world of compliance and hierarchy.

> Following Durkheim's reasoning, Roger Caillois argues that festivals transgress the boundary of mundane reality opening a space wherein participants become renewed and reemerge prepared, recharged and ready to re-enter society with a zest for everyday life. In this view, the festival is a venting system wherein individuals momentarily break from stasis and that rupture enables them to return and reinstate the very stasis from which they initially sought reprieve.[44]

Discipline, conformity, a focus on sin, a need for control—all of these were elements that conjoined between the Protestant Reformation and the rise of industrial society in a move that devoided the world of mystery and put the onus on the individual rather than the community. Millennials witness the fruits of shifts of past centuries and question the bland, homogenous world they inherited and are no longer willing to simply follow the doctrine without any transcendent event or experience that engages and enlivens them.

Aspiring to a spirituality that is embodied and relevant for the world they face, the Gen Z generation questions everything and seek ways to transcend the boundaries of the structured life that requires little creativity. They have lived indoors for fear of assaults and predators, and they have followed a linear trajectory of schooling that requires much of their time during the formative years when social experimentation might aid them in finding their allies and place in society.[45] Gen Z grew up in a post 9/11 world, filled with economic uncertainty, mass school shootings, political polarization, and a heightened awareness of identity politics. "These factors have led Gen-Zers to have a more pragmatic view of the world than millennials, manifested as a higher prevalence of risk

44. Lucia, *White Utopias,* 22.

45. For an in-depth look at Gen Z attitudes and challenges, see Bethune, "Gen Z More Likely to Report Mental Health Concerns"; Parker and Igielnik, "On the Cusp of Adulthood."

aversion, financial frugality, and an expectation that they will need to work harder than the generation that preceded them."[46] Rampant materialism and the easy availability of commodities to satisfy their desires has left young generations floundering for meaning in a fear-based world. Rejecting this normative complacency, a subset of young people seeks to reinvent themselves and the systems that are failing post-modern society. A recent Los Angeles Times article explained,

> Today, young people still seek the things that traditional organized religion may have provided for their parents or grandparents: religious beliefs, yes, but also a sense of community, guidance, purpose and meaning. But it can be hard for young people to find those things in their parents' religions. So they're looking elsewhere. On top of that, a lot of younger people feel alienated by mainstream religion—by attitudes toward LGBTQ people and women, by years of headlines about scandals and coverups, or by the idea that anyone who isn't part of that religion is inherently bad or wrong.[47]

Thus, rituals such as Burning Man and festival culture in general, allow for a sense of play, an unstructured creative world to engage with their peers and experience life directly. As UCLA anthropologist Megan Heller explored in a podcast, "The difference, in our society at least, in American society, is that the things we put in the ritual bucket are the ideas and commitments and groups of people that we acknowledge to be important. And play is associated with the ideas and symbols and commitments that we think of as powerful, having a strong effect on us, but not necessarily admirable."[48] For example, the Burning Man rituals involve the transformational quality of fire, thought to produce the alchemical quality of purity through the dissolution of old patterns out of which an altered consciousness emerges bursting with potential for creative and world-changing endeavors. The fire carries the capacity to dissolve negative patterns, unwanted memories, habits and emotional states, and provide an opening for rebirth and recalibration that allow participants to view the world with fresh eyes and open hearts.

Anthropologists Jean and John Comaroff argue that rituals have appeal to subaltern populations as a form of empowerment, given the rapid

46. Talmon, "Generation Z."

47. Roy, "How Millennials Replaced Religion With Astrology and Crystals."

48. Magister, "The Connection Between Ritual, Art, and Play."

changes of modernity. They view ritual as an instrument of resistance that both makes remakes "social facts and collective identities" and gives voice to cosmologies or contests dominant discourses.[49] Paradoxically, however, ritual events have also increasingly become tourist attractions for disenchanted people seeking in other cultures signs of "a disappearing real."[50]

As Caveat Magister explained in the Burning Man blog, radical ritual includes "Experiences of awe and wonder, flow states, connecting to parts of your psyche (and perhaps through them, the universe? Who knows?) that you don't understand. These are all things that are important to us . . . the things in life that we strive for and value and cherish . . . but that are also most hard to come by."[51] Ritual provides a way to set priorities in life, to determine what is important and conversely what is not and creates space for community-building, something our society places little emphasis on.

The Emerging Church

Interestingly, the Emerging Church attempts to provide some of these opportunities for Christians. Yet despite the burgeoning Christian music scene and a number of outdoor Christian music festivals, particularly in the Eastern half of the United States like Atlanta Fest in Georgia, Creation Festival in Pennsylvania, Next Fest in Fayetteville, North Carolina, and SonRise Music Festival in Virginia Beach, Virginia, there is little media coverage and few artists that get the publicity that would make them a household name. Christian festivals are much more structured with a stage and audience participation, but the other activities are things like skateboarding and dirt bikes. The culture is more like a county fair, with extended families gathering for picnics and little in the way of individual soul searching, though Randall Reed has interviewed millennials at the Wild Goose Festival in North Carolina, which is described as a Spirit, Justice, Music and Arts Festival inspired by some of the transformational festivals mentioned in this chapter.[52] This mirrors reflections by John Morehead, who writes:

49. Comaroff and Comaroff, *Modernity and Its Malcontents*, xi–xxxvii.

50. Horton, "Maintaining Hispano Identity," 252, quoting Mary M. Crain.

51. Magister, "Perform at Your Own Risk."

52. Reed, "The Problem of Anti-Institutionalism," 166–67.

> The kind of Christian community that is waiting to be built in the twenty-first century West must be radically different than what many conservative evangelicals are likely to be comfortable with if it is to resonate with Burning Man as a Bohemian arts-inspired community. A robust Christian community in this context must be qualitatively different as a sacred space that encourages social experimentation and which embraces the values and ideals of self-expression, creativity, festivity, sensuality, art, care for the environment, and which challenges rampant consumerism.[53]

For Christianity to remain relevant in the twenty-first century, the tradition would be wise to reconsider the implications of Weber's *The Protestant Ethic and the Spirit of Capitalism*. Young people do not see the fruits of their labors as an end goal. How does this equate with "the earning of more and more money, combined with the strict avoidance of all spontaneous enjoyment of life"[54] when the divide between haves and have nots is increasingly visible? Millennials want to engage in a life lived to its fullest, without regard for income and status. Many are opting for world travel, socially engaged internships, and minimalist lifestyles.

More than half a century has passed since Eliade wrote about the value of initiation and sacred experience. Even at that time, he was aware that Christianity was losing its connection to the sacred. He wrote:

> As for the Christianity of the industrial societies and especially the Christianity of the intellectuals, it has long since lost the cosmic values that it still possessed in the Middle Ages. We must add that this does not necessarily imply that urban Christianity is deteriorated or inferior, but only that the religious sense of the urban population is gravely impoverished. The cosmic liturgy, the mystery of nature's participation in the Christological drama, have become inaccessible to Christians living in a modern city. Their religious experience is no longer open to the cosmos.[55]

Perhaps it is time for the church to return to the significance of its rituals and its connection to direct experience. Perhaps young people should have the opportunity to experience the rites of passage of a wilderness

---

166–67.

53. Morehead, "BURN, BABY, BURN, Christendom Inferno."

54. Weber, *The Protestant Ethic*, 53.

55. Eliade, *The Sacred and the Profane*, 178–79.

solo experience or engage in rituals that allow for hierophanies to occur so that the connection between heaven and earth can become explicit once again.

In their article "Emerging Christianity and Religious Identity," Katherine Moody and Randall Reed noted that many young people raised in evangelical churches are turning away from institutions they find "judgmental, hypocritical, and homophobic; shallow, consumerist and individualistic; exclusivist and intolerant; and both separated from culture and science and too invested in politics."[56] Millennials and Gen Z observe a world that is divisive, on the verge of climate catastrophe and needing structural reformation in institutions from the church to government to corporations. They seek a community to engage with in an embodied holism that meets them at the depth of their inquiry and develops individual and societal solutions. They want an actual spiritual experience, not just someone reciting words devoid of connection. This may be an ongoing challenge for the Emerging Church. As John Morehead notes:

> As for the Christianity of the industrial societies and especially the Christianity of the intellectuals, it has long since lost the cosmic values that it still possessed in the Middle Ages. We must add that this does not necessarily imply that urban Christianity is deteriorated or inferior, but only that the religious sense of the urban population is gravely impoverished. The cosmic liturgy, the mystery of nature's participation in the Christological drama, have become inaccessible to Christians living in a modern city. Their religious experience is no longer open to the cosmos.[57]

Pandemic Postscript

In the middle of completing this chapter, the COVID-19 virus effected global travel, gatherings of all types, and many of the goods and services we have come to rely on. Festivals were cancelled or postponed, and some groups created online alternatives through Zoom or other platforms. Hugging, handshakes and large gatherings were off limits. Many people found themselves in self-imposed quarantine because of underlying

56. Moody and Reed, "Emerging Christianity and Religious Identity," 35.

57. Eliade, *The Sacred and the Profane*, 178–79.

health conditions that made it dangerous to interact with the public. Festival culture came to an abrupt halt.

As I write this epilogue, people are experiencing quarantine fatigue and bringing a third wave of the virus to their communities by ignoring mask mandates and social distancing orders. Sadly, churches are among the worst offenders, ignoring the rules and demanding in-person worship services as their Constitutional right. In April 2020, when the pandemic was surging, some pastors were defiant to public health orders.[58]

But over time virtual services became normative and this may change the way parishioners attend services in the future. It may be years before we return to a time when we can gather comfortably in large groups, and my own sense is that this is a time to engage personal inner work. It is a time for reflection on how we want to inhabit the world. Will we acknowledge the role of humans in climate change that has disrupted weather patterns resulting in droughts, fires, floods, unpredictable temperature swings and pollution levels in air, food, and water that are unsustainable? Will we acknowledge the genocides, the colonizing mindset of empire, the separation of races and classes and all the trauma and pain this has caused? Perhaps we must struggle to reveal the interconnectedness of all beings and all life in order to develop the virtues of gratitude and humility so that we can meet each other once again on a more level playing field. Festivals will change as a result of this year of housebound seclusion. We can look forward to a revision of sacred spectacle, hopefully one that is more inclusive and profound.

Bibliography

Alfred, Taiaiake. *Peace, Power, Righteousness: An Indigenous Manifesto*. 2nd ed. New York: Oxford University Press, 2009.
Ateljevic, Irena. "Visions of Transmodernity: A New Renaissance of Our Human History?" *Integral Review* 9 (2013) 200–219. https://integral-review.org/visions-of-transmodernity-a-new-renaissance-of-our-human-history/.

58. In Arkansas, Pastor Chad Gonzales of Awaken Church defied demands to end services. His declaration of Jesus as a coronavirus victim was based on the belief that Jesus took away every sin and disease on the cross, a particularly powerful message for Easter. Similarly, Pastor Tony Spell of the Life Tabernacle Church in Louisiana was arrested for holding large services. Spell declared his intention to hold large Easter services and insisted that he will never yield to this "dictator law." Even more chilling was his statement that "true Christians do not mind dying." See Turley, "Why the Government Can Shut Down Church Gathering During Pandemic."

Bain, Katie. "I Tried to Find Spiritual Enlightenment at a Music Festival." *Vice*, September 14, 2017. https://www.vice.com/en/article/a3kdd8/i-tried-to-find-spiritual-enlightenment-at-a-music-festival.

Bethune, Sophie. "Gen Z More Likely to Report Mental Health Concerns." American Psychological Association, January 2019. https://www.apa.org/monitor/2019/01/gen-z.

Black Rock City Census. "BRC Census Population Analysis, 2013–2019." http://blackrockcitycensus.org/sociodemo.html#age.

Bloom Connections. "Lightning in a Bottle." http://bloomconnections.com/Lightning-in-a-Bottle.

Bottorff, David Lane. "Emerging Influence of Transmodernism and Transpersonal Psychology Reflected in Rising Popularity of Transformational Festivals." *Journal of Spirituality in Mental Health* 17 (2015) 50–74.

Burning Man Project. "Burning Man 2017: Radical Ritual." *Burning Man Journal*, December 16, 2016. https://journal.burningman.org/2016/12/black-rock-city/participate-in-brc/burning-man-2017-radical-ritual/.

Comaroff, Jean, and John L. Comaroff. *Modernity and Its Malcontents: Ritual and Power in Postcolonial Africa*. Chicago: University of Chicago Press, 1993.

Davis, Erik. "Beyond Belief: The Cults of Burning Man." In *AfterBurn: Reflections on Burning Man*, edited by Lee Gilmore and Mark Van Proyen, 15–42. CounterCulture Series. Albuquerque: University of New Mexico Press, 2005.

Deloria, Vine, Jr., with Philip J. Deloria. *The World We Used to Live In: Remembering the Powers of the Medicine Men*. 2nd ed. Golden, CO: Fulcrum, 2016.

Doucette, Kitt. "7 Wildest Transformational Festivals." *Rolling Stone*, May 11, 2016. https://www.rollingstone.com/culture/culture-lists/7-wildest-transformational-festivals-68486/.

Eisenstein, Charles. *Sacred Economics: Money, Gift, and Society in the Age of Transition*. Berkeley: North Atlantic, 2011.

Eliade, Mircea. *The Sacred and the Profane: The Nature of Religion*. Translated by Willard R. Trask. New York: Harcourt, Brace & World, 1959.

Gilmore, Lee. "Fires of the Hearth: Ritual, Pilgrimage and Transformation at Burning Man." In *AfterBurn: Reflections on Burning Man*, edited by Lee Gilmore and Mark Van Proyen, 43–64. CounterCulture Series. Albuquerque: University of New Mexico Press, 2005.

———. *Theater in a Crowded Fire: Ritual and Spirituality at Burning Man*. Berkeley: University of California Press, 2010.

Horton, Sarah. "Maintaining Hispano Identity through the Santa Fe Fiesta: Re-Appropriating Key Symbols and Resisting Anglo Dominance." *Kiva* 66 (2000) 249–65.

Jain, Andrea R. *Selling Yoga: From Counterculture to Pop Culture*. Oxford: Oxford University Press, 2015.

Johner, Andrew. "Transformational Festivals: A New Religious Movement?" In *Exploring Psychedelic Trance and Electronic Dance Music in Odern Culture*, edited by Emília Simão, Armando Malheiro da Silva, and Sérgio Tenreiro de Magalhães, 58–86. Hershey, PA: IGI Global, 2015.

Jones, S.T. *The Tribes of Burning Man: How an Experimental City in the Desert Is Shaping the New American Counterculture*. San Francisco: Consortium of Collective Consciousness, 2011.

Leung, Jeet Kei. *Transformational Festivals: Jeet Kei Leung at TEDxVancouver*, 2011. TEDx Talks. https://www.youtube.com/watch?v=Q8tDpQp6moA.

Lucia, Amanda J. *White Utopias: The Religious Exoticism of Transformational Festivals*. Berkeley: University of California Press, 2020.

MacColl, Margaux. "Statistics on Gen Z & Activism Show They Want to Get Involved, They Just Need To Know How." *Bustle*, May 2, 2019. https://www.bustle.com/p/statistics-on-gen-z-activism-show-they-want-to-get-involved-they-just-need-to-know-how-17179280.

Magister, Caveat. "The Connection between Ritual, Art, and Play." *Burning Man Journal*, March 29, 2017. https://journal.burningman.org/2017/03/philosophical-center/the-theme/the-connection-between-ritual-art-and-play/.

———. "Perform at Your Own Risk: What We've Learned About Radical Ritual." *Burning Man Journal* August 2017. https://journal.burningman.org/2017/08/philosophical-center/spirituality/perform-at-your-own-risk-what-weve-learned-about-radical-ritual/.

Marsh, Sarah. "Boom in Wellness at Festivals as Young People Swap Hedonism for Yoga." *The Guardian*, August 2, 2019. http://www.theguardian.com/culture/2019/aug/02/health-not-hedonism-the-festivals-putting-wellness-at-their-heart.

Menakem, Resmaa. *My Grandmother's Hands: Racialized Trauma and the Pathway to Mending Our Hearts and Bodies*. Las Vegas: Central Recovery, 2017.

Mercadante, Linda. *Belief without Borders: Inside the Minds of the Spiritual but Not Religious*. Oxford: Oxford University Press, 2014

Moody, Sarah, and Randall Reed. "Emerging Christianity and Religious Identity." *Journal for the Scientific Study of Religion* 56 (2017) 33–40.

Morehead, John W. "BURN, BABY, BURN, Christendom Inferno: Burning Man and the Festive Immolation of Christendom Culture and Modernity." *The Ooze: Conversations for the Journey*, December 14, 2006.

Nickles, David. "Festivals, Politics, Change." *The Nexian*. September 9, 2014. https://the-nexian.me/home/knowledge/128-festivals-politics-and-change.

Parker, Kim, and Ruth Igielnik. "On the Cusp of Adulthood and Facing an Uncertain Future: What We Know about Gen Z so Far." *Pew Research Center's Social & Demographic Trends Project* (blog), May 14, 2020. https://www.pewsocialtrends.org/essay/on-the-cusp-of-adulthood-and-facing-an-uncertain-future-what-we-know-about-gen-z-so-far/.

Pew Research Center. "America's Changing Religious Landscape." *Pew Forum*, May 12, 2015. https://www.pewforum.org/2015/05/12/americas-changing-religious-landscape/.

Reed, Randall W. "The Problem of Anti-Institutionalism in Millennials." In *The Emerging Church, Millennials, and Religion*. Volume 1: *Prospects and Problems*, edited by Randall W. Reed and Michael G. Zbaraschuk, 166–87. Eugene, OR: Cascade.

Roy, Jessica. "How Millennials Replaced Religion With Astrology and Crystals." *Los Angeles Times*, July 10, 2019. https://www.latimes.com/health/la-he-millennials-religion-zodiac-tarot-crystals-astrology-20190710-story.html.

Saad, Layla. *Me and White Supremacy: Combat Racism, Change the World, and Become a Good Ancestor*. Naperville, IL: Sourcebooks, 2020.

St John, Graham. "Blazing Grace: The Gifted Culture of Burning Man." *NANO : New American Notes Online* 11 (July 2017). https://nanocrit.com/issues/issue11/ Blazing-Grace-The-Gifted-Culture-of-Burning-Man.

Talmon, Geoffrey A. "Generation Z: What's Next?" *Medical Science Educator* 29, December 1, 2019, 9–11.

Taylor, Charles. *A Secular Age.* Cambridge: Harvard University Press, 2007.

Taylor, Mia. "Inside One of the Year's Biggest Trends: Wellness Festivals via the Bhakti Fest." *TheStreet,* September 30, 2016. https://www.thestreet.com/lifestyle/travel/ inside-one-of-the-year-s-biggest-trends-wellness-festivals-via-the-bhakti-fest-13755111.

Thomassen, Bjørn. *Liminality and the Modern: Living Through the In-Between.* Surrey, UK: Ashgate, 2014.

Turley, Jonathan. "Why the Government Can Shut Down Church Gathering during Pandemic." *The Hill* (blog), April 11, 2020. https://thehill.com/opinion/ judiciary/492332-why-the-government-can-shut-down-church-gatherings-during-pandemic.

Turner, Victor. "Betwixt and Between: The Liminal Period in Rites de Passage." In *The Forest of Symbols: Aspects of Ndembu Ritual,* 93–111. Ithaca, NY: Cornell University Press, 1967.

———. *The Ritual Process: Structure and Anti-Structure.* New Brunswick: Aldine Transaction, 2011.

Weaver, Hilary N. *Trauma and Resilience in the Lives of Contemporary Native Americans: Reclaiming Our Balance, Restoring Our Wellbeing.* New York: Routledge, 2019.

Weber, Marx. *The Protestant Ethic and the Spirt of Capitalism.* Translated by Talcott Parsons. New York: Scribner, 1958.

PART 2

Curating and Enduring Through Change

4

Gender, Anxiety, and Millennial Romantic Lives

Embracing Agency through Intentional Improvisation

LAINE WALTERS YOUNG

Abstract

Stressed out by a "predictive horizon of impermanence" in a volatile global economy, millennial young adults hesitate to make sacrifices or commitments to adult intimates, leading to long lives of deformalized relationships and untrodden interpersonal ethical territory. This chapter reviews how millennials reiterate differential and unequal gendered approaches to combining lives, responsibilities, and earnings, revealing them to be retrenching in practice from their own professed egalitarian ideals. It draws attention to millennials' neoliberal values of self-reliance and authenticity and suggests that attempts to actualize these values leads to pursuit of symptom relief and personal responsibility that traps them into enacting a relativism, which, as an existential predisposition, is hesitant to pass judgement and keeps their life goals more modest than otherwise. The chapter concludes prescriptively, proposing that millennials can find an ethical way forward by identifying and claiming their desires through a process of postmodern improvisation which entails further developing their skills of self-reflection, systematic assessment, and interpersonal communication in order to develop a proficiency of self-advocacy and ethical acumen.

Young adults (ages eighteen to thirty), loosely concurrent with the millennial generation until a few years ago, make up the most educated yet, often beset by student loans and uncompleted degrees, also the most financially challenged generation in recent memory.[1] This combination of factors sets them up for a high-stakes game of life in terms of the widening gap between the chances of achieving social survival or succumbing to a failure of financial balance and familial prospects, which produces intensive and pervasive feelings of anxiety.[2] Young adults experience tension between feeling the need to obtain an elusive, yet all important, sense of security and worrying that the future will be difficult to keep up with in terms of rapid change in a globalized knowledge economy.[3] This tension encourages a feeling of constantly needing to cultivate and present themselves as having a diverse and potentially malleable portfolio of skills and abilities that apply to the working world but also the life of family and partnership.[4] In concrete implications, this improvisational portfolio mentality mixes with chances of a much longer life span than in the past resulting in people spending a majority of their lives "single," or non-married.[5] Millennials in their twenties and early thirties feel they need to keep their options non-committed on relational fronts in order to survive the vicissitudes of an unpredictable, rapidly changing economy. They feel as if relational attachments would foreshorten their own freedom and ability to survive in a raucous world.[6] In sum, they do

1. Pew Research Center, "Millennials On Track"; Rattner, "We're Making Life Too Hard."

2. This era is one in which the psyche associates the human being first and foremost with vulnerability rather than with hope and resilience. Among the reasons for this existential anxiety is the presence and production of "fear entrepreneurs," who have grown expert at profiting off and encouraging people to fear at new levels compared to ever before, Bingaman, *Treating the New Anxiety*, 2–3.

3. The United States Census reports that on average contemporary young adults will change jobs eleven times between the ages of eighteen and forty-four; seven to eight of those switches will occur between the ages of eighteen to twenty-seven, Syed and Mitchell, *Handbook of Emerging Adulthood*, 90.

4. Psychologist Varda Konstam notes that if Emerging Adults felt like they could prepare for and know the future, they would readily take the advantage. They are not nihilists in the least, but deeply postmodern in their sense that all of life is change and fluidity. Konstam, *Romantic Lives*, 322; Hallman, *Millennial Teachers*, x.

5. In 2014, the American population became majority "single." See, Miller, "Single Americans," 1.

6. Willoughby and James note that most millennials are looking for a partner who will "cause the least disruption in their daily lives." Willoughby and James, *Marriage*

not see relational commitments as, overall, providing more to them in stability and support than they risk costing in burdens.[7]

Much of the ecclesial and cultural studies worlds, however, have failed to keep up theoretically with what this means or how these simultaneous needs for security and flexibility feed into each other on a deeply cultural level.[8] I suggest, drawing upon the work of psychologists and ethicists who are keenly attending to the super modern age of an overabundance of rapid change,[9] millennial men and women are doubtful of progress in the reliability of themselves and others as providers and agents of happiness, and they are hyperconscious of trying to find the true and the reliable. Out of these psycho-existential currents created by real material and physical instability, millennials retrench. They particularly retrench on gender issues, hoping for flexibility and egalitarianism in their romantic partnerships,[10] but finding themselves up against structural constraints about which gender is likely to make more money, with women predicting in the end that they will be felled from egalitarian ambition by so many things.[11] Many millennials report that, while they

---

Paradox, 106.

7. Freitas, *Consent*, 90–91; Christian ethicist Jennifer Beste found her students were more interested in avoiding the stress that relationships can bring, but they were too scared of this for reasons of vulnerability, Beste, *College Hookup Culture*, 162. Today in the young adult lexicon is the term "to catch feelings," which describes an experience of discovering interest in someone unexpectedly. This surprise is often associated with the fact that by default, one is not supposed to care or be interested in another romantically, thus to "catch feelings" has an air of inappropriate shame about it, "Catch Feelings," *Urban Dictionary*.

8. Such persons must also come to understand how postindustrial increase in levels of precariousness influences the worldview, psychology, and behavior of young adults as a baseline level of stress and anxiety that complicates the already tenuous human developmental position they have as emerging adults who are trying to find their place in the world by virtue of their age as budding adults in charge of themselves and their future. This means that they have combining intensities to deal with in terms of developmental stage of life and generational cohort. This intensity is something that may smooth out as they age but will likely shape the foundations of adult life for them forever after.

9. Bingaman, *Treating the New Anxiety*, 19.

10. Counselors Rik Rusovick and Carmen Knudson-Martin note that young adult Americans approach their intimate relationships as a peer relationship these days, but that does not mean there are not underlying gender inequality ideologies at work, Rusovick and Knudson-Martin, "Gender Discourse," 284.

11. Miller, "The Ambition Collision," 3; Gender sociologist Barbara Risman notes that women still "age up" into a pay gap for a variety of reasons, many of them not in

believe in equal rights for men and women, they are more interested in prioritizing an arrangement of work and care that they hope or feel will be less stressful than that of the two-career households they experienced growing up.[12]

Male and female millennials try to stay open and malleable themselves in an unpredictable world to best prepare themselves for a contradictory form of nimbleness that gives them the best chance at stability. They are stressed and anxious at the numbers of changes they anticipate in life. And they doubt the durability and possibilities that marriage could be equally beneficial to both men and women, such that, while a majority of millennials say they want egalitarian and flexible intimate partnerships between the genders, their experience of relationships in college and their plans on how to take care of themselves financially belie that they do not expect a true partnership of equals to come out in the social wash of their lives.

Most poignantly, research by family studies and human development researchers Brian Willoughby and Spencer James, in their 2017 book *The Marriage Paradox: Why Emerging Adults Love Marriage Yet Push It Aside*, tangibly and undeniably reveal what other research has indicated in less clear terms: that young adult millennials do not believe that a committed intimate partnership, such as marriage, will keep them from drowning in life's rough waters. In part, millennials infer that adult partners are more likely to restrict them from making the necessary changes to keep up with life. When asked about why they feel this way, they generally cite the specter of having grown up with high rates of divorce in their communities,[13] how often people including themselves have let them down,[14] and how they are hesitant to ask all but the "right person" to make sacrifices on their behalf.[15] It can be summarized that

---

their control, Risman, *Where Millennials Will Take Us*, 4; Christian ethicist Jennifer Beste makes it clear in her book *College Hookup Culture* that she finds a significant decline in gender equality in comparison to college students of generations past when it comes to sex and negotiating the terms of intimate relationships, Beste, *College Hookup Culture*, 101.

12. Carslon, "A View from Above," cited by Risman, *Where the Millennials Will Take Us*, 5; Filipovic, *The H-Spot*, 36.

13. McGuire, "Millennials' Perceptions," 8, 31; Pew, "Millennials: A Portrait," 53.

14. Silva, *Coming Up Short*, 83.

15. Crossley, *Finding Feminism*, 41; Konstam, *Romantic Lives*, 7, 69–70.

many contemporary young adults doubt the benefit of formalized, committed partnerships over other models of living.[16]

It is curious however, what kind of connections and commitments contemporary young adults feel will *help* their lives, including children, and what connections and commitments, such as impersonal organized religion or a needy spouse, will *hinder* them. Contemporary young adults are so wedded to the individual life trajectories that they already see for themselves that they are, as Willoughby and James put it, looking for a partner who will "cause the least disruption in their daily lives."[17] Yet, there are significant contradictions to what is allowed to cause a disruption in one's personal life that puts the issue back on the distrust of partnership. For instance, this generation often finds children more reliable companions than spouses. Millennials report a relational wholeness gained from parenting, not from partnership. They also believe that dissolving a relationship that is not a formal one is less emotionally and materially damaging to children.[18]

The dependency of children means they are clearly in need of care in a way that is hard to ignore and which also means children are unlikely and unable to walk away from the relationship like a divorcing spouse who can financially support themselves and knows how to do laundry. This difference between committing to a child and committing to a spouse speaks to an underlying current that fear of abandonment and the fear of broken reliance on another are the real issues for why adults do not want to commit to partnership but will to parenthood. Breaking apart the old adage that "first comes love, then comes marriage, then comes the baby with the baby carriage," as part of a larger U.S. social trend across demographics, millennials continue to deem having children as desirable and possible even when they do not feel the same way about marriage.[19] Forecasting the end before they engage in much of a start, millennial young adults do not expect to manage it all, and, if necessary, are prepared to drop long-term, romantic commitments to maintain a grip on everything else.[20]

16. Silva, *Coming Up Short*, 65–70.

17. Willoughby and James, *Marriage Paradox*, 106; Kefalas et al., "More than Being Together," 863.

18. Silva, *Coming Up Short*, 65–70.

19. For more on this, see Hertz, *Single by Chance*; Alcorn, "Millennials Want Children"; Wang and Taylor, "For Millennials Parenthood Trumps Marriage," 3.

20. Willoughby and James, *Marriage Paradox*, 80.

I describe young adult millennials as obsessed and driven by a "predictive horizon of impermanence" in which they expect that their lives will undergo constant change and responsibility in a variety of ways.[21] British psychologist Kirk A. Bingaman has noted that this anticipation of such rapid and abundant change makes it difficult to attach meaning to anything, for there are always new and ground-shaking events to process the very next day.[22] This psychological milieu requires millennials to figure out how to remain loose and flexible even as they yearn for something in their lives with staying power.[23] The contradictions between these two desires result in a hardened reliance on the self and its own trajectory as the most reliable path to security, consistency, and authenticity, since the involvement of significant others is generally seen as further subjecting a person to the unknown future and its myriad ways for things to go wrong and fail. This suspicion of the strength and sustenance possible from bilateral commitment has subtle but profound ethical import. What millennials expect and desire in an ethics of intimacy deserves to be generously explored for its underlying reasoning and associated currents of confluence.

In this chapter, I argue that neoliberal values of self-reliance and authenticity drive millennials to engage in a postmodern improvisational style of pulling together disparate sources of information and beliefs to guide their action toward meeting these values.[24] Sociologist Jennifer Silva identifies the contemporary trends of unpredictability and risk as contributing to young adults' search for authenticity. She writes of her generation, "the more our futures seem uncertain and unknowable, and the more individualistic we are forced to become, the greater our need

21. For instance, only one-third of the millennial workforce will find themselves in "steady staff" positions compared to gig economy, entrepreneurial, or varying shift work, O'Reilly and Vella-Zarb, "Meet the Future."

22. Bingaman, *Treating the New Anxiety*, 6–9. Bingaman writes, "Anxiety, therefore, is anticipatory, an unconsciously preemptive strategy to maintain a semblance of control by heading potential threats off at the proverbial pass before they ever occur or become reality," 10.

23. This yearning is also seen in the research of Kate McGuire, who writes about how millennials admire the steadfastness and longevity of their grandparents' relationships, McGuire, "Millennials' Perceptions," 61.

24. Bingaman cites that the three main features of postmodernity include an incredulity towards all metanarratives, a perceived saturation of all narratives with issues of power and dominance (making people more suspicious of the balance or imbalance of power, and a celebration of difference (which also comes with a resistance to judge that which is different. Bingaman, *Treating the New Anxiety*, 18.

to find and express our authentic selves."[25] When these values of self-reliance and authenticity are understood as the motivating factors for behavior, then it is more possible to trace how the ways in which gender as a social identity of possibility and constraint mixes with self-reliance and authenticity and results in certain behaviors that look more like an Eriksonian idea of pseudo-intimacy, an inhibition against the full giving of the self, rather than true intimacy.[26] I use self-reliance as a concept because self-reliance is affiliated with where one draws a sense of security. Self-reliance speaks to a new configuration of what is considered the ultimate unit of responsibility—the self—a sobering view of the human spirit which has little concern for the possible heights of freedom more commonly associated with the concept of individualism.

Authenticity also relates to a reliance on the self. Authenticity in this sense is derived from giving substantial authority and validity to that which is personally experienced, rather than any external source no matter how reputable. This self of experience also cannot easily commit to the future, for that will not be the same self as made the initial commitment. In this frame of mind, it is understandable that millennial young adults consider pre-existing frameworks such as marriage, no matter how romantically or ethically attractive, to be relatively inauthentic as a guideline for their contemporary intimate life because it predetermines major aspects of life ahead of the actual living of it. This seems a logical inconsistency, and therefore a falsity, to a contemporary young adult.

I also argue that the increase of deformalized relationships into their thirties amongst millennial young adults in the U.S. and worldwide, for all their debatable ethical potentials and pitfalls, is the outcome not only of anxiety about self and security, but also a generative, affirmative quest to be true to self and others more than ever before.[27] Thus, deformalized committed intimacy on behalf of the quest for greater authenticity results in a phenomenon which is hard to sociologically or ethically evaluate at face value in terms of its overall benefit or disadvantage. Yet it is quite

25. Silva, *Coming Up Short*, 74.

26. Leading researchers on Emerging Adulthood, developmental psychologist Laura Padilla-Walker and her colleagues note that there is little research on gender's effect of marriage in emerging adulthood because most of the intimacy literature for the life phase focuses on casual sexual relationships. Padilla-Walker et al., "Positive Relationships," 226; Kroger and Marcia, "The Identity Statuses," 31–54; Orlofsky, "Intimacy Status," 111–33, cited by Pratt and Matsuba, *Life Story*, 230; Pratt and Matsuba, *Life Story*, 46; Erikson, *Identity*, 135–36, cited by Pratt and Matsuba, *Life Story*, 230.

27. Chambers, *Sociology of Family Life*, 4, 41.

possible that this quest to be true to the self results in an epistemology that weighs more seriously human experience and allows for more rapid and rigorous critique as to whether or not the narratives of the past suf-ficiently befit and speak to the moment of the present and future. If I am successful in persuading people that these are in fact irrefutable drives for contemporary young adults, then the question becomes best what to do about making these more than unconscious intuition but rather a form of agency that can be consciously discussed and cultivated despite of—in fact in response to—the impermanence and insecurity of the world.

As Presbyterian pastor, MaryAnn McKibben Dana, writes in her book, *God, Improv, and the Art of Living*, that improvisation starts with a "yes" to the situation at hand in which we first accept what we cannot change in order to then respond appropriately to what is right in front of us.[28] It thus requires deep attention to the other and the moment at hand to be successful.[29] This has a pragmatic realism to it, and a form of concrete, intense relationality that a lived ethics requires. Furthermore, cultivating a view of life as lots of little moments of ethical response, can bring down a person's level of fear and anxiety about messing up and equip them to better respond to change when it comes.[30] I suggest that aiding contemporary young adults in the awareness of these drives and how they can be leveraged more consciously is something that those who study and work with young adults, like myself, can and should do.

How The Marriage Paradox relates to Where the Millennials Will Take Us on Gender

In *The Marriage Paradox*, Willoughby and Spencer critically contribute to the extant literature on contemporary young adults by postulating that cognition about marriage in the minds of young adults affects how they live out their twenties.[31] Specifically, rather than millennials dismissing marriage as a value outright as some reports might make it seem, the authors describe the millennial struggle to grapple with what marriage might mean in their lives as something "very real and personal."[32] Wil-

28. Dana, *God, Improv*, 18.
29. Dana, *God, Improv*, 70, 73.
30. Dana, *God, Improv*, ix.
31. Willoughby and James, *Marriage Paradox*, x.
32. Willoughby and James, *Marriage Paradox*, x.

loughby and James find, consonant with other research, that millennials still deeply respect and value marriage and all that might come with it. This very respect leads them to enter into the arrangement with greater consideration and discernment than those in generations past.[33]

Given the pressure that millennials feel in general, however, and the demands of mundane "adult" married life they perceive awaits them, millennials largely date for fun and exploration while in their twenties. Thus, they screen and pursue dating partners based on those who can entertain them.[34] Pressures to use college as a time for exploration and yet also safeguard and prepare for a fluid future has resulted in people declaring they do not have time for nor interest in more serious relationships. They feel like they already have too much responsibility. What intimate interactions do exist at college are often alcohol-influenced. Christian ethics professor and ethnographer of young adults Jennifer Beste, in collaboration with her students, finds that how college students interact in alcohol-soaked environments bears little resemblance to how they would handle opposite sex, romantic, or sexual interactions in a sober context. Yet, even when sober, she finds that contemporary young adults flounder when it comes to discerning the sexual ethics guidelines by which they might live.[35] At parties, contemporary young adults want their behavior to be "no strings attached," meaning that they would prefer to pretend as if their behavior in this context will not have consequences or require an expectation of follow-up in the context of their sober, weekday lives. They engage in behavior that they think will help relieve stress.[36]

As many scholars like Willoughby and James report, contemporary young adults simply do not conceive of dating as direct preparation or vetting for marriage until the end of the decade.[37] Willoughby and

33. Willoughby and James, *Marriage Paradox*, xvi.

34. Gortner, *Varieties of Personal Theology*, 303–4; Willoughby and Spencer, *Marriage Paradox*, 13, 89–90; Bogle, *Hooking Up*, 121; Dietz, "Boost your Confidence," 6.

35. Beste, *College Hookup Culture*, 162, 169. Beste devotes the second half of her book to taking what her students have learned from observing their own college party and hookup culture and putting it in conversation with Roman Catholic ethicist Margaret Farley's guidelines for Just Love, as well as Roman Catholic theologian Johann Metz's idea of poverty of the spirit. See also King, *Faith with Benefits*.

36. Beste, *College Hookup Culture*, 152; In 2016 *The Journal of Brain and Behavior* published a study that indicated that women are twice as likely as men to suffer from severe stress and anxiety, *The Journal of Brain and Behavior* (2016) cited by Salam, "Having It All," 2; see also Wong, "There's a Stress Gap."

37. Willoughby and James, *Marriage Paradox*, 89–90; For instance, Konstam,

James note that as the prospect of marriage becomes more realistic as age and stability are acquired, millennials switch from simply seeking dating partners to dating in order to screen potential marriage partners.[38] When it comes to criterion for potential marriage partners, their criteria shifts away from a partner that is exciting to one that is dependable and capable.[39] Psychologist Varda Konstam writes that emerging adults told her that they discovered—with experience—that it was important to have the ability to rest and be real in the relationship. They noted that to be self-conscious all the time is unsustainable.[40] These young adults also reported learning that a true intimate relationship takes time, investment, and energy. As one respondent put it, she now sees that a romantic partner must be "more than a hobby."[41] Konstam's respondents described a good relationship as involving a daily caring of the other person's day-to-day life, including its inherent stresses, joys, and fears.[42]

Why this level of understanding about what it takes to have a durable, rewarding relationship is not immediately obvious to young adults may reveal a lack of relational skills, and a deeper ethical doubting of what to expect and invest in an intimate other. Willoughby and James and Konstam see one of the generational changes appearing in contemporary young adults they studied is that they are overall less willing to make sacrifices in general, and for each other, and do not expect it from a partner.[43] This holds true, to some degree, at any stage of the relationship.[44] Willoughby and James write that "For many [contemporary young adults], the idea of having a partner on which to rely, someone to help

---

writing after Willoughby and James, and likely partially in response to them as they published books in the same Oxford series, finds that amongst contemporary young adults there is a common belief that dating couples should not have to make sacrifices for each other, but marital couples absolutely should, Konstam, *Romantic Lives*, 93.

38. Willoughby and James, *Marriage Paradox*, 89–90.

39. Willoughby and James, *Marriage Paradox*, 12–4, 90–92.

40. Konstam, *Romantic Lives*, 31.

41. Konstam, *Romantic Lives*, 92.

42. Konstam, *Romantic Lives*, 10.

43. Konstam, *Romantic Lives*, 7. In general, millennials approach large concepts like sacrifice like they do marriage; they do not ascribe to them automatically as true and beneficial narratives without having some sense of the details and context of how such concepts might play out specifically in their lives. For instance, Konstam found that only a small minority of her respondents outright considered sacrifice to be an obligation of an interpersonal relationship. Konstam, *Romantic Lives*, 77.

44. Willoughby and James, *Marriage Paradox*, 16.

you through the ups and downs of life, sounds almost like a fairytale."[45] They are always planning for contingencies and fall back options, but not ones that necessarily involve leaning on each other, regardless of gender. Where gender does come into play in terms of Life Plan Bs, Gerson describes men and women having similar desires for a fluid egalitarianism between men and women partners.

Both genders describe themselves as wanting sufficiency for themselves; however, women define sufficiency as the ability to take care of themselves and children without relying upon a male partner, and men see sufficiency as the ability to still take care of a family, but to have the freedom not to do so if desired. When male and female partners find themselves unable to achieve this fluid reliance upon each other and exchange of domestic and financial responsibilities, women become the persons more likely to take care of domestic responsibilities while men prioritize financial earning and career prospects.[46] Many millennials report that, while they believe in equal rights for men and women, they are more interested in prioritizing an arrangement of work and care that they hope or feel will be less stressful than that of the two-career household they experienced growing up.[47]

Part of this involves an expectation for greater egalitarianism than in partnerships past. Feminist sociologist Kathleen Gerson notes of young adults she interviewed for her book *The Unfinished Revolution*, "Most of my interviewees hope to create lasting, egalitarian partnerships, but they are also doubtful about their chances of reaching this goal . . . Far from rejecting the value of commitment, almost everyone wants to create a lasting marriage or marriage-like relationship."[48] Both men and women, expect to work and contribute at home in their future romantic relationships. Gerson quotes Michael, a 26-year-old African American raised by his working-class single mother:

> I don't want the fifties type of marriage, where I come home
> with a briefcase and she's cooking. She doesn't have to cook. I
> just want her to have a career of her own. I want things to be
> comfortable. And somewhere down the line, if I lose my job or
> things start going crazy in the marriage, I want to be able to
> set my goals, and she can do what she wants, because we both

45. Willoughby and James, *Marriage Paradox*, 37.

46. Gerson, *The Unfinished Revolution*, 102–5.

47. Carlson, "A View from Above"; Risman, *Where the Millennials will Take Us*, 55.

48. Gerson, *The Unfinished Revolution*, 10–11.

> have this economic base and the attitude to do it. That's what
> marriage is about.[49]

While the ability for everyone being able to "do what they want" is a new definition of marriage, most family studies research supports the idea that younger generations desire relationships of flexibility, in terms of gender and prospects of work-home engagement being more flexibly divided.[50]

Hence, the desire and expectation of partnership is flexibility, not erasure of gender roles as if a point on a political manifesto. Gerson notes that the young people she interviews want adaptable, equitable relationships. Respondent Amy had to say:

> I want a fifty-fifty relationship, where we both have the potential
> of doing everything. Both of us working, and in dealing with
> kids, it would be a matter of who has more flexibility with regard
> to their career. And if neither does, then one of us will have to
> sacrifice for one period, and the other for another.[51]

This alternating sacrifice, while backed up by sociological research on work-life precarity and the most likely way for heterosexual couples to survive a constantly shifting economy structure, is often hard to achieve.

Bonnie Cushing's and Monica McGoldrick's research shows that once young adults become parents, whatever values of egalitarianism they may or may not have espoused and practiced earlier, raising children shifts couples back to more traditional divisions of labor, with women typically taking on more hours per week of responsibilities than men.[52] While millennials have been too young as a generational cohort until now to pass through into child-raising time, the gap between the expectations of a respondent like Amy that responsibilities and burdens can alternatively shift between heterosexual partners and the lack of that in past tradition exposes a substantial hurdle for millennials to overcome in making their expectations break through past practice in new reality. Gerson highlighted that whether her couples were in traditional or "reversed" care-work relationships, it was important to note that most couples hoped for a more integrated and equal balance than they had

---

49. Gerson, "Moral Dilemmas," 16.

50. Mason and Lu, "Attitudes," 39–57; Zuo and Tang, "Breadwinner Status, 29–43, cited by Kohlman and Krieg, "Introduction," xv.

51. Gerson, "Moral Dilemmas," 16.

52. Cushing and McGoldrick, "The Differentiation of Self and Faith," 255.

been able to achieve.[53] Work-life sociologist Alison Pugh, however, who had a closer focus on class, found that working-class persons in particular would most prefer a traditional model but fear it is not economically sustainable.[54]

Research shows that, overall, a gendered alternation of reliance is a stated ideal for many young adults. Yet while it does in fact lead to success in the gig and knowledge economies of the present, it does not bear out in actual practice for most young adults as they progress down the partnership road.[55] With men making more than women in most partnerships, it has been clear that women are the ones who sacrifice free hours, and career advancement to take care of children and to protect the male partner's ability to financial provide if such a need arises.[56] This is in part because research indicates that persons have mixed feelings about progressing with equity if it comes at the cost of other values such as stress relief, financial reward, and getting along with peers.[57] And, if it is not clear already by this point in the chapter, millennials feel themselves under considerable stress and anxiety.

Even for those who profess belief in some degree of egalitarianism, Gerson's research in 2010 finds that contemporary young adults are reticent for men to trade in career stability and advancement in order to increase their responsibility at home, even if the household is economically stable out of fear that the situation will not last.[58] Weighing in on this from her own research, Pugh found that somewhat "counterintuitively," men's greater employment insecurity may make couples prioritize men's jobs because women, as more marketable yet less well paid, are more likely to get a job somewhere somehow.[59]

---

53. Gerson, "Different Ways, 167.

54. Pugh, "Introduction,"14.

55. See Pugh, *Tumbleweed Society* and *Beyond the Cubicle*.

56. Such a need today includes women staying home to care for children while they are distance learning during the COVID-19 pandemic, whereas many fewer men have given up their jobs to do the same. See Cohen and Hsu, "Pandemic Could Scar" and Hsu, "Even the Most Successful."

57. This stall is identified by researcher of millennial feminism Alison Dahl Crossley as in part because the generation has been cultivated to be apolitical precisely through a belief that individualism and it associated privatization must be valorized at all costs, Crossley, *Finding Feminism*, 5.

58. Gerson, *The Unfinished Revolution*.

59. Pugh, *Beyond the Cubicle*, 10.

These choices are made, in part, because a continuing parenthood career penalty leads to reluctance among intimate partners to truly practice an egalitarian partnership across spheres of work and home.[60] For instance, since women are still expected to first and foremost be mothers, even though their marriage attractiveness now includes earning potential as a factor, they receive less resistance at work and in society to continuing to take on the majority of the care-work at home.[61] Relatedly, in terms of self-reliance weighed against the resources envisioned as necessary for committing to a family, Gerson finds that men feel more apprehension than women do about the prospect of financially making ends meet for a family in comparison to simply taking care of themselves.[62] Thus, men and women both view family as requiring something more from them that is required of them on their own, but what and how it is required, and if it is an equal demand, involve consideration of how gender plays out in their particular social situation.

If they are able to sustain themselves on their own, women who cannot find a partner with whom they can expect to have an egalitarian intimate relationship will fall back on notions of autonomy and financial security rather than settle for a partnership which might involve too much compromise and inequality. Pugh and Silva independently insinuate that women will go it alone when necessary because they have trouble trusting men.[63] This often has to do with questions around financial "providership," safety, and fidelity, but also include how much support and decision-making responsibility they will receive from such potential husbands.

Research shows that one of the drivers of cohabitation, particularly among working-class persons, is that reluctance for men to give women decision-making and influencing power after they become wives.[64] Despite the fact that men often find themselves in a disadvantaged position of "providership" compared to that of generations past, Sarah M. Corse and Jennifer Silva note, "Neither the working-class or middle-class men

---

60. On average, while millennial women have approximate pay equity with millennial men, a financial penalty in terms of earnings of mothers versus fathers appears in this generation when the women enter their thirties. O'Connor, "Millennials Avoid Gender Pay Gap."

61. Risman, *Where the Millennials Will Take Us*, 47.

62. Gerson, *The Unfinished Revolution*, 159, 164.

63. Pugh, "Introduction," 14; Silva, *Coming Up Short*, 11.

64. Sassler and Miller, *Cohabitation Nation*, 2–3, 9, 10, 188.

we spoke with valued their intimate relationships as a specific hedge against the downside in the realm of work."[65] To do so would require being vulnerable, and to rely upon women to occasionally take the lead as a strategy for familial survival.

Rather than for most men and women to see this as a viable option, however, men see the need to spend all the more energy and effort building an earning power safety net against economic need, rather than assume that women with whom they partner can provide financially for them if they are not able to do so for themselves. Women, however, are still socialized—and believe—that they should take care of themselves and their children or be able to rely upon a male partner for the bulk of financial sustenance. To envision that women might need to take the financial lead is something only a small minority of families and partnerships, what Gerson calls "reverse traditional" relationships, can entertain or accomplish.

Gerson's findings and those of many others reveal that young adult women in heterosexual relationships are still bearing—and expected to bear—more of the emotional, domestic, and care work of their partnerships and families at the sacrifice of their employment prospects and other aspects of their personal self-fulfillment, at least compared to the sacrifices, compromises, or reduced career ambitions of their male partners. But furthermore, they do so in somewhat complicit agreement with their male partners that it should stay that way until economic and social fortunes allow it to cost less to risk loosening the grip on male providership.

Echoing a good deal of what Gerson published in 2010, sociologist Barbara Risman notes in her 2018 book *Where the Millennials Will Take Us: A New Generation Wrestles with the Gender Structure* that while millennials are progressively liberal in attitudes, advancing and sticking by gender politics may not be as salient for them as other values.[66] She reports that, regardless of what any particular millennial individual espoused in terms of gender politics, across the board what they had in common was experiences of significant "gender policing" in which persons respond negatively when men or women are not acting within the relevant gender role the person expects.[67] Out of four ideal types of

65. Corse and Silva, "Intimate Inequalities," 299.

66. Risman, *Where the Millennials Will Take Us*, 57.

67. Risman, *Where the Millennials Will Take Us*, 5.

gender role ideology which Risman developed through her analysis of one hundred and sixteen multi-method interviews with millennials in the Chicago area, she finds that the largest category, at 40 percent, are the *Straddlers*.[68] These are persons for whom gender equity aspirations and practices are wildly inconsistent, and possibly even contradictory, across their life stories and interview anecdotes. For instance, family and peer pressure often cause millennial men and women to conform to established gender-role behavior despite their espoused attitudes for egalitarianism and gender-role fluidity.

On the whole, *Straddlers* are often unsure where they stand on gender issues.[69] Risman identifies that categories of progressive gender champions, whom she labels as *Innovators* and *Rebels*, are much smaller in numbers than the *Straddlers*, yet have an outsized cultural impact in part because they actively seek to change things.[70] Her fourth category, *True Believers*, believe that men and women are different and therefore ought to have different roles, often citing religious teachings for their thoughts.[71]

Shaping Factors and Driving Values: The Psychology of the Authentic Millennial Self

It is hard to grasp how millennials view the world, what they prioritize, what they consider possible and probable, and what they end up doing with their lives, without understanding the depth to which millennials are a product of their material and psychological environment. Millennials have never known an economic-cultural system other than neoliberalism, categorized as a shift toward ever greater deregulation, privatization and financialization which began in 1979, the year before the first of the millennial generation were born. Therefore, millennials are more likely than previous generations to naturalize neoliberal values and patterns as simply "the way life is."

Many popular commentators describing millennials at large have noted that some millennial shock and anxiety likely comes from the uptick in sudden, mass violence by homegrown terrorists, such as the

---

68. Risman, *Where the Millennials Will Take Us*, 214.

69. Risman, *Where the Millennials Will Take Us*, 6.

70. Risman, *Where the Millennials Will Take Us*, 5.

71. Risman, *Where the Millennials Will Take Us*, 5.

Columbine high school students who shot up their school, or the Saudi Arabian Muslim extremists who flew into the Twin Towers on 9/11. This has added to a sense of unpredictability in terms of the chances of a sudden, locally concentrated, human-instituted violence that irreparably changes the lives of those affected.[72] Yet violence is not the only contemporary influence in making millennials anxious about security. In his book *Caring for Souls in a Neoliberal Age*, pastoral theologian and counselor Bruce Rogers-Vaughn identifies neoliberalism as the main factor in "shaping how, why, and to what degree individuals suffer" by encouraging people to seek "symptom relief and personal responsibility rather than communion, wholeness, and meaning-making."[73] Millennials exhibit this encouragement, living lives often turned inward and toward mental and emotional escape.

As a psychological drive, this compulsion toward self-reliance and authenticity for contemporary young adults operates largely unconsciously, fueled by anxiety about physical, financial, and psychological security. If asked, millennials would say that they largely have no other logical choice but to pursue these values. To back up this point, I commonly engage sociologist of contemporary culture Jennifer Silva's study of working-class millennials as illustrative of self-reliance's financial and therapeutic implications. In *Coming Up Short: Working-class Adulthood in an Age of Uncertainty*, Silva notes that today self-reliance is bolstered and defined by an idea that one can, and should, achieve psychological maturity through individualistic, therapeutic means.[74] Seventy percent of her respondents viewed themselves as their greatest risk and potential pitfall in life.[75] Thus, getting oneself right psychologically is particularly important, since in the minds of millennials psychological immaturity serves as the leading factor in keeping one from surviving and thriving.

Silva remarks that her respondents report that they are not willing to help others who are in need. They also do not expect to be helped

72. This type of terror and atrocity is becoming predictable enough for the generation which follows millennials, as evidenced by the political mobilization efforts by some student survivors of the 2018 Stoneman Douglas High School shooting in Florida.

73. Rogers-Vaughn, *Caring for Souls*, 6, 16.

74. Silva, *Coming Up Short*, 128.

75. Silva, *Coming Up Short*, 138.

themselves,[76] even by doctors when they are in medical need.[77] Yet, despite this evidence to the contrary, it cannot be said that they are becoming jaded and wholly unconnected from themselves and each other. Amidst this sense of privatization there is a sense of ethical authority in the individual and a drive to connect with others in what they describe as an authentic, embodied way.

Spiritual director and author of the book *Hungry Souls, Holy Companions: Mentoring a New Generation of Christians* Patricia Hendricks writes that contemporary young adults are postmoderns who value personal experience as authoritative over abstract belief. She notes, "the postmodern thinker is more open to learning about religion through stories and experience rather than theological constructs."[78] He or she is also skeptical of authority, particularly external authority.[79] These characteristics of postmodernism undergird millennials' distaste for labels, institutions, and predetermined frameworks precisely because they are impersonal.[80] In a nutshell, a quest for authenticity that can only be defined personally and through experience makes structures and forms that are not created through personal experience no longer matter for millennials. Thus, organized religion through churches and denominations, relationship frames such as marriage, and labels in general are all forms of larger association which millennials actively reject or evade.

Secularism scholars Joseph O. Baker and Buster G. Smith describe contemporary culture at large as moving toward "personal authenticity."[81] Yet what this buzzword means in terms of belief and behavior deserves to be unpacked. When used by befuddled members of older generations, authenticity is ridiculed as some hoped after but evasive and ambiguous level of truth. However, authenticity can and does mean more than "truth." Its etymology and millennial usage point to this. According to the *Merriam-Webster Dictionary*, authenticity primarily means worthy of acceptance as truthful. Yet I find it important to note that a synonym of authentic is obsolete.[82] Authentic is what is relevant, as well as what is

76. Silva, *Coming Up Short*, 98.

77. Silva, *Coming Up Short*, 140.

78. Hendricks, *Hungry Souls*, 2.

79. Hendricks, *Hungry Souls*, 3.

80. Pew, "Most Millennials Resist."

81. Baker and Smith, *American Secularism*, 67.

82. "Authentic," *Merriam-Webster Dictionary*.

true. When used by and about millennials, it indicates a certain intensity of connection inductively determined through first-hand, eclectically sourced, embodied experience.

Shenandoah Nieuwsma, commenting on the epistemology of millennials, describes their quest for authenticity as a form of hyper-subjectivity. For them, something must be personally believable to be compelling and thus true. In this realm of hyper-subjectivity, facts and rationality no longer matter to the degree that they used to, because personal experience can bump all other factors. In typical subjectivity, hearing data and analysis is filtered through personal points of reference, Nieuwsma notes, but this new form of hyper-subjectivity is about filtering something through personal reference not just to draw personal connections to it but rather to evaluate and draw a verdict on its utter veracity.[83] Nieuwsma notes that while weak hyper-subjectivity leads to a resistance to judge that results in toleration, strong hyper-subjectivity leads to difficulty finding common ground between people and their claims because rationality cannot be appealed to.[84] When the term authentic is used by and about millennials, it indicates a certain intensity of connection inductively determined through first-hand, eclectically sourced, embodied experience. This helps explain why some behaviors and ways of being are more meaningful to millennials than to others.

Young adults are often shown to be unwilling to judge the actions of others, which they attribute to a sense of cosmopolitanism that can also be a positive force for tolerance and supportive engagement with others rather than a harbinger of moral relativism. Yet this lack of judgment does not automatically nor necessarily equate to mean that young adults cannot make decisions for themselves and have no guiding values. Contemporary young adults are simply content to make their own choices without dictating that others act the same way, notes Konstam.[85] In fact, as they seek not to judge others, they all the more search for internal, personalized sources of authority and responsibility from which to judge and discern. As religion scholars Julian Galette and Jaco Hamman put it, millennials believe strongly in the "priesthood of all believers," that all persons should have access to the divine and be able to facilitate this for

---

83. Nieuwsma, "Certain of the Uncertain," 6.

84. Nieuwsma, "Certain of the Uncertain," 7.

85. Konstam, *Romantic Lives*, 323.

others, regardless of official ordination and training.[86] This helps explain why some behaviors and ways of being are more meaningful to millennials than others.

Contemporary young adults are already improvising and flexible in how they approach spirituality and religion, yet beyond the work of Presbyterian minister MaryAnn McKibben Dana, mentioned at the beginning of the chapter, few scholars of religion or philosophers frame shifts in the religious landscape of the U.S. in this way. However, there are a few excellent studies and commentaries in recent literature on what it means to be spiritually authentic for the 35 percent of millennials who have been categorized as either Spiritual but Not Religious (SBNR), or religiously unaffiliated, that does describe what makes up the spirituality of this semi-ambiguous category of believing non-believers.[87]

Elizabeth Drescher, in her 2016 book *Choosing Our Religion: The Spiritual Lives of America's Nones*, articulates that there are four main aspects of contemporary spirituality: 1) family, 2) friends, 3) food, and 4) Fido.[88] She finds that a focus on the practices of Spiritual But Not Religious reveals a story of what they do believe in: "'spirituality' as it is variously articulated, moves through the lives of the nones as they craft stories that 1) are embedded in everyday life; 2) center primarily on relationships rather than individualistic pursuits or institutionalized rituals; and 3) are composed of practices focused on the integration of body, mind, and spirit."[89] More cosmopolitan, non-judgmental forms of spirituality have taken hold recently, argues Drescher, a view which is backed up by the findings in Linda Mercadante's *Belief without Borders: Inside the Minds of the Spiritual but not Religious*.

While religion scholars or members or organized religion often lob accusations that "a belief without borders" is internally or traditionally inconsistent, Mercadante argues that hybridity and syncretism of spiritual ideas, practices, and identities is seen by contemporary persons as highly appropriate and natural.[90] Drescher and Mercadante's scholarship offer the most detailed case studies illuminating trends in millennial spiritual life as an involving an individualistic, narrow realm of concern

---

86. Cited in Young, *Young Adults, Intimacy, and Mutuality*, 70.

87. Lipka, "Millennials Increasingly are Driving Growth."

88. Drescher, *Choosing our Religion*, 43.

89. Drescher, *Choosing our Religion*, 51.

90. Mercadante, *Belief without Borders*, 72.

and intermittent engagement. Yet this same research also indicates such strong contemporary value-orientations toward actualization, collaboration, relationality, and participation that millennials cannot be written off as hopelessly relativistic or immoral.[91]

Jolene Erlacher's *Millennials in Ministry* highlights how millennials value expediency, immediacy, and justice above other concerns.[92] This fuels their impatience with traditional church structures and hierarchies in favor of prioritizing teamwork, collaboration, and tolerance whether inside or outside the church. Erlacher observes that millennials have radical respect and value for the individual before them, which is not discounted because of rank, position within the organization, or other factors.[93] Often churches, as collective structures, are seen by millennials as not as good as other forces for tending to the individual, so they seek other means for achieving this end.

Deformalization and Improvisation:
Understanding the Subtlety of Millennial Agency

Social science scholars studying changes to contemporary mainstream cultural behavior have described cultural trends away from formalized intimacy and organized religion broadly as deinstitutionalization.[94] As I allude to earlier in this chapter, more recent scholarship has furthered categorization of these trends by describing it as de-formalization. Deformalization involves a diversification of shape to behavior and ideas and includes, therefore, a bit by default, less shape to inhibit future changes to whatever form a behavior or concept has taken. For instance, as more people cohabitate rather than marry, their relationship no longer follows a semi-standard process of religious vows proclaimed publicly at a singular time and place. To some degree, these relationships of cohabitation are thus easier to dissolve since they involve less change to form: no legal name changes, no automatic court proceedings over division of assets, common property, and responsibilities for children, no need for

91. See Hendricks, *Hungry Souls*; See Erlacher, *Millennials in Ministry*.

92. Many books attempt to grapple with and describe the nuances of millennial inconstancy in engaging with organized religion. For examples of such, see Johnstone and Root, *Embedded Faith* and Lane, *Lessons in Belonging*.

93. Erlacher, *Millennials in Ministry*, 10–11.

94. Cherlin, "The Deinstitutionalization of American Marriage," 848–861; Pew Research Center, "Millennials in Adulthood."

an annulment or other response from religious authorities. These legal and social ties are part of what it means to have a formal relationship in the first place.

There is much debate over the implications of the informality, or at least loosened form of cohabitation. Scholars of religion Christian Smith and Patricia Snell seem to bemoan the foolishness of contemporary young adults in their research for believing that cohabitation serves as anything approximate to a test-run for marriage.[95] Yet researchers of contemporary cohabitation Maureen Baker and Vivienne Elizabeth note that cohabitation has become as prevalent as it is because it is highly convenient, financially prudent, and, ironically, does not require much communication, commitment, negotiation, cooperation, or forethought about how or where one wants to live since the situation is presumed to be temporary, nor does it necessarily signify an advanced level of commitment in the relationship (although it often does).[96]

As I have attempted to illustrate with examples from their intimacy, gender, and spiritual practices, I believe relying upon categories of deinstitutionalization and deformalization as sufficient descriptors of social trends leaves a considerable gap in describing and theorizing about millennials. To address this gap, I point to millennials navigating their lives through an improvisational process. This improvisation as a theory of action seems consistent with millennials' expectation of change, their belief in self-reliance and authenticity, and their resistance to pre-existing or formalized frameworks.

In my extensive literature review on contemporary young adults, social theorists Luke Howie and Perri Campbell stand alone in helping me expound upon this idea of improvisation. They deem the self of contemporary young people as a "guerilla self," a form of fighting back against a system organized against them through using the terms of the system against to eke out some space for substantive living.[97] Howie and Campbell elaborate:

> Guerrilla selfhood is a term used to designate types of identity that require participation *through* resistance, institutionalization *through* the appearance of not being institutionalized and individualism *in the midst of* a failure of individualism. In

95. Smith and Snell, *Souls in Transition*, 62.

96. Baker and Elizabeth, *Age of Cohabitation*, 6, 8, 14, 147; Sassler and Miller, *Cohabitation Nation*, 18–19, 178–79.

97. Howie and Campbell, *Crisis and Terror*, 76.

building this concept we draw on literature where the guerrilla metaphor has been deployed to signify moments where *the
weapons of the system are turned upon themselves*. It is, we argue,
a style of thinking the exercises imagination and resists attempts
to exterminate ambivalence . . . The guerrilla self is ravaged by
uncertainty and doubt. But it is hopeful.[98]

Such nuanced action of tweaking the rules rather than outright, organized
resistance can seem like nothing more than giving into over-preening
individualism. Often the distinguishing line between capitulation to the
pressures and subverting them to find breathing room for hope is hard
to see clearly.

As pastor Dana notes, improvisation starts with a "yes" to the situation at hand in which we first accept what we cannot change in order
to then respond appropriately to what is right in front of us.[99] It thus
requires deep attention to the other and the moment at hand to be successful.[100] This has a pragmatic realism to it, and a form of concrete,
intense relationality that a lived ethics requires. Dana emphasizes that
the process of improvisation may not know the end game, but there are
certainly patterned rules and response to rely upon in order to develop
a momentary plan.[101] This understanding that one can respond in a patterned way to the unknown can provide the hope and resilience that
Bingaman says is necessary to treat super modern anxiety.[102] He writes
that the level of anxiety people are facing may not be disproportionate to
what we are facing in the restructuring of our world and the undercutting
of its reliability.[103] Yet the best way to have hope in the system is to pursue
response with ever greater intentionality and particularity, to get better at
attaching an intensity of meaning to things at the very time that the speed
of things seems to make that impossible.[104]

Yet social science research indicates that a flexibility of response,
while holding onto an internal moral core in how one relates to personal
commitments, is what persons need to cultivate in order to weather the
winds of economic challenge successfully in a neoliberal environment.

98. Howie and Campbell, *Crisis and Terror*, 76.

99. Dana, *God, Improv*, 18.

100. Dana, *God, Improv*, 70, 73.

101. Dana, *God, Improv*, ix.

102. Bingaman, *Treating the New Anxiety*, 3.

103. Bingaman, *Treating the New Anxiety*, 10.

104. Bingaman, *Treating the New Anxiety*, 20, 26, 29.

Pugh, in her books *The Tumbleweed Society* and *Beyond the Cubicle: Job Insecurity, Intimacy and the Flexible Self*, has done the most careful and precise work in this area. She parses out how the infidelity of a neoliberal economy does and does not affect relational stability within the home and a stable sense of self, largely depending on factors that are often based in socioeconomic situation.[105]

Other work-life researchers who have published in the past ten years have also reiterated the importance of flexibility in approaching how to manage workforce and domestic care needs. Echoing the work of Gerson mentioned earlier, feminist sociologist Joan C. Williams notes that workplace policies and ideals continue to encourage women in a heterosexual partnership to do more than half of the domestic management and men to do the majority of the financial providing in terms of security and dollars. She sees this as a result of a self-reinforcing, interlocking system of gender and class. In line with Gerson, Williams notes that a rigid ideal of a masculine worker remains at the center of today's economic and culture system. This obstinate ideal, and its accompanying financial and policy reality, disincentivizes people from taking risks toward a better gendered, better work-life balance than they currently have.[106]

Concluding Remarks

In the final pages of her book, Konstam encourages researchers to understand that while intimate relationships have always been risky, the amount of risk contemporary young adults feel in general because of their position in a neoliberal economy causes a "perfect storm" of screening relationships with extra care.[107] I would say that they are critically evaluating what partnership adds to their "risk portfolio" or "profile," as the amount of risk one feels and how this factors into evaluation of potential partners is a complex compilation of interactions which include their geographic location, age, possible dependents, desire to have children in the future, student loan debt, job prospects, anticipated future moves for education, work, or family, family support, psychological and physical health, and financial stability.

105. Pugh, *Tumbleweed*; Pugh, *Cubicle*.
106. Williams, *Reshaping*, 2–5, 107, 149.
107. Konstam, *Romantic Lives*, 331, 337.

I therefore conclude that in order to make room for greater fluidity in gender and work-life balance, among other reasons, millennials can embrace improvisation as an ethical style and process.[108] There is some evidence that this is occurring in a public, shared spaces in which millennials programmatically offer themselves a guided sense of self-reflection and collaborative processing in order to advance and better articulate their ethics, questions, and desires around intimacy and sex.[109] In particular, millennials are forming their own forums and writing their own educational materials about how to date and determine sexual interest, evaluate one's desires, and communicate with a partner effectively.[110] They are writing and self-publishing books about the importance of confidence in dating, how to handle online profile anxiety and digital ghosting (suddenly no longer maintaining contact with someone with whom one was formerly in frequent contact),[111] and how to try to live a casual romantic life in order to grow personally, among other things.[112]

Thus, rather than stumbling through a process of improvisation for lack of a better choice, sans significant political and economic change toward a non-neoliberal society, millennials can continue and, with greater intentionality, further develop skills of self-reflection, systematic assessment, and interpersonal communication to eke out the best living space they can in a turbulent, neoliberal world. Beste and Freitas both note in their direct work with college students at the time that there is a yawning need for reflective spaces in which millennial men and women, in college and afterwards, can realize that the norms they unconsciously enact in their sexual practices to feel free and wanted are ultimately re-inscribing—if not fully regressing—inequalities of power dynamics between the sexes.[113] Furthermore, Beste and Freitas each argue, despite young adults'

108. For more on how this might be done, see Wells, *Improvisation;* Jenkins, "Incompetent Christians"; Young, *Black Queer Ethics.*

109. While there are a handful of books which address the wide variety of spirituality and religiosity of contemporary young adults, there is no extant academic text or study that covers a similarly wide and novel span of millennial intimacy beyond marriage.

110. See Roth and Schmiedt, *Millennial Sex Education.*

111. See Nochman et al., *Left Swipes and Love.*

112. See Perry, *Available.*

113. Beste, *College Hookup,* 101; Freitas, *Consent,* 42, 85; Feminist scholars have noted that women achieving and maintain sexual agency, at least of some sort, is seen as crucial to the development of new femininities, Attwood, "Through the Looking Glass," 203.

default responses to stress as numbing themselves to go with the flow, young adults are perfectly capable of engaging in discussions of sexual ethics and desire.[114] In fact, drawing on Beste and Freitas I argue that identifying and claiming authentic desire for sex and relationship is the first step in figuring out the "yes" in an improvisational-style sexual ethic so that a following step of what to do about that desire can be deduced.

In brief, intentionally embracing improvisation entails the ability to do both situational and personal assessments of experience and of the personal priorities garnered from that experience. It calls one to develop skills of assertion and communication to articulate these experiences for self and others in such a way that desires can be pursued and methods of getting there defended, or, if not functional, assessed as such, and revised. It requires an acceptance of the fact of human vulnerability and its particular psychological intensity during young adulthood, as deeply uncomfortable as this may be.[115] Along the way this improvisational navigational method requires honesty about the constancy and changes of identity, as well as that its agents subject themselves to risk, scandal, and vulnerability that comes with going after life in a way the world as it has been thinks is improbable in its ambiguity. This improvisational style may or may not reinforce self-reliance, but it will, hopefully, be authentic and fruitful in a way which we can all champion.

In contrast to previous generations, contemporary young adults believe that life will be a juggle and a stretch economically and emotionally to such a degree that self-reliance is the only sound strategy for security and fulfillment both now and in the long term.[116] At the psycho-spiritual level this same underlay of self-reliance is often expressed as a desire to be "authentic." As I have stated in this chapter, this predictive horizon

114. Beste, *College Hookup*, 242–53; Freitas, *Consent*, 78; Freitas believes rigorous discussion is needed to "empower [contemporary young adults] to unpack, critique, and become more self-aware" of what assumptions and narratives college students are operating out of, as well as how this matches up against their own desires and religious concerns." She argues that only this level of engagement can begin to meet the complexity of sexuality and of the ethics of consent, Freitas, *Consent*, 138, 47, 46, xii.

115. Freitas' most recent book is about the current impulse driven by social media in college life to seem perfect and invulnerable. See Freitas, *The Happiness Effect*. The pressing undercurrent of what prohibits young adults from having the psychological and emotional space to reflect upon their values and their actions and seek a different path indicates that it is essential to offer them anxiety and stress management mechanisms.

116. Pew Research Center, "Millennials in Adulthood"; McGuire, "Millennials' Perceptions"; Crossley, *Finding Feminism*.

of needing to be self-reliant and wanting to be authentic has considerable implications for millennial behavior and expectations in terms of intimacy and family commitments as they move through their twenties and thirties. For instance, instead of seeing marriage as a universal moral framework for all serious romantic, sexual, and procreative relationships, millennials have moved toward a diversification of intimate and non-intimate connections.[117] They are living singly for longer, dating casually, using birth control with less stigma than in the past, procreating on their own, and cohabitating in record numbers.

Rather than simply another expression of a long cultural trend toward greater and greater individualism, however, self-reliance and authenticity become interpellated with each other as values, feeding into and defining each other in such a way as to create something much more. I argue this point in part because this radical sense of subjectivity seems accompanied by a poignant combination of grief, confidence, and desire for connection that defies many of the positive feelings of freedom and independence commonly associated with individualism. Instead, the repercussions of a deeper dive into the self as locus of responsibility and authenticity is as ethically unproven as it is a non-negotiable reality.

Bibliography

Alcorn, Katrina. "Millennials Want Children, But They're Not Planning on Them." *New York Times*, January 8, 2014.

Attwood, Feona. "Through the Looking Glass? Sexual Agency and Subjectification Online." In *New Femininities: Postfeminism, Neoliberalism, and Subjectivity,* edited by Rosalind Gill and Christina Scharff, 203–14. New York: Palgrave Macmillan, 2011.

"Authentic." *Merriam-Webster Online Dictionary.* https://www.merriam-webster.com/dictionary/authentic.

Baker, Joseph O., and Buster G. Smith. *American Secularism: Cultural Contours of Nonreligious Belief Systems.* Religion and Social Transformation Series. New York: New York University Press, 2015.

Baker, Maureen, and Vivienne Elizabeth. *Marriage in an Age of Cohabitation: How and When People Tie the Knot in the Twenty-First Century.* Oxford: Oxford University Press, 2014.

Beste, Jennifer. *College Hookup Culture and Christian Ethics.* Oxford: Oxford University Press, 2018.

Bingaman, Kirk A. *Treating the New Anxiety: A Cognitive-Theological Approach.* Lanham, MD: Aronson, 2007.

---

117. See Chambers, *Sociology of Family Life.*

Bogle, Kathleen A. *Hooking Up: Sex, Dating, and Relationships on Campus*. New York: New York University Press, 2008.

Carlson, Daniel. "A View from Above: How Structural Barriers to Sharing Unpaid Work at Home May Lead to 'Egalitarian Essentialism' in Youth." Online Symposium published by the Council on Contemporary Families. http://contemporaryfamilies.org/4-carlson-egalitarian-essentialism-in-youth/.

"Catch Feelings." *Urban Dictionary*. https://www.urbandictionary.com/define.php?term=catch%20feelings.

Chambers, Deborah. *The Sociology of Family Life: Change and Diversity and Intimate Relations*. Malden, MA: Polity, 2012.

Cherlin, Andrew J. "The Deinstitutionalization of American Marriage." *Journal of Marriage and Family* 66.4 (2004) 848–61.

Cohen, Patricia, and Tiffany Hsu. "Pandemic could Scar a Generation of Working Mothers." *New York Times*, June 3, 2020. https://www.nytimes.com/2020/06/03/business/economy/coronavirus-working-women.html.

Corse, Sarah M., and Jennifer M. Silva. "Intimate Inequalities: Love and Work in the 21st Century." In *Beyond the Cubicle: Job Insecurity, Intimacy, and the Flexible Self*, edited by Allison J. Pugh, 283–303. New York: Oxford University Press, 2017.

Crossley, Alison Dahl. *Finding Feminism: Millennial Activists and the Unfinished Gender Revolution*. New York: New York University Press, 2017.

Cushing, Bonnie, and Monica McGoldrick. "The Differentiation of Self and Faith in Young Adulthood: Launching, Coupling, and Becoming Parents." In *Human Development and Faith: Lifecycle Stages of Body, Mind, and Soul*, edited by Felicity Kelcourse, 244–58. 2nd ed. St. Louis: Chalice, 2015.

Dana, MaryAnn McKibben. *God, Improv, and the Art of Living*. Grand Rapids: Eerdmans, 2018.

Dietz, Max. "Boost Your Confidence and Get the Girl." In *Left Swipes & Love: A Millennial's Guide to Hookups, Dating, and Tinder*, edited by Amanda Nachman and Daniel Kuhn. College Park, MD: College Magazine, 2016.

Drescher, Elizabeth. *Choosing our Religion: The Spiritual Lives of America's Nones*. New York: Oxford University Press, 2016.

Erikson, Erik. *Identity, Youth, and Crisis*. New York: Norton, 1968.

Erlacher, Jolene Cassellius. *Millennials in Ministry*. Valley Forge, PA: Judson, 2014.

Filipovic, Jill. *The H-Spot: The Feminist Pursuit of Happiness*. New York: Nation, 2017.

Freitas, Donna. *Consent on Campus: A Manifesto*. New York: Oxford University Press, 2018.

———. *The Happiness Effect: How Social Media Is Driving a New Generation to Appear Perfect at Any Cost*. New York: Oxford University Press, 2017.

Gallete, Julian, and Jaco Hamman. "Practicing Table Fellowship for Spiritual Nurture." In *Millennial Narrative: Sharing a Good Life with the Next Generation*. Nashville: Abingdon, 2019.

Gerson, Kathleen. "Different Ways of *not* having it all: Work, Care, and Shifting Gender Arrangements in the New Economy." *Beyond the Cubicle: Job Insecurity, Intimacy, and the Flexible Self*, edited by Allison J. Pugh, 155–77. New York: Oxford University Press, 2017.

———. "Moral Dilemmas, Moral Strategies and the Transformation of Gender: Lessons from Two Generations of Work and Family Change." 1998 Sociologists for Women in Society Feminist Lecture reprinted in *Gender and Society* 16 (2002) 8–28.

———. *The Unfinished Revolution: How a New Generation Is Reshaping Family, Work, and Gender in America.* New York: Oxford University Press, 2010.

Gortner, David T. *Varieties of Personal Theology: Charting the Beliefs and Values of American Young Adults.* Burlington, VT: Ashgate, 2013.

Hallman, Heidi. *Millennial Teachers: Learning to Teach in Uncertain Times.* New York: Routledge, 2017.

Hendricks, Patricia. *Hungry Souls, Holy Companions: Mentoring a New Generation of Christians.* Harrisburg, PA: Morehouse, 2006.

Hertz, Rosanna. *Single by Chance, Mothers by Choice: How Women are Choosing Parenthood without Marriage and Creating the New American Family.* New York: Oxford University Press, 2006.

Holmes, Erin Kramer, Geoffrey Brown, Kevin Schafer, and Nate Stoddard. "Healthy Transitions to Family Formation." In *Flourishing in Emerging Adulthood*, edited by Laura M. Padilla-Walker and Larry J. Nelson, 70–97. New York: Oxford University Press, 2017.

Howie, Luke, and Perri Campbell. *Crisis and Terror in the Age of Anxiety: 9/11 and the Global Financial Crisis.* New York: Palgrave MacMillan, 2017.

Hsu, Andrea. "Even the Most Successful Women Pay a Big Price in Pandemic." *All Things Considered.* National Public Radio. October 20, 2020. https://www.npr.org/2020/10/20/924566058/even-the-most-successful-women-are-sidelining-careers-for-family-in-pandemic?fbclid=IwAR1WvoowhOXE15QRJqreHaMO7AJAk8lzOJSSSHNE9uYif75sO7LGW6RnuCY.

Jenkins, Willis. "Doing Theological Ethics with Incompetent Christians: Social Problems and Religious Creativity." In *Lived Theology: New Perspectives on Method, Style, and Pedagogy*, edited by Charles Marsh, Peter Slade, and Sarah Azaransky, 54–66. New York: Oxford University Press, 2017.

Johnstone, Carlton, and Andrew Root. *Embedded Faith: The Faith Journeys of Young Adults within Church Communities.* Eugene, OR: Wipf and Stock, 2013.

Kefalas, Maria J., Frank F. Furstenberg, Patrick J. Carr, and Laura Napolitano. "Marriage Is More Than Being Together": The Meaning of Marriage for Young Adults." *Journal of Family Issues* 32 (2011) 845–75.

King, Jason. *Faith with Benefits: Hook Up Culture on Catholic Campuses.* New York: Oxford University Press, 2017.

Kohlman, Marla, and Dana B. Krieg. "Introduction: Intersectional Dynamics of Gender, Family and Work." In *Notions of Family: Intersectional Perspectives*, edited by Marla Kohlman, Dana B. Krieg, and Bette J. Dickerson, ix–xxv. Bingley, UK: Emerald Group, 2013.

Konstam, Varda. *The Romantic Lives of Emerging Young Adults: Moving from I to We*, edited by Larry Nelson. New York: Oxford University Press, 2019.

Kroger, Jane, and James E. Marcia. "The Identity Statuses: Origins, Meanings, and Interpretations." In *Handbook of Identity Theory and Research*, edited by Seth Schwartz, Koen Luyckx, and Vivian Vignoles, 31–54. New York: Springer, 2011.

Lane, Erin. *Lessons in Belonging from a Church-Going Commitment-Phobe.* Downers Grove, IL: InterVarsity, 2015.

Lipka, Michael. "Millennials Increasingly Are Driving Growth of 'Nones.'" Pew Research Forum Fact Tank: News in the Numbers series. Pew Research Forum. May 12, 2015. http://www.pewresearch.org/fact-tank/2015/05/12/millenials-increasingly-are-driving-growth-of-nones.

Mason, Karen O., and Yu-Hsia Lu. "Attitudes toward Women's Familial Roles: Changes in the United States, 1977–1985." *Gender and Society* 2 (1988) 39–57.

McGuire, Kate. "Millennials' Perceptions of How Their Capacity for Romantic Love Developed and Manifests." Master's thesis, Smith College School for Social Work, 2015.

Mercadante, Linda A. *Belief without Borders: Inside the Minds of the Spiritual but not Religious.* New York: Oxford University Press, 2014.

Miller, Lisa. "The Ambition Collision: This Is What Happens to Ambition in Your Thirties." *Cut*, September 6, 2017.

Miller, Rich. "Single Americans Now More Than Half the US Population." *Chicago Tribune*, September 10, 2014. http://www.chicagotribune.com/news/nationworld/chi-single-americans-population-20140910-story.html.

Nieuwsma, Shenandoah. "Certain of the Uncertain: Reflections on Millennial Epistemology and the Emerging Church." In *Emerging Church, Millennials, and Religion*. Volume 1: *Prospects and Problems*, edited by Randall Reed and G. Michael Zbaraschuk, 3–14. Eugene, OR: Cascade Books, 2018.

Nochman, Amanda, Daniel Kuhn, and College Magazine. *Left Swipes & Love: A Millennial's Guide to Hookups, Dating and Tinder.* College Park, MD: College Magazine, 2016.

O'Connor, Sarah. "Millennials Avoid Gender Pay Gap Until their 30s." *The Financial Times*, Jan. 4, 2017. Academic OneFile.

O'Reilly, Brian, and Karen Vella-Zarb. "Meet the Future." *Fortune* 142.3 (July 24, 2000) 144–68.

Orlofsky, Jacob L. "Intimacy Status: Theory and Research." In *Ego Identity: A Handbook for Psychosocial Research*, edited by James Marcia et al., 111–33. New York: Springer, 1993.

Padilla-Walker, Laura M., Madison K. Memmott-Elison, and Larry J. Nelson, "Positive Relationships as an Indicator of Flourishing During Emerging Adulthood." In *Flourishing in Emerging Adulthood*. Emerging Adulthood Series, edited by Laura M. Padilla-Walker and Larry J. Nelson, 212–36. New York: Oxford University Press, 2017.

Perry, Matteson. *Available: A Memoir of Heartbreak, Hookups, Love and Brunch.* New York: Scribner, 2016.

Pew Research Center. "Millennials: A Portrait of Generation Next." February 2010.

———. "Millennials in Adulthood: Detached from Institutions, Networked with Friends." March 2014.

———. "Millennials on Track to be the Most Educated Generation to Date." March 17, 2015. https://www.pewresearch.org/fact-tank/2018/03/16/how-millennials-compare-with-their- grandparents/ft_millennialsworkforce_031715_v3/.

———. "Most Millennials Resist the 'Millennial' Label." September 3, 2015. https://www.pewresearch.org/politics/2015/09/03/most-millennials-resist-the-millennial-label/.

Pratt, Michael W. and M. Kyle Matsuba. *The Life Story, Domains of Identity, and Personality Development in Emerging Adulthood: Integrating Narrative and Traditional Approaches.* New York: Oxford University Press, 2018.

Pugh, Allison J. *Beyond the Cubicle: Job Insecurity, Intimacy and the Flexible Self.* New York: Oxford University Press, 2017.

———. "Introduction." In Pugh, Allison J. ed., Beyond the Cubicle: Job Insecurity, Intimacy and the Flexible Self, 1–23. New York: Oxford University Press, 2017.

————. *The Tumbleweed Society: Working and Caring in an Age of Insecurity*. New York: Oxford University Press, 2015.

Rattner, Steven. "We're Making Life Too Hard for Millennials." Opinion. *New York Times*, July 21, 2015.

Risman, Barbara J. *Where the Millennials Will Take Us: A New Generation Wrestles with the Gender Structure*. New York: Oxford, 2018.

Rogers, Holly, and Margaret Maytan. *Mindfulness for the Next Generation: Helping Emerging Adults Manage Stress and Lead Healthier Lives*. New York: Oxford University Press, 2012.

Rogers-Vaughn Bruce. *Caring for Souls in a Neoliberal Age*. New Approaches to Religion and Power Series. New York: Palgrave Macmillan, 2016.

Roth, A. Lea, and Nastassja Schmiedt. *Millennial Sex Education: I've Never Done This Before*. 2nd ed. Online. Spring Up, 2015.

Rusovick, Rik, and Carmen Knudson-Martin. "Gender Discourse in Relationship Stories of Young American Couples." In *Couples, Gender, and Power: Creating Change in Intimate Relationships*, edited by Carmen Knudson-Martin and Anne Rankin Mahoney, 275–96. Thousand Oaks, CA: Springer, 2009.

Salam, Maya. "Does 'Having It All' Mean Doing It All?" Gender Letter. *New York Times*, December 7, 2018.

Sassler, Sharon, and Amanda Jayne Miller. *Cohabitation Nation: Gender, Class, and the Remaking of Relationships*. Oakland: University of California Press, 2017.

Silva, Jennifer. *Coming Up Short: Working-Class Adulthood in an Age of Uncertainty*. New York: Oxford University Press, 2013.

Smith, Christian, and Patricia Snell. *Souls in Transition: The Religious and Spiritual Lives of Emerging Adults*. Oxford: Oxford University Press, 2009.

Syed, Moin, and Lauren L. Mitchell. "How Race and Ethnicity Shape Emerging Adulthood." In *The Oxford Handbook of Emerging Adulthood*, edited by Jeffrey Jensen Arnett, 87-104. Oxford Library of Psychology. Oxford: Oxford University Press, 2016.

Wang, Wendy, and Paul Taylor. "For Millennials Parenthood Trumps Marriage." Pew Research Forum. 2011.

Wells, Samuel. *Improvisation: The Drama of Christian Ethics*. Grand Rapids: Brazos, 2004.

Williams, Joan C. *Reshaping the Work–Family Debate: Why Men and Class Matter*. Cambridge: Harvard University Press, 2010.

Willoughby, Brian, and Spencer James. *The Marriage Paradox: Why Emerging Adults Love Marriage Yet Push It Aside*. New York: Oxford University Press, 2017.

Wong, Kristin. "There's a Stress Gap between Men and Women: Here's Why It's Important." *New York Times*, November 14, 2018.

Young, Laine Walters. "Young Adults, Intimacy, and Mutuality in Late Modernity: Contemporary Updates to Theological, Psychological, and Marginalized Perspectives on Relationship Ethics." PhD diss., Vanderbilt University, 2019.

Young, Thelathia Nikki. *Black Queer Ethics, Family, and Philosophical Imagination*. New York: Palgrave Macmillan, 2016.

Zuo, J., and S. Tang. "Breadwinner Status and Gender Ideologies of Men and Women regarding Family Roles." *Sociological Perspectives* 43 (2000) 29–43.

5

Millennials, Secularization, and Catholic Sexual Abuse Crisis

A Generational Examination and Reflection

Daniel Rober

Abstract

The Catholic sexual abuse crisis has been a defining event in the lives of millennial Catholics. This chapter looks at the church affiliation of millennial Catholics through the prism of this event. First, it explores the event itself and its emergence in the life cycle of this generation, with particular emphasis on how it impacted their parents and older peers. Second, it examines the evidence for how it has directly impacted the religious lives of millennials. Third, it examines questions of how the church can move forward to engage millennials and avoid the sectarianism of being a church only of the highly intentional, which has not traditionally been the preferred Catholic mode of belonging to the church. The chapter concludes that church leaders and theologians need to focus on these questions with regard to millennials in order to have a credible institutional future.

The secularization of millennials and the rise of religious nones among young people have been much remarked upon and demonstrated through sociological and other evidence.[1] One of the institutions most affected by this dynamic, particularly in the U.S., has been the Roman Catholic Church, which has also been bleeding members of earlier generations.[2] For millennials coming of age within that institution, perhaps the single most trenchant event in terms of overall impact has been the sexual abuse crisis in the church as it played out in the media beginning in 2002.[3] Recent aftershocks related to this crisis serve to underscore the way in which it has defined the Catholic Church for a generation.[4]

This chapter explores secularization and changing religious identities of Catholic millennials through the lens of the Catholic sexual abuse crisis. It will examine the dynamics that have played out in Catholic families, communities, and institutions with respect to religious belonging. In addition to disaffiliation, it will also examine the counterexample of millennials who have become very devout Catholics, during this period, as well as other nones who have been the subject of outreach by the church: what are their motivations and how does this crisis affect their relationship to the church?

This chapter will proceed in three sections. First, it will examine the event of the sexual abuse crisis in the span of the millennial generation, who ranged from their early twenties to elementary school years when it broke out in 2002. In so doing, it will examine responses from the previous two generational cohorts, given their influence on millennials as parents and older peers. The sexual abuse crisis of 2002 fundamentally changed the culture of the U.S. church in a way that has profoundly affected the faith lives of millennial Catholics. Second, it will examine Catholic patterns of disaffiliation through Albert Hirschman's classic framework of institutional belonging. Finally, in dialogue with scholars such as Kate Dugan who have examined Catholic youth evangelization as well as other groups such as the "Nuns and Nones" initiative, it will look at personal narratives of Catholic young adults and their relationship to the church.

1. Drescher, *Choosing our Religion*, 30: "To claim 'None' as the label for one's spiritual identity is to refuse to participate in the normative system of religious identification, where labels suggest general agreement with beliefs, values, and practices that distinguish one religious institution from another."

2. Pew Research Center, "America's Changing Religious Landscape."

3. Boston Globe, *Betrayal*.

4. *National Catholic Reporter,* "Open Letter to the US Catholic Bishops."

Millennials in a Changing World

Millennial Catholic life must be understood in terms of the millennial generation's overall identity, both with respect to other generations and with respect to particular characteristics and events that have shaped it. Malcolm Harris, a millennial journalist who has chronicled his own generation's development particularly in response to the 2008 Recession and its aftereffects, has defined this generation's identity in terms of the role of human capital in its development.[5] This emphasis has changed parenthood such that many millennials grew up experiencing what Harris calls "an unprecedented lack of unsupervised time," which he views as a denial of the chance to "build selves without adult oversight."[6] Harris notably places little emphasis on religion, mostly remarking upon it in terms of millennial declines in religiosity vis-à-vis previous generational cohorts.[7] Intriguingly with regard to the subject of this chapter, Harris notes declining rates of sexual abuse against children for the millennial cohort, particularly on its younger end. This decline, important in its own right, also may impact this generation's view of the Catholic sexual abuse crisis. Harris does not attribute causality to religion in this area, but it tracks with his emphasis on millennial cultivation of self and the resulting risk aversion. Such risk aversion, combined with the reputation of the Catholic Church as an unsafe place for children, may affect millennial choices concerning religious upbringing and socialization of their own children.

Donna Freitas, whose sociological work has engaged directly with millennials in areas such as social media and sex on college campuses, has also commented extensively on the way in which millennials, particularly younger millennials, have increasingly been defined—and found ways to define themselves—in terms of social media use and the culture that it creates. Freitas portrays a social world in which young people feel compelled to use social media yet at the same time express revulsion about its effects in their own lives.[8] This culture, particularly its emphasis on

---

5. Harris, *Kids These Days*, 5.

6. Harris, *Kids These Days*, 6.

7. Harris, *Kids These Days*, 193.

8. Freitas, *The Happiness Effect*, 10: "That students are aware they are splitting themselves in twothat they somehow *have* to do this to operate effectively and safely online—has been particularly fascinating and worrisome to me."

authenticity as well as the defense of reputation, has repercussions for how millennials engage with institutions such as the church.

Millennials thus have been raised and socialized amid large-scale social changes, particularly in the areas of technology and social media but also in the broader society, and they have arguably lived through multiple paradigms. Within the Catholic context, millennials have also lived through different iterations of what it means to be Catholic. They have been raised by parents and grandparents embodying "Vatican II" and "post-Vatican II" ideas and experiences of church, to use terms employed by Mary Ellen Konieczny in her important study of Catholic parish life.[9] They have also, in Eugene Kennedy's terms, experienced both "Type I"—highly institutionalized Catholicism, and "Type II"—a more free-spirited, anti-institutional approach often tied in to "spiritual but not religious" experiences.[10] As such, they have been implicated in versions of "retraditionalization," as Konieczny describes efforts to rediscover aspects of tradition that were lost particularly in the Catholic experience of the Second Vatican Council and its aftermath.[11]

Millennials, then, even as a "large" generation, stand in a kind of liminal generational space in which their experiences have bridged the gap between one era and another, largely defined by the growth of the Internet, the prevalence of cell phones, and the use of social media. Within the Catholic context, they also bridge an era constituted in many ways by the rise of the sexual abuse crisis as defining event in church life. It is to that issue that this chapter now turns.

Millennials in Relation to the Sexual Abuse Crisis

From a sociological perspective, the millennial generation represents a split demographic with respect to the Catholic sexual abuse crisis. Older

9. Konieczny, *The Spirit's Tether*, 71: "The outlook and attitudes of a particular generation dominates the shared perspective at each congregation, with different generation units of other cohorts finding their place within this dominant perspective."

10. Kennedy, *Tomorrow's Catholics*, 9: "Culture One is intrinsically dependent on the church *as institution* for its existence. Culture Two is intrinsically dependent on the church *as mystery* and only extrinsically dependent on it as institution."

11. Konieczny, *The Spirit's Tether*, 72: "Nearly all of the Vatican II and post-Vatican II generation Catholics at Assumption defined their Catholic belonging in opposition to experiences of childhood and present practices of the post-Conciliar church, with worship figuring prominently among them."

millennials, born in the 1980s, experienced a church in which this crisis had not yet become a major national issue. While a number of important studies had been written about this topic, it was arguably more of a "back-burner" issue for those who were not directly affected.[12] The Boston sexual abuse revelations beginning in 2002, and subsequent "aftershocks" that have continued up until the present in Philadelphia and other places, changed this situation by making the sexual abuse crisis something to be reckoned with by almost all practicing Catholics in the United States if not the entire developed world.[13]

For many millennials, then, particularly younger millennials, the Roman Catholic sexual abuse crisis is not one in which they were primarily victims or potential victims (who were more likely of their parents' or grandparents' generation) but rather an encompassing reality of the church into which they were born and baptized (or not baptized, sometimes for this very reason).[14] As such, this scandal occupies a distinct place for millennials particularly compared to older cohorts.[15]

The sexual abuse crisis thus looms for millennials as a pre-indictment of the church's credibility from a moral and institutional perspective. This view of the church means that millennials are less likely to have a "first naiveté" when it comes to the church or religious realities; they are more likely to have been presented with a less exalted, perhaps more realistic but also potentially more cynical, vision of the church from the beginning.[16] This shift has important implications for the formation of a religious imaginary among young adults.

The effects of the sexual abuse crisis, however, have not happened in a vacuum. They have occurred in the context of widespread dissatisfaction with church teaching in other areas, particularly concerning gender and sexuality.[17] They have also taken place in a time of cultural

12. Jenkins, *Pedophiles and Priests*; Berry, *Lead Us Not Into Temptation*; Sipe, *Sex, Priests, And Power: Anatomy of a Crisis*.

13. Weigel, *The Courage to Be Catholic*, is emblematic of this issue in that it situates the sexual abuse crisis in terms of doctrinal orthodoxy and fidelity. This approach is characteristic of Weigel's overall trajectory of thought, influenced by certain aspects of John Paul II's pontificate and teaching.

14. Grossman, "Baptism Rates Slide."

15. Saint Mary's, *Going, Going, Gone*, 32: "Church scandals, specific Church teachings, or personalities within the Church seem to be less important in decisions regarding affiliation than many may assume."

16. Ricoeur, *Symbolism*, 350

17. Rober, "Sex, Secularity and Cognitive Dissonance."

fragmentation within the church, where traditional patterns of organizing have given way to ideological grouping and self-segregation.[18] The sexual abuse crisis, then, has been a destabilizing force within an already-destabilizing institution—a particularly deep crisis given that the institution's identity particularly since the nineteenth century has been wrapped up in notions of historical stability and continuity.

For millennials, then, the sexual abuse crisis does not constitute a horrible aberration within an otherwise "normal" experience of the church, but rather a central part of their experience of the church. Michele Dillon, a sociologist who has tracked issues surrounding Catholicism and internal dissent for decades, has argued that doctrinal activism from the "moderately religious" has been key to positioning the church vis-à-vis secular culture.[19] The following section will explore demographic changes and interrogate whether the kind of activism described by Dillon might be less relevant for millennials than it was for prior generational cohorts.

Religious Patterns and the Institutional Church: Exit and Voice

The second decade of the twenty-first century has witnessed a "crisis of institutions." Institutions of all kinds—governments, universities, and churches, particularly the Catholic Church—have loomed large in this crisis. The sexual abuse crisis represents the most important institutional crisis in the contemporary Catholic church, but not the only one. It indeed has been weaponized for the purposes of other institutional battles, particularly by well-funded American enemies of Pope Francis.[20] In the contemporary Catholic church, then, the sexual abuse scandal sits at the middle of various interconnected conflicts concerning sexuality and institutional power in particular. It also coincides with demographic decay of the church in the Western world.

The economist Albert Hirschman noted that the decay of institutions and states follow certain kinds of patterns. Hirschman particularly identifies exit, voice, and loyalty as three major reactions to crises in

18. See Bruce, *Parish and Place*, 50. Bruce describes how the itinerant nature of American Catholics in the 20th century that meant "prioritizing purpose over place."

19. Dillon, *Postsecular Catholicism*, 24.

20. Senéze, *Comment L'Amérique Veut Changer de Pape*.

institutions. These ideas, while formulated to address economic realities, function well particularly in the U.S. religious context, where religious life has followed market patterns in certain respects.[21] Exit means that, "Some customers stop buying the firm's products or some members leave the organization," resulting in membership decline and correction by management.[22] Voice, meanwhile, expresses a situation in once customers or members "express their dissatisfaction directly" whether to management or to another authority capable of offering some remediation. Hirschman details the way in which these expressions of dissatisfaction differ in varying contexts, particularly as exit has been viewed as almost treasonous in some situations.[23] I think these ideas, which bear some resemblance to Finke and Stark's rational choice theory noted above, are particularly helpful for understanding the situation of Catholic millennials precisely in that recent decades have evinced an increasing tendency toward the "exit" option among Catholics generally and younger Catholics in particular.

Within previous generational cohorts, this threefold dynamic balanced itself somewhat differently. During the generation following the Second Vatican Council and the disillusionment felt by many laypeople with *Humanae Vitae* (the 1968 document reaffirming church teaching against the use of artificial birth control), all of these patterns can be discerned very clearly.[24] Demographic data certainly show that exit was a real possibility for many Catholics, even as Garry Wills and others have expressed that often former Catholics were uncomfortable in new church surroundings.[25] Catholic identity thus ran deep for this generation, even among those who were deeply unsatisfied with the state of the church.

Voice also found expression through new possibilities of dissent and "loyal opposition" to the church, both in journalism and in the form of lay groups such as Call to Action or later Voice of the Faithful.[26] For Catholics of older generations, particularly the "baby boom" cohort, these periodicals and structures have allowed for articulating a vivid sense of how Catholics can maintain a robust sense of religious identity

21. Finke and Stark, *The Churching of America*.
22. Hirschman, *Exit, Voice, and Loyalty*, 4.
23. Hirschman, *Exit, Voice, and Loyalty*, 17.
24. Tentler, *Catholics and Contraception*; McClory, *Turning Point*.
25. Wills, *Bare Ruined Choirs*, 15.
26. Dillon, *Catholic Identity*.

while simultaneously expressing profound dissatisfaction with how the church is run. Michele Dillon has described this phenomenon in terms of "interpretive autonomy," such that, "The typical self-identified Catholic, therefore, is one who disagrees with Church teaching on sexual and other issues and continues to stay Catholic."[27] Tricia Bruce argues that for older Catholics, the sexual abuse scandal in fact created "a cultural moment during which a critique of the Catholic Church was publicly accepted and expected," particularly in highly Catholic contexts such as Boston where the scandal first became major national news.[28]

Demographic data thus suggest an increasing use of the "exit" option on the part of millennial Catholics and their younger "Generation Z" peers currently coming of age. The *Going, Going, Gone* survey, an important recent survey of Catholic young adults (most of them from Generation Z) conducted by the St. Mary's Press Research Group, suggests that many young people begin internally disaffiliating from the church as teenagers, perhaps before they are able to prevail on parents to prevent themselves from being taken to church but nevertheless decisively.[29] This data shifts from stereotypes that the college years—when attendance patterns have typically dropped off due to newfound independence particularly among residential college students—as crucial to loss or retention of young adults.

Millennial Catholic socialization has thus run through rather than around the sexual abuse crisis. Stephen Bullivant has described this pattern in terms of what he calls "Credibility Enhancing Displays," or CREDS, which strengthen a sense of belonging to the church. In the absence of such credibility, the sexual abuse scandal represents a version of a "Credibility Undermining Display" or CRUD.[30] While perpetrated by a small minority of priests (with a more substantial number of bishops involved), this event, particularly its coverup, has shaken faith in the church as an institution. Rather than simply undermining the credibility of particular priests or bishops most egregiously involved, it has the broader effect of undermining faith in the institution as a whole.

27. Dillon, *Postsecular Catholicism*, 23.

28. Bruce, *Faithful Revolution*, 172.

29. Saint Mary's, *Going, Going, Gone*, 42: "The median age for when formerly Catholic teens and young adults left the faith in 13. Nearly four in ten (39 percent) report leaving between ages 13 and 17."

30. Bullivant, *Mass Exodus*, 227.

Recent surveys have shown perhaps surprisingly robust overall religious patterns among Catholic twentysomethings.[31] According to Clydesdale and Garces-Foley's research, there still exists among young people a subset of "cradle Catholics," from whom "family, ethnicity, and religion are tightly intertwined."[32] The young adult Catholic *milieu*, according to their survey, is defined particularly by community, with this being a major priority among young adults in choosing a parish.[33] This community can take on various forms depending on who is seeking it, but for most it "combines socializing and sharing faith experiences with people like them."[34]

This discussion of community contrasts, however, with the overall data, which show that it is relatively rare to find youths who identify strongly with Catholic faith communities as an important part of their lives.[35] Indeed, the *Going, Going, Gone* data indicates that for many youth community fails to get them through "disruptive" events in their life such as deaths in the family.[36] Similarly, data does seem to reflect disillusionment with community, and further show a departure from the traditional "life-cycle effect" in which departed youth might be expected to return to raise their own children.[37]

Returning to Hirschman's categories, then, it would appear that for millennials, the "voice" option has lost some of its appeal as compared to prior generations. The *Going, Going, Gone* study notably describes its "dissenter" category in terms of those who have actively left the church.[38] This reflects a lessened sense that there might be a home within the church for those who disagree with its doctrines. Several reasons might be proposed for this shift. Lower levels of Catholic education among Catholics may account in part for it, given Christian Smith's finding that Catholic high schools have a positive effect on future engagement with the church.[39] Greater policing of orthodoxy in the church, particularly during the John Paul II and Benedict XVI eras, may have given many young Catholics a

31. Clydesdale and Garces-Foley, *The Twentysomething Soul*.

32. Clydesdale and Garces-Foley, *The Twentysomething Soul*, 53.

33. Clydesdale and Garces-Foley, *The Twentysomething Soul*, 62.

34. Clydesdale and Garces-Foley, *The Twentysomething Soul*, 63.

35. Smith et al., *Young Catholic Americans*, 100.

36. Saint Mary's, *Going, Going, Gone*, 36.

37. Saint Mary's, *Going, Going, Gone*, 32.

38. Saint Mary's, *Going, Going, Gone*, 21.

39. Smith et al., *Young Catholic Americans*, 248.

more black-and-white sense of identity compared to earlier generations. The overall declining influence of religion and Christianity in particular in the U.S. must also be taken into account here.

It is clear, then, from Clydesdale's and other studies that robust communities of Catholics do exist among millennials, but the question is, what kind of communities? Will such communities be able to carry forward effectively what Kennedy calls "Type II" Catholicism, absorbing the spirit of the Gospel while relying less on the institution than the church has in the past? Or will the very fragility of contemporary Catholicism in the U.S. context make this more challenging?

Moving Forward

This third section will look at questions of where the church can move forward from here, focusing particularly on questions of sexuality and of social capital. Given that the church appears hamstrung by the hypocrisy of its teaching vis-à-vis its members' practice regarding sexuality, this creates a particularly challenging situation in that areas of church teaching and practice indirectly related to the sexual abuse crisis become caught up in it. In another vein, the sexual abuse crisis and related decline in practice on the part of many millennials has also kept them from benefitting from the social capital that tends to attach itself to religious practice. This shift, in turn, affects the shape of the church itself, possibly moving it in a more sectarian direction.

Katherine Dugan's work on the Fellowship of Catholic University Students (FOCUS) demonstrates what a sectarian version of millennial Catholic belonging looks like.[40] This organization cultivates a strong Catholic identity among Catholic young adults using techniques closely related to those employed by Evangelical churches. Its story is in many ways a success—drawing many youth into a relationship with the church and cultivating an ethos of "dynamic orthodoxy."[41] This ethos owes much to the example and inspiration of Pope John Paul II, whose papacy was characterized by charismatic evangelization combined with an emphasis on doctrinal orthodoxy.

40. Dugan, *Millennial*, 17: "FOCUS missionaries represent a millennial-generation interpretation of postconciliar U.S. Catholicism."

41. Dugan, *Millennial*, 12: "FOCUS intentionally aims to intervene in this process of identity formation in order to shape emerging adults as dynamically orthodox Catholic adults."

Like John Paul II's papacy, however, the FOCUS story has a dark side or blind spot when it comes to the sexual abuse crisis, as is notable in Dugan's book where this issue scarcely arises among the enthusiastic missionaries to whom she speaks. This blind spot can be seen most especially in the sexual abuse revelations at the Franciscan University of Steubenville, perhaps the headquarters of the "dynamic orthodoxy" described in Dugan's book.[42] Many millennial Catholic leaders attended the school and many more have attended summer youth conferences sponsored by the university around the United States. The revelations, involving abuse of students by Franciscan priests working at the school, have been notable for the way in which the administration and its notable defenders have attempted to ignore or continually hide it.[43] This repeats the pattern of other notable conservative Catholic figures or institutions involved in sexual abuse scandals in the United States.

On the other side of the ideological spectrum within the church, broadly speaking the "liberal" wing of the church, the "Nuns & Nones" project constitutes an important initiative for putting millennials into contact with the church. This project contrasts sharply in tone and audience with FOCUS and other such examples. The project describes itself on its website as "an alliance of spiritually diverse millennials, women religious, and key partners working to create a more just, equitable and loving world."[44] The tenor of the project accords with the overall trajectory of women religious after Vatican II toward an engagement with the world that works—consciously or otherwise—on the margins of the institutional church.[45]

The Nuns & Nones project, interestingly, does not define itself in terms of response to the sexual abuse crisis, although notably many news articles about the project have set it against this backdrop. Given that the sisters are clearly seeking to provide an open space for conversation, it makes sense to avoid pre-loading particular contexts into the conversation. It provides a space for "voice," in Hirschman's terms, while presupposing a thinner account of what that voice might entail than Catholic

---

42. Dugan, *Millennial*, 27. FOCUS had its origins in figures such as Curtis Martin and Scott Hahn who are associated with Franciscan University.

43. Morson, "Franciscan University Vows to Stop Sexual Assault," *National Catholic Reporter.*

44. The Nuns and Nones Project, para. 1.

45. Prejean, *River of Fire.*

periodicals and organizations that have fostered such a dynamic among older generations.

FOCUS and the Nuns & Nones project in many ways represent poles of millennial engagement with the church, although they are of course not constituted in opposition to one another. They carry forward, in many ways, the political battles that have taken place in the church since the Second Vatican Council (1962–65) while notably shifting the ground away from the centers of power in the church. Both of these groups engage millennials on a more grassroots level, through evangelization or open discussion, respectively.

What these examples both emphasize is that millennial engagement with the church is increasingly shifting away from classic institutional models in which the local parish and the local bishop constituted one's primary place of interface with the church. Donna Freitas has commented in this regard that for many young Catholics, particularly women, the challenge has been "to widen their scope of *where* one shows one's commitment to Catholicism," since traditional channels are often either closed and unwelcoming or otherwise unappetizing.[46] This widening of scope, I would argue, is likely to be the general trend for millennials moving forward. This trend is reflected also in Tricia Bruce's research on Catholic parishes, which demonstrates the increasing shift away from the dominance of the territorial parish and toward the revival of the "personal parish" reflecting the needs of particularly constituted communities.[47] Much of this would likely have resulted without the sexual abuse crisis, but I would argue that the damaging effect of the abuse crisis on territorial parishes has contributed to this set of issues.[48]

Millennial Catholics will relate to their church (or, in many cases, other churches they might join later) with a wariness that other generations acquired only over time. For those who stay, or indeed convert, that wariness is offset by other factors, particularly belief in the truth of Catholic teachings and the community of faith that can be found in the church. The intentionality of such religious belonging, however, which does not necessarily connote to a particular set of ideological positions within the church (except perhaps a more polarized set of them overall) distinguishes itself sharply from more traditional Catholic modes

46. Freitas, "Afterword," 236.
47. Bruce, *Parish and Place*.
48. Seitz, *No Closure*.

of belonging and points to a smaller church in the future.[49] Such a shift would represent a major change in the composition of the Catholic community, and possibly a more sectarian direction for it. Avoiding this fate will require articulating a new idea of Catholic identity and belonging.

Conclusion: The Sexual Abuse Crisis as Defining Event

The sexual abuse crisis and its ramifications are the defining event for the religious lives of Catholic millennials, and that the ongoing response to this set of issues will likely determine millennial engagement with Catholic beliefs, practices, and institutions moving forward. It is thus particularly important for theologians and church leaders to think about what kind of church they hope to emerge from the throes of this crisis. In my conclusion, I will engage with Massimo Faggioli's important theological discussion of these issues and tie it into the demographic and other data I have presented above.

Massimo Faggioli has written that the sexual abuse crisis in Catholicism constitutes a crisis for theology. In this sense, he builds on his own previous work concerning how theology as a discipline fits within the body of the church.[50] Faggioli particularly fixates on the way in which the sexual abuse crisis has become a crisis for ecclesiological paradigms of reform, particularly those that came out of the Second Vatican Council.[51] He describes a "hermeneutic of systemic distrust" as characterizing the life of the church today.[52] The church is "paying a high price" as Faggioli puts it, for not sufficiently dealing with issues surrounding clericalism in the twentieth century.[53] It is thus a reckoning with unfinished business of Vatican II and the postconciliar era.

---

49. This is a descriptive rather than prescriptive point. This question has been central to Catholic theological debates, notably engaged by Joseph Ratzinger/Pope Benedict XVI, whose approach to this issue sometimes seemed to bridge this gap. See Ratzinger, *Faith and the Future*, 104: "As a small society, she will make much bigger demands on the initiative of her individual members."

50. Faggioli, "A Wake-Up Call to Liberal Theologians" and "Endangered Species."

51. Faggioli, "The Catholic Sexual Abuse Crisis," 582: "The paralysis of the institutional church in articulating the structural changes needed in light of the Catholic abuse crisis is a subset of the more general paralysis of the institutional church *tout court* that has been typical of the last few decades."

52. Faggioli, "The Catholic Sexual Abuse Crisis," 584–85.

53. Faggioli, "The Catholic Sexual Abuse Crisis," 588.

Faggioli's work contrasts with and yet complements the conclusions to Stephen Bullivant's recent study on disaffiliation, which represents a center-right approach to some of the same issues. In his conclusion, Bullivant questions whether subsequent events in the church mean that the Second Vatican Council, with its mandate to open the church to dialogue with the modern world, was in fact a failure.[54] Faggioli would clearly not concede this point, but he does point out that the frameworks put in place by Vatican II—particularly its emphasis on the role of the laity and of more horizontal structures of power within the church such as synods and conferences of bishops—are not necessarily functioning as effectively or credibly as they did at that time. The retrenchment of clericalism during the John Paul II era combined with the eroding credibility of clerical structures among the laity has led to a situation in which Pope Francis and other leaders have sought to revive these reform measures perhaps too late to make an impact on a critical mass of laypeople.

I would argue, echoing Faggioli, that the sexual abuse crisis constitutes a key touchstone for millennial thinking about the church. While previous generations, specifically the "World War II" generation who led the church in the 1960s and 1970s particularly, set the crisis in motion, it has had an acute effect on the experience of the church for millennials. This crisis and its aftereffects must inevitably be a part of the picture for any millennial project of theology or church reform. Whether or not it has had a causal effect on disaffiliation—I think based on the evidence above that the matter is ambiguous—it is likely that it will be seen as the watershed moment in the church's loss of credibility among this generation.

The biggest challenge presented by the sexual abuse crisis, returning to Hirschman's categories, is its contribution to the rise of "exit" as dominant strategy for millennials in regard to Catholicism, rather than "voice" or "loyalty." If the paradigms for remaining faithful to the tradition, whether as a loyalist or a dissident, no longer make sense, this will lead to a more sectarian version of the church centered more around the model of FOCUS or Weigel's "Evangelical Catholicism" than a broader "people's church" model inclusive of everyone.[55] Michele Dillon's discus-

---

54. Bullivant, *Mass Exodus*, 263: Bullivant argues that Catholics chose to assimilate just as the broader culture "started rapidly to become less orthodoxly believing, less regularly practicing, and ultimately, less religiously identifying."

55. Weigel, *Evangelical Catholicism*. For discussion of the issue of "People's Church," see Rahner, *The Shape of the Church to Come*.

sion of differences between young white and Hispanic Catholics (the latter of whom are now the majority generationally) concerning political issues around immigration in particular should be alarming as a sign of how the church's social teaching is being taught and received.[56]

I have argued throughout this chapter that for millennials, the sexual abuse crisis is now part and parcel of the Catholic Church's institutional identity. In many ways, particularly on questions of safety, transparency, and accountability, this has been and will continue to be, a good thing. On the other hand, it has led in many ways to further polarization within the life of the church and less perceived space to carve out versions of Catholicity in between highly identity-based conservative spaces and alienated ones. The challenge for millennial Catholic theologians and for millennial Catholics more broadly is to articulate anew a vision of being Catholic amid the complexities of a church that has too often failed to live up to its claims.[57]

Bibliography

Berry, Jason. *Lead Us Not into Temptation*. Garden City, NY: Doubleday, 1992.
Boston Globe Investigative Staff. *Betrayal*. Boston: Back Bay, 2003.
Bruce, Tricia Colleen. *Faithful Revolution*. New York: Oxford University Pres, 2011.
———. *Parish and Place: Making Room for Diversity in the American Catholic Church*. New York: Oxford University Press, 2017.
Bullivant, Stephen. *Mass Exodus*. New York: Oxford University Press, 2019.
Clydesdale, Tim, and Kathleen Garces-Foley. *The Twentysomething Soul*. New York: Oxford University Press, 2019.
Dillon, Michele. *Catholic Identity: Balancing Faith, Reason, and Power*. Cambridge: Cambridge University Press, 1999.
———. *Postsecular Catholicism*. New York: Oxford University Press, 2018.
Drescher, Elizabeth. *Choosing Our Religion*. New York: Oxford University Press, 2016.
Dugan, Kate. *Millennial Missionaries*. New York: Oxford University Press, 2019.
Faggioli, Massimo. "'The Catholic Sexual Abuse Crisis as a Theological Crisis: Emerging Issues." *Theological Studies* 80 (3) 572–89.
———. "Endangered Species." *Commonweal*, December 17, 2018. https://www. commonwealmagazine.org/endangered-species-0.
———. "A Wake-Up Call to Liberal Theologians." *Commonweal*, May 16, 2018. https:// www.commonwealmagazine.org/wake-call-liberal-theologians
Finke, Roger, and Rodney Stark. *The Churching of America 1776–2005*. New Brunswick, NJ: Rutgers University Press, 2005.
Flanagan, Brian. *Stumbling in Holiness*. Collegeville, MN: Liturgical, 2018.

56. Dillon, *Postsecular Catholicism*, 31.

57. Brian Flanagan, *Stumbling in Holiness*, offers a good starting point for these reflections.

Freitas, Donna. "Afterword." In *From the Pews in the Back*, edited by Kate Dugan and Jennifer Owens, 234. Collegeville, MN: Liturgical, 2009.

———. *The Happiness Effect*. New York: Oxford University Press, 2019.

Grossman, Cathy Lynn. "Baptism Rates Slide Despite High-Profile Boosts." *Religion News*, October 22, 2013. https://religionnews.com/2013/10/22/baptism-rates-slide-despite-high-profile-boosts/.

Harris, Malcolm. *Kids These Days: Human Capital and the Making of Millennials*. New York: Little, Brown, 2017.

Hirschman, Albert O. *Exit, Voice, and Loyalty*. Cambridge: Harvard University Press, 1970.

Jenkins, Philip. *Pedophiles and Priests*. New York: Oxford, 1996.

Kennedy, Eugene. *Tomorrow's Catholics/Yesterday's Church: The Two Cultures of American Catholicism*. Ligouri, MO: Triumph, 1995.

Konieczny, Mary Ellen. *The Spirit's Tether*. New York: Oxford University Press, 2013.

McClory, Robert. *Turning Point*. New York: Crossroad, 1995.

Morson, Jenn. Franciscan University Vows to Stop Sexual Assault, but Victims Need Convincing." *National Catholic Reporter*, October 9, 2018.

The Nuns and Nones Project. https://www.nunsandnones.org/.

National Catholic Reporter. "Open Letter to the US Catholic Bishops: It's Over." November 9, 2018. https://www.ncronline.org/news/opinion/open-letter-us-catholic-bishops-its-over.

Pew Research Center. "America's Changing Religious Landscape." May 12, 2015. https://www.pewforum.org/2015/05/12/americas-changing-religious-landscape/.

Prejean, Helen. *River of Fire*. New York: Random House, 2019.

Rahner, Karl. *The Shape of the Church to Come*. Translated by Edward Quinn. New York: Seabury, 1974.

Ratzinger, Joseph. *Faith and the Future*. San Francisco: Ignatius, 2009.

Ricoeur, Paul. *The Symbolism of Evil*. Translated by Emerson Buchanan. Boston: Beacon, 1967.

Rober, Daniel. "Sex, Secularity, and Cognitive Dissonance: Catholics and Conscience in the Wake of 1968." In *"You Say You Want a Revolution,"* edited by Sandra Yocum, Elena Procario-Foley, and Susie Paulik Babka, 84–95. Maryknoll, NY: Orbis, 2019.

Saint Mary's of Minnesota. *Going, Going, Gone*. Winona, MN: Saint Mary's, 2018.

Seitz, John C. *No Closure: Catholic Practice and Boston's Parish Shutdowns*. Cambridge: Harvard University Press, 2011.

Senéze, Nicholas. *Comment L'Amérique Veut Changer de Pape*. Montrouge Cedex: Bayard, 2019.

Sipe, Richard. *Sex, Priests, and Power: Anatomy of a Crisis*. New York: Brunner/Mazel 1995.

Smith, Christian, Kyle Longest, Jonathan Hill, and Kari Christofferson. *Young Catholic Americans*. New York: Oxford University Press, 2014.

Tentler, Leslie Woodcock. *Catholics and Contraception: An American History*. Ithaca, NY: Cornell University Press, 2004.

Weigel, George. *The Courage to Be Catholic*. New York: Basic, 2002

———. *Evangelical Catholicism*. New York: Basic, 2014.

Wills, Garry. *Bare Ruined Choirs*. Garden City, NY: Doubleday, 1972.

6

The Spiritual Turn in Canada

"Spiritual but not Religious"
Canadian Millennials

GALEN WATTS

Abstract

More ethnically diverse, socially progressive, and digitally aware than any generation in history, millennials stand at the vanguard of cultural transformation in North America. This transformation has been identified as a "Spiritual Revolution," and understood as a generational shift away from institutional religion, towards a more privatized and personal spirituality. Given that millennials will play a significant role in shaping the political and moral landscapes of the future, it is imperative that scholars of religion come to understand the socio-political character of this emerging form of religiosity. This chapter contributes to this endeavor through qualitative research with Canadian millennials who self-identify as SBNR, making the case that self-spirituality can be understood as a form of virtue theory, with attendant ethics.

Introduction

More ethnically diverse, socially progressive, and digitally aware than any generation in history, millennials stand at the vanguard of cultural transformation in North America.[1] This transformation has been identified as a "Spiritual Revolution,"[2] and understood as a generational shift away from institutional religion, towards a more privatized and personal spirituality.[3] According to a study commissioned in 2012 by the *National Post* nearly one quarter of Canadian millennials consider themselves "Spiritual but not Religious" (SBNR),[4] and a 2013 Pew Research Center report found rising religious disaffiliation in Canada to be the result of a generational shift.[5] These empirical findings support the widely noted conclusion that, "All signs point to the 'spiritual, not religious' self-definition as becoming more of a reality of our time."[6] Given that millennials will play a significant role in shaping the political and moral landscapes of the future, it is imperative that scholars of religion come to understand the socio-political character of this emerging form of religiosity. This chapter is an attempt to contribute to this endeavor.

My analysis is based on qualitative data collected from in-depth semi-structured interviews with fifty Canadian millennials who self-identify as SBNR conducted over five years.[7] These are the findings of a doctoral research project on the politics of the "spiritual turn,"[8] as it relates to the millennial generation (born between 1980–2000) in Canada. The chapter will proceed as follows. First, I introduce the discourse that informs what goes by "spirituality" among Canadian millennial SBNRs— which I call, following Paul Heelas, "self-spirituality."[9] I offer a brief sketch of its history, identifying what I take to be its primary historical tributaries. Second, I suggest that self-spirituality can be understood as

---

1. Greenberg and Weber, *Generation We*; Winograd and Hais, *Millennial Momentum*.

2. Heelas and Woodhead, *Spiritual Revolution*.

3. Starkey, *God, Sex, and Generation X*; Fuller, *Spiritual, But Not Religious*; Wuthnow, *After the Baby Boomers*.

4. Johnson, "Polling Religion in Canada."

5. Pew Research Center, "Canada's Changing Religious Landscape."

6. "Ask the Religious Experts." See also Mercadante, *Belief Without Borders*.

7. For more on methods see Watts, "On the Politics of Self-Spirituality."

8. Houtman and Aupers, "The Spiritual Turn."

9. Heelas, *The New Age Movement*.

a form of virtue theory, with attendant ethics. I outline what I take to be its core ethics and then briefly discuss their historical antecedents. Third, I discuss the ideological nature of this discourse, as well as some of the socio-political implications that follow from it. I then conclude by outlining some implications my analysis holds for the study of religion, more generally.

The Discourse of Self-Spirituality

> Spirituality is something you believe in, whereas I feel like religion is imposed upon you. —Nathalie

> Like why should I have to go through Jesus? God is in me. —Charlene

> Spirituality to me is more about exploration and freedom, and just being who you are. —Emir

Only in the last half-century has the SBNR moniker risen to prominence. Though scholars disagree about what "spirituality" sans religion actually signifies, an emerging consensus has taken shape within the study of religion. This consensus holds that underlying much of what goes by "spirituality" today entails a specific cultural-cum-religious discourse.[10] Paul Heelas once deemed this new religious form "self-spirituality" because it *sacralizes the self*.[11] As the above quotations are meant to illustrate, my research participants seem to be in unanimous agreement about what their "spirituality" orbits around, and where they look for guidance—that being, the *true self* within. Heelas deems this a *self-ethic*, the basic idea of which is that the true self is the source of moral and epistemological authority. Thus, one of my SBNR research participants asserted, "Spirituality is something *you* believe in, whereas I feel like religion is imposed upon you." While another proclaimed, "I need to look within myself to do anything." In *Spiritual but not Religious: Understanding Unchurched America* historian Robert Fuller argues the SBNR disposition points "to a psychological process whereby individuals can apprehend, and become

---

10. See Forman, *Grassroots Spirituality*; Lynch, *The New Spirituality*; Heelas, *Spiritualities of Life*; Hanegraaff, *New Age Religion and Western Culture*; Houtman and Aupers, "Religions of Modernity"; Campbell, *The Easternization of the West*.

11. Heelas, *The New Age Movement*.

inwardly connected to, an immanent divinity."[12] In other words, SBNRs view their true self as a conduit of the supernatural or God. Of course, they largely eschew this language. For SBNRs—who borrow primarily from the New Age and Human Potential movements—the true self is generally spoken of as one's "Higher Self" and understood as a byproduct of Nature or the Universe. Furthermore, self-spirituality endorses an *experiential epistemology*. In this, it continues a long-standing strand within the Western tradition—its "third way."[13] We can classify this epistemic stance as "the belief that there is no authority external to the individual qualified to judge the nature of truth."[14] Thus an SBNR research participant who dabbles in Buddhist meditation told me, "for me it's your own truth," while a member of a Twelve Step group said, "I found it was more encouraging to find the truth within myself." This helps to explain why self-spirituality so often leads its adherents to gravitate towards, and find inspiration in, testimonies, personal narratives, and autobiographical anecdotes; where and when individuals can "identify" or "relate" to other's experiences self-spirituality is strongest. Heelas informs us, "Truth, not surprisingly for those who see themselves as spiritual beings, *must*—at least, first-and-foremost—come by way of one's own experience."[15] In fact, the more intense, ecstatic, esoteric, powerful, or effervescent the experience, the more authoritative. As Émile Durkheim would have predicted, self-spirituality is made real in moments that break with the expectations of ordinary life. For SBNRs, "spirituality" is signaled in moments of quiet contemplation or unexpected bliss—be it while in meditation, climbing a mountain, or dancing at a rave.

It follows that, contra their self-image, SBNRs are neither traditionless, nor wholly unique.[16] In fact, they collectively (albeit unknowingly) subscribe to self-spirituality, a cultural-cum-religious discourse that is both comprehensive and coherent.

Much work has been done recently to trace the history of self-spirituality.[17] Philosopher Charles Taylor argues its popularity is the result

12. Fuller, *Spiritual, But Not Religious*, 143.

13. Hanegraaff, *New Age Religion and Western Culture*.

14. Campbell, *The Easternization of the West*, 134.

15. Heelas, *The New Age Movement*, 21.

16. Watts, "Missing the Forest for the Trees."

17. Fuller, *Spiritual but not Religious*; Tacey, *The Spirituality Revolution*; Schmidt, *Restless Souls*; Gottlieb, *Spirituality*; Carrette and King, *Selling Spirituality*.

of the "massive subjective turn of modern culture."[18] He characterizes this turn by a kind of "inwardness" or "interiorization." Moreover, like a number of others,[19] Taylor traces the high value placed on self-expression and self-realization within the spiritual milieu to the Romantics and their "philosophy of nature as source."[20] Indeed, self-spirituality is profoundly romantic. Social historian Elline Kay Eskenazi writes, "For God, Romantics exchanged the individual person. For an abode of the sacred, they exchanged nature. And for a diabolical force, Romantics exchanged society and social convention."[21] These romantic notions deeply influenced the development of what Catherine Albanese calls metaphysical religion. Most notably, during the eighteenth century, Unitarians, Universalists, and Transcendentalists propagated what Albanese calls, "self-culture," as they followed "a spiritual logic," that had its intellectual roots in antiquity, "from outer to inner."[22] This was a logic that had been percolating for quite some time. These new religious movements gave birth to a number of offshoots such as Spiritualism, Theosophy, New Thought, and other nineteenth-century metaphysical religions that have profoundly shaped self-spirituality.

Among other things, they were precursors to the New Age Movement, which came of age during the 1960s and 70s counterculture and is closely associated with the baby boomer generation—the generation that raised millennials. Indeed, New Age ideas and practices, which, even in the movement's heyday were interminably difficult to pin down, let alone map out, have since seeped into contemporary western consciousness.[23] Put another way, directly following the counterculture, "the New Age was stepping aside for a new and exoteric spiritual America"[24]—one that has only become ever more diffuse and eclectic. It is for this reason that Taylor suggests we are today living in a "spiritual super-nova, a kind of galloping pluralism on the spiritual plane."[25] While perhaps true, today's

---

18. Taylor, *The Ethics of Authenticity*, 26,

19. Thomas, "Spiritual but Not Religious"; Heelas, *Spiritualities of Life*; Jacobs, "Spirituality."

20. Taylor, *Sources Of the Self*, 373.

21. Eskenazi, "The Roots of New Age Spirituality," 126.

22. Albanese, *A Republic of Mind and Spirit*, 161.

23. Hanegraaff, *New Age Religion and Western Culture*.

24. Albanese, *A Republic of Mind and Spirit*, 514.

25. Taylor, *A Secular Age*, 300.

spiritual super-nova displays for more cultural coherence than most (including Taylor) realize.

One would be remiss not to mention the importance of the rise of psychology and what sociologist Robert Bellah and coauthors call "therapeutic culture" in shaping self-spirituality.[26] In the late nineteenth century, the well-known American scholar William James, sought to map out the route to "Saintliness," what he viewed as the essential task of religion.[27] In his *Varieties of Religious Experience*, James both carries forward and extends the subjective turn of modern culture, positing that there is an "experiential core to religion that underlies all of the various creeds and rituals associated with religious organizations."[28] Moreover James's pragmatism reduced religion to *what it did* for individuals, thereby giving scientific legitimacy to the romantic idea that "anything that is subjectively experienced as real must therefore be regarded as real."[29] Sociologist Wade Clark Roof concurs. He argues, "[o]f all his penetrating insights into religious psychology, James's comment on the power of a religious experience to redeem and vivify—to fill an empty interior world—is especially fitting to our time."[30]

Lastly, it is important to note that all of this paved the way for what Paul Heelas and Linda Woodhead call "subjective wellbeing culture," the "most widespread cultural expression" in the West today.[31] It is a cultural expression which can be characterized by the significant value it ascribes to "being treated as a uniquely valuable person, finding out about oneself, expressing oneself, discovering one's own way of becoming all that one can (reasonably) be."[32] There is little doubt that subjective wellbeing culture owes much to Romantic thought. Heelas and Woodhead propose that the rising popularity of self-spirituality is largely the result of a wider cultural trend towards valuing "self-expression," "personal fulfillment" and "subjective well-being" taking place in the West.[33] Thus it is worth

---

26. Bellah et al., *Habits of the Heart*, 119.

27. James, *The Varieties Of Religious Experience*.

28. Fuller, *Spiritual but not Religious*, 56.

29. Hanegraaff, *New Age Religion and Western Culture*, 227.

30. Roof, *Spiritual Marketplace*, 16.

31. Heelas and Woodhead, *Spiritual Revolution*, 83.

32. Heelas and Woodhead, *Spiritual Revolution*, 81.

33. Heelas and Woodhead, *Spiritual Revolution*, 79.

noting that self-spirituality is generally at home in contemporary mainstream cultural currents.

In sum, we can see that while my research participants Nathalie, Charlene, and Emir are no doubt distinct, they nevertheless belong to a timeworn and shared religious tradition, which has longstanding roots in North America, and multiple historical precursors. Moreover, the SBNR orientation, contra the self-understanding of existing SBNRs, derives much of its appeal from sharing deep elective affinities with the wider culture.

The Ethics of Self-Spirituality

We should view the spiritual turn as the culmination of a long historical move inwards. Self-spirituality is a spirituality that *sacralizes the self*; it is the logical culmination of the massive subjective turn. Scholars began paying attention to this emerging religious form in the wake of the counterculture—what sociologist Robert Wuthnow aptly called the "Consciousness Reformation."[34] Conservative commentators have generally denounced it, arguing that its rejection of traditional religious institutions amounts to a soft relativism that it is antithetical to a moral life. Self-spirituality, with its attendant individualism, the argument goes, leads to either narcissism or hedonism, or both. For example, Reverend Lillian Daniel argues that self-spirituality, "fits too snugly with complacency,"[35] while Martin E. Marty dismisses "religionless spirituality" as "banal" and "solipsistic."[36] Others have disparaged SBNRs for their "promiscuity of belief,"[37] condescendingly representing the way they approach religion as a "pick and mix" style.[38] What these criticisms are blind to, I maintain, is not only the shared cultural logic informing the SBNR disposition, but also the distinct ethical imaginary at work.

In this section, I will make a case for thinking about the kind of ethicality inherent to self-spirituality as one centered on virtue. Virtue ethics is concerned with character development rather than the following of categorical moral axioms. It presupposes a substantive and teleological

---

34. Wuthnow, *The Consciousness Reformation.*
35. Cited in Oppenheimer, "Examining the Growth."
36. Cited in Schmidt, *Restless Souls*, 284.
37. Webster, *Dispirited*, 44.
38. Carrette and King, *Selling Spirituality*, 128.

account of human flourishing, which the individual attains by cultivating the necessary virtues. Self-spirituality as is expressed by Canadian millennials can be understood as a form of virtue ethics, endorsing the following virtues: self-reliance, acceptance of difference or tolerance, empathy, emotional courage and resilience, and compassion. These are grounded in a substantive conception of human flourishing, framed as a process of *self-realization*. Although couched in a therapeutic register, this conception of flourishing involves certain ethical principles. In fact, permeating what we might call the spiritual milieu—itself encompassing a broad range of schools of thought and practice—are a number of core ethics that, collectively, serve to enable the individual to *realize their true self*. These four core ethics include an ethic of self-responsibility, an ethic of authenticity, an ethic of productivity, and an ethic of self-awareness.[39] In what follows I will outline and explicate each ethic respectively.

In one way or another, for my research participants the spiritual life involves taking responsibility for oneself. Whether it be one's own happiness, success, past trauma and pain, or simply one's daily attitudes, self-spirituality locates responsibility in the individual. For SBNRs "religion" is a kind of crutch—a form of negative dependency that keeps one from being truly independent, autonomous, and self-reliant. One SBNR participant asserted, "for me, spirituality is an individual task," adding, "one of my main personal philosophies is that like, if you want to be happy, *you* have to work for it." Across the board, my research participants emphasized the importance of self-reliance, that is, relying on and looking to their true self in order to determine their courses of action. They also stressed the need to avoid blaming others for one's own failures and troubles. The reasoning informing this *ethic of self-responsibility* is quite simple: to the extent that moral and epistemological authority lies within the self, one must always look within and rely on one's own inner resources.

The view that self-reliance is a virtue is, as Bellah and coauthors have pointed out, a part of the Euroamerican cultural tradition.[40] Indeed, American poet and Transcendentalist Ralph Waldo Emerson wrote a famous essay entitled, "Self Reliance" exalting the individual who stands by their own conscience in contrast to those who follow the dictates of society. And this theme was taken to its extreme by Henry David Thoreau, a

39. Watts, "On the Politics of Self-Spirituality."
40. Bellah et al., *Habits of the Heart*, 55–6.

friend of Emerson, in his classic *Walden*. These representative figures can be said to have been carrying on a tradition of self-responsibility that has come to define the North American imaginary. This general orientation, toward autonomy and individual freedom, is found frequently among SBNRs. For instance, one SBNR participant stated, "you constantly have to be accountable for yourself." Self-spirituality therefore implies an obligation to take responsibility.

Tied to this is an *ethic of authenticity*, which conceives of societal norms and institutions as corrupting or oppressive. An SBNR research participant explained her decision to leave the church as follows: "It just felt like a judgmental hypocritical environment, that wasn't allowing me to be free to be who I am." And similarly, when asked what it means to be SBNR, another participant responded: "I think it's about . . . not wanting to be confined to a box, or confined to someone else's construction of what I should be." It remains a core precept in my research participants' accounts that we all have within us a true self which reflects *who we really are*. Taylor refers to this as an *expressivist* conception of human life.[41] On this view, the ultimate purpose of life is to fulfill one's own nature, which "means espousing the inner élan, the voice or impulse" *within*, however that is understood.[42] In other words, an expressivist view of the human condition postulates that each self has its own distinct potential—what is commonly called the "true self" but goes by many names—which is an imperative for each individual to realize. Thus, to be authentic implies abiding by a part of oneself that is not externally enforced, that exists prior to, or at least separate from, cultural and social norms. These norms are equated with what many of my participants call the "ego." Furthermore according to self-spirituality the true self is conceived as *presocial* in nature. This means that to the extent that one is self-consciously taking on external roles or trying to live up to expectations derived from society, one is not being true to oneself. Thus, an SBNR participant relayed that when she feels "least spiritual" is when, "I'm conscious of myself as the external me." While another said, "I feel terrible pretending to be something that I'm not."

I call the third ethic an *ethic of productivity*. Within self-spirituality, "'personal growth' can be understood as the shape 'religious salvation'

---

41. Taylor, *The Ethics of Authenticity*.
42. Taylor, *Sources of the Self*, 347.

takes."[43] Paradoxically, it is generally accepted by SBNRs that one ought to engage in a constant process of work upon oneself in order to realize who one truly is. For example, a research participant shared, "You don't really get any holidays from spirituality." For this SBNR, the virtues come as the result of continuous self-work—one learns to become more compassionate through practices of visualization and emotional discipline; one learns to become braver by facing one's fears or stepping outside of one's comfort zone; one learns to be more tolerant and empathetic by reflecting upon the suffering of others. Crucially, self-spirituality holds that the true self is the embodiment of virtue, thus to the extent that one is cultivating the virtues, one is also getting closer to realizing one's true self.

The fourth and final ethic is an *ethic of self-awareness*. Hanegraaff explains, "Spiritual development means getting in touch with, and aligning oneself with one's Higher Self rather than with one's limited personality."[44] One of my participants asserted, "I think it is to know yourself. That is the deepest spiritual practice." Consider: if the *telos* of life is to realize the self that one truly is, then one must first become aware of *who that is*. This may be achieved in a variety of ways, but fundamentally it requires *going within*—engaging in self-reflection in order to develop "self-awareness." It is here where the conception of the self-informing self-spirituality becomes critical. Recall that according to self-spirituality the true self is *presocial* in nature, or ontologically independent of social institutions and traditions. It is therefore a non-situated self, wholly unencumbered by external ties. Accordingly, gaining self-awareness entails delineating those parts of one's self that are believed to be socially and culturally imposed, from those which are natural to, or reflective of, one's *true self*. This can only be accomplished through a process of introspection (often aided by meditation), which requires disengaging, or stepping back, from one's thoughts and feelings in order to assess them "objectively." This process of disengagement is necessary to achieving self-awareness, and also, necessary to identifying one's true self. However, as opposed to the Buddhist conception of no-self as true self, instead, we find a Romantic conception of the self as supposedly historical and wholly original to the individual. Yet, interestingly, what becomes equated with the true self is prone to fluctuation; for instance, one's gender may be viewed at one moment as

43. Hanegraaff, *New Age*, 46.
44. Hanegraaff, *New Age*, 211.

essentially who one is, and at another moment be merely a contingent aspect of one's self. Or, one's sexuality may be viewed at one point as expressing one's true self, and at another wholly external to who one truly is. This pragmatic essentialism is endemic to self-spirituality. Moreover, it is this self-conception, which remains the basis upon which the ideological framework of self-spirituality is built.

The Political Character of Self-Spirituality

There is perhaps no value more sacred to self-spirituality than *individual liberty*. What this amounts to in practice is, first and foremost, a commitment to allowing individuals to "listen to the voice within" and "follow their heart"—that is, *negative freedom*. This derives from the ethic of authenticity: in order to realize one's true self, individuals require a protected space within which to do so. Moreover, self-spirituality as expressed by Canadian millennials is fundamentally egalitarian, even democratic in nature. As Eeva Sointu and Linda Woodhead suggest, it recognizes "the uniqueness—and unique worth—of each and every individual."[45] Evincing the protestant principle, and sharing in the Emersonian celebration of "individuality," self-spirituality rejects all attempts to order, tame, or control the true self.[46] This is especially evident among SBNR Canadian millennials. For instance, when asked why she left the church of her youth a research participant replied, "So I could actually determine my own freedom." Similarly, another told me that while she enjoys visiting different religious communities, what she detests is when they "put an ultimatum on me." Another relayed, "from my understanding, there is no legitimate way of praying to God. Everyone can pray to God in his own way." SBNRs rail against what they perceive as external norms and regulations. Because they hold self-realization in such high esteem, they give great weight to the value of *self-expression*, that is, the freedom to express, and be recognized as, one's true self. A research participant explained, "When I think of religion, it's very obviously . . . tainted and very limiting; placing limitations on life and life experiences, whereas spirituality to me is a bit more about exploration and freedom, and just being who you are."

In turn, Canadian SBNR millennials exhibit a strong cosmopolitanism, rooted in an ethical liberalism. Although predominantly socially

45. Sointu and Woodhead, "Spirituality, Gender, and Expressive Selfhood," 273.
46. Schmidt, *Restless* Souls, 33.

progressive in their political views, they tend to value individual freedom of choice above all else. Their self-spirituality is informed by both an ethical and epistemological individualism. What is right for one individual may not be right for another; *what is right is what is true to oneself.* This is a byproduct of the sacralization of the self. When my research participants make decisions about what to do, they do not appeal to a sacred text, but rather look within for guidance. What their gut tells them, or what their intuition reveals, is what orients them. Among these millennials human nature is understood as benevolent, and therefore human ills are understood to be the result of poor social structures or social conditioning. The corollary of this is that they are deeply suspicious of institutions and their authority. Because they view institutions as corrupting of their true self, they tend to develop little attachment to them. This is not to suggest, however, that SBNRs are entirely anti-social. As I outline below, some of my research participants were steadfastly committed to communities of various kinds. However, most were not members of a religious institution. They tended to see these as ultimately hotbeds of corruption, greed and fear mongering, entirely at odds with an authentic spiritual life. Having said this, some of my research participants were affiliated with a religious institution of liberal background. Yet these participants did not justify their institutional affiliation on the basis of loyalty to the religious institution itself. Instead, they spoke of *feeling* connected or close to specific individuals whom they knew at their place of worship; for these SBNRs what mattered were the relationships, not the religious institution itself.

As might be expected, these Canadian millennials are incredibly receptive and respectful of difference—be it ethnic, gendered, or sexual in nature. Their epistemological framework, which places authority in their own selves, also encourages them to let others be who they truly are—their true selves. On many occasions, my research participants would say, "that isn't what I would want, but if that's who they are, I'm not going to judge." This liberal attitude towards difference once again highlights how important freedom of choice is among this cohort. However, this is not a mere moral relativism. John Stuart Mill's famous harm principle was deeply ingrained in their discourses; one could choose to do whatever one wanted, so long as it did not infringe on the liberty of, or harm, another. Indeed, the denigration of "religion" often derived from the assumption that religious people were not respectful of other's rights to choose for themselves what to do or who to be. Again, self-spirituality, at its most basic, adheres to an ethical liberalism.

We can conclude that self-spirituality sacralizes individual liberty in the following senses: because it views social institutions and norms as stifling individuals' authenticity, it challenges and contests external constraints that are believed to regulate or deform the true self. On these grounds, it champions negative freedom. However, because it conceives of social institutions and norms as *aspects of the self*—the "ego"—it endorses a conception of positive freedom that requires individuals to shed these aspects in order to become truly free. Thus, we can conclude with cultural sociologists Dick Houtman and Stef Aupers that self-spirituality "can be understood as a veritable religion of modernity because its participants collectively sacralize the long-standing modern value of individual liberty, and especially the ideal of an authentic self that distances itself from allegedly alienating institutions and traditions."[47]

The Socio-Political Implications of Self-Spirituality

There are a multitude of socio-political implications that follow from this, but given my limited space, I will only discuss three. First, if my analysis is correct, it is clear that self-spirituality, at least as it is expressed by Canadian millennials, is fundamentally liberal. Its ethicality is substantially liberal, endorsing what I take to be liberal virtues: self-reliance, acceptance of difference or tolerance, empathy, emotional courage and resilience, and compassion.[48] Moreover, the conception of the self endorsed, in many ways, reflects the conception of the self operationalized in liberal political theory.[49] The notion of an unencumbered self lies at the heart of, for instance, Rawlsian political liberalism, and provides the basis for the liberal reverence for individual rights.[50] This being the case, it follows that self-spirituality is prey to the same kinds of weaknesses as liberal theory. The prioritization of individual liberty, if pushed too far, can lead to a devaluing and corrosion of the very institutions that make it possible. My SBNR research participants seemed to take for granted that the liberal democratic state will always be there to protect their right

47. Houtman and Aupers, "Religions of Modernity," 15.

48. Macedo, *Liberal Virtues*.

49. See Rawls, *A Theory of Justice*.

50. Sandel, *Liberalism and the Limits of Justice*.

and freedom to *be their true selves*, and they saw no reciprocal obligation to protect or sustain the state's legitimacy. Thus, in devaluing the role of institutions and traditions in shaping the true self, both self-spirituality and liberal theory risk undermining the social conditions upon which they rest.

Second, the SBNR reverence for autonomy and individual freedom may undermine the development of collectivity. Critics have contended that one of the most troubling aspects of self-spirituality is its seeming worship of the individual at the expense of the community.[51] Yet this claim lacks nuance and oversimplifies the truth. While I agree with critics that self-spirituality can hamper the creation of community, I also believe it can and does inform communal commitment.

As critics have noted, self-spirituality can in some instances impede the cultivation of community—be it cultural, religious, or political. In such cases we see how the SBNR disdain of conformity can fuel an instinctual rejection of any attempt to explicitly unite them around a shared cause or commitment. Taylor helpfully sheds light on why this might be: in describing the religiosity of those who adhere to a romantic expressivism he writes, "The religious life or practice that I become part of not only must be my choice, but must speak to me; it must make sense in terms of my spiritual development as I understand this."[52] In turn, for many SBNRs, their commitment to a community is dependent upon a contingent sense of belonging, largely based in subjective feeling. Thus, they may *feel* deeply connected to a specific group of people, but as soon as their feelings change the justificatory basis of the community disappears. And if confronted with such a situation, given the ethic of authenticity, the SBNR cannot make sense of continuing their loyalty. To offer an illustrative example: when I asked one of my research participants why she had attended so many different communities without ever spending more than a few weeks at each—Buddhist, Christian, Hindu—she replied that it was because she just never "felt at home" in any of them. Like her, a number of others I spoke to could not make sense of committing to a religious community. For these SBNRs, the spiritual life is self-evidently about flexibility and mobility; the soul is restless and ought not be tied down.

---

51. See for example Daniel, *When 'Spiritual but Not Religious' Is not Enough*.
52. Taylor, *Varieties of Religion Today*, 94.

Yet there are still others who do not fit this description. Among this group of SBNRs, self-spirituality in fact serves to underpin and sustain commitment to a distinct community. Such cases exhibit the following two features. First, the discourse of self-spirituality and its attendant ethics were institutionalized at the community. Thus, talk of self-realization, the virtues of self-reliance, emotional courage, and compassion, and practices of self-cultivation were normalized. Examples include: yoga studios, meditation classes, alternative medicine offices, self-help workshops, and artistic groups. In such spaces, SBNRs tend to feel quite comfortable. This is because the *lingua franca* is self-spirituality. Second, these SBNR individuals learned to associate *becoming their true selves* with joining and participating in their respective community. I found this among, for instance, Twelve Step members, community organizers, and some artists. These people did not view commitment to their respective communities as a burden, or as an impediment to self-realization. On the contrary, for these SBNRs, becoming *who they truly are* was seen to *depend* upon their sustained commitment to these communities. As one Twelve Step member put it, "I discovered my true self in the rooms of Alcoholics Anonymous. It is there where I feel most authentic." And similarly, an artist explained, "Once I entered the theatre world, I found my people. I found myself." It follows that self-spirituality is not necessarily at odds with community, but in fact can be institutionalized and therefore serve to engender community. But in order for this to occur, individuals must come to associate their true self with the community they have joined— which does not always occur.

Third, self-spirituality always risks producing a certain degree of anomie. Due to the intense pressure placed on the SBNR individual to remain self-reliant, whilst remaining suspicious of institutions, many experience, at one time or another, a deep sense of social isolation. This might seem odd, given that self-spirituality adheres to a strong ethicality, and in fact can be understood as a kind of virtue theory. It can be explained by returning to the distinction I make above, between those SBNRs who subscribe to self-spirituality bereft of community, and those who belong to a community that has institutionalized self-spirituality as its authoritative discourse. Again, I will focus on the more familiar case and then examine the other kind.

Among those SBNRs who subscribe to self-spirituality but lack any supporting community, they experienced tremendous difficulty retaining the conviction of their beliefs and living up to them. In these cases, it becomes clear how the SBNR valorization of self-reliance and autonomy can stifle an individual's ability to summon and sustain the motivation necessary to adhere to their own ethical standards. For this type of SBNR, the spiritual life is one of continual and consistent fits and starts—a few months of intense devotion to cultivating the virtues, followed by many more of waning enthusiasm and commitment. Moreover, feelings of isolation and loneliness are not uncommon. When bereft of institutionalization, there is something about self-spirituality that is incredibly personally demanding, and yet deeply isolating. Placing epistemological authority in the self, the SBNR individual is left to his or her own devices in a world that can seem without meaning.[53] As a result, this type of SBNR can end up frantically searching within for signs of divine providence, of cosmic significance, to be reassured that they are not alone. Much like the early Calvinists who sought cosmic reassurance in their pecuniary achievements, the institutionally bereft SBNR individual searches within for feelings or intuitions that all is well. But feelings and intuitions are far less tangible than material goods, and for this reason suffering can be especially difficult for them to cope with. Suffering in the form of depression, anxiety, or addiction were incredibly common among this kind of SBNR individual.

Interestingly, it is often for reasons of this nature that a number of my SBNR research participants decided to join and become active in a distinct community where self-spirituality was institutionalized. One of the most powerful examples of this are those in Twelve Step programs such as Alcoholics Anonymous (AA). These SBNR millennials described in vivid detail the pain of anomie, attempting to engage in spiritual searching on their own.[54] What they found at AA was a communal space where self-spirituality was institutionalized—thus where a goal of self-realization was normalized—yet where they could engage in self-work in the company of supportive others. These SBNR AA members spoke confidently about realizing their true self through *commitment* to the Twelve Step group. In turn, for such individuals, participation in AA satisfies both their need for autonomy and community.

53. Watts, "Recovering Enchantment," 41–42.
54. Watts, "Recovering Enchantment," 46–49.

Conclusion: Implications for the Study of Religion

What implications might this analysis hold for the study of religion, more generally? First, I would argue that self-spirituality, as I have presented it here, is not unique to the millennial generation in Canada, nor is it unique to those who self-identify as "spiritual but not religious." In fact, I would argue that it is far more prevalent than the number of individuals who self-identify as SBNR would suggest. This is for two reasons.

First, as Fuller has noted, unchurched traditions like those that inform self-spirituality have begun to shape in significant ways the dominant forms of religiosity in the West.[55] Second, self-spirituality is largely disseminated through mainstream cultural products and the wider subjective wellbeing culture (e.g. Hollywood Films, popular books and television, and other pop cultural mediums).[56] It is for this reason that individuals can both subscribe to self-spirituality whilst struggling with anomie; there is sufficient institutional support in the wider society to give plausibility to the discourse of self-spirituality, yet void of concrete participation in a community the SBNR individual is likely to suffer from social isolation. In turn, I hypothesize that self-spirituality will continue to grow in adherents (if one can use this term) long into the future. Of course, self-spirituality, like all discourses, will change from context to context. What I have described in this chapter is the way in which self-spirituality is interpreted and made manifest among Canadian millennials specifically. I cannot speak to the ways in which cohorts of other age groups or cultural contexts might apply it. It seems to me self-spirituality, given its underlying cultural structure, allows for a wide and diverse array of expressions.

Second, my analysis should provoke scholars of religion to be skeptical of religious affiliation as presented in large-scale surveys. I say this because some of my research participants identified as "Christian," "Jewish," and even "Muslim" despite adhering to what I am calling "self-spirituality." This suggests that religious affiliation, as presented in surveys, may reveal little about an individual's worldview. Of course, this is a common critique made by qualitative researchers. I mention it merely to reaffirm its validity.

Lastly, I believe my analysis helps to illuminate the tensions that inform much of the recent debates surrounding the spiritual turn. Once we

55. Fuller, *Spiritual but not Religious.*
56. Watts, "On the Politics of Self-Spirituality."

accept that self-spirituality is fundamentally liberal in nature, as it prizes individual rights and freedoms (especially freedom of choice), we can begin to make sense of why there have been so many conservative attacks launched at it. It has been a longstanding conservative critique of liberalism that it weakens the binds of tradition and communal authority, placing too much authority on the individual. This illuminates how the study of spirituality has, in large part, acted as a theoretical battleground for conservative and liberal social commentators. While conservatives are quick to denounce self-spirituality for what they view as a lackluster and ultimately individualistic stance towards religion, many liberal commentators celebrate what they view as the triumph of individual autonomy in the face of outdated tradition. In this chapter, I have adopted something like a middle position. I have argued that while conservative concerns about self-spirituality are not misplaced, they underestimate the degree to which self-spirituality can be institutionalized (for instance, at Twelve Step groups) in order to reconcile a self-ethic and an ethic of community.

Bibliography

Albanese, Catherine L. *A Republic of Mind and Spirit: A Cultural History of American Metaphysical Religion.* New Haven: Yale University Press, 2007.

"Ask the Religion Experts: What Does 'Spiritual, Not Religious' Mean?" *The Ottawa Citizen,* October 31, 2013. https://ottawacitizen.com/Life/Faith%20&%20 Ethics/ask-the-religion-experts-what-does-spiritual-not-religious-mean/ wcm/7b1df69e-fd23-4ccd-bd96-35a7a6bd0f5d.

Bellah, Robert N., Richard Madsen, William M. Sullivan, Ann Swidler, and Steven Tipton. *Habits of the Heart: Individualism and Commitment in American Life.* Berkeley: University of California Press, 1985.

Campbell, Colin. *The Easternization of the West: A Thematic Account of Cultural Change in the Modern Era.* Boulder, CO: Paradigm, 2007.

Carrette, Jeremy, and Richard King. *Selling Spirituality: The Silent Takeover of Religion.* London: Routledge, 2005.

Daniel, Lillian. *When "Spiritual But Not Religious" Is not Enough: Seeing God in Surprising Places, Even the Church.* New York: Jericho, 2013.

Eskenazi, Elline Kay. "The Roots of New Age Spirituality in United States Social History." PhD diss., California Institute of Integral Studies, 2010.

Forman, Robert K. *Grassroots Spirituality.* New York: Imprint Academic, 2004.

Fuller, Robert C. *Spiritual, But Not Religious: Understanding Unchurched America.* New York: Oxford University Press, 2001.

Gottlieb, Roger S. *Spirituality: What It Is and Why It Matters.* New York: Oxford University Press, 2013.

Greenberg, Eric H., and Karl Weber. *Generation We: How Millennial Youth Are Taking Over America and Changing Our World Forever.* Emeryville, CA: Pachatusan, 2008.

Hanegraaff, Wouter J. *New Age Religion and Western Culture: Esotericism in the Mirror of Secular Thought*. Leiden: Brill, 1996.

Heelas, Paul. *The New Age Movement: The Celebration of the Self and the Sacralization of Modernity*. Oxford: Blackwell, 1996.

———. *Spiritualities of Life: New Age Romanticism and Consumptive Capitalism*. Malden, MA: Blackwell, 2008.

Heelas, Paul, and Linda Woodhead. *The Spiritual Revolution: Why Religion Is Giving Way to Spirituality*. Malden, MA: Blackwell, 2005.

Houtman, Dick and Stef Aupers. "Religions of Modernity: Relocating the Sacred to the Self and the Digital." In *Religions of Modernity: Relocating the Sacred to the Self and the Digital*, 1–30. International Studies in Religion and Society 12. Leiden: Brill, 2010.

———. "The Spiritual Turn and the Decline of Tradition: The Spread of Post-Christian Spirituality in 14 Western Countries, 1981–2000." *Journal for the Scientific Study of Religion* 46 (2007) 305–20.

Jacobs, Anne C. "Spirituality: History and contemporary developments—An evaluation." *Koers: Bulletin for Christian Scholarship* 78.1 (2013) 1–12.

James, William. *The Varieties of Religious Experience*. 1901. Reprint, New York: First Vintage, 1990.

Johnson, Richard. "Polling Religion in Canada." *National Post*, Dec. 21, 2012. http://news.nationalpost.com/2012/12/21/polling-religion-in-canada/.

Lynch, Gordon. *The New Spirituality: An Introduction to Progressive Belief in the Twenty-first Century*. London: Tauris, 2007.

Macedo, Stephen. *Liberal Virtues: Citizenship, Virtue, and Community in Liberal Constitutionalism*. Oxford: Clarendon, 1991.

Mercadante, Linda A. *Belief without Borders: Inside the Minds of the Spiritual but not Religious*. New York: Oxford University Press, 2014.

Oppenheimer, Mark. "Examining the Growth of the 'Spiritual but not Religious.'" *New York Times*, July 19, 2014. https://www.nytimes.com/2014/07/19/us/examining-the-growth-of-the-spiritual-but-not-religious.html.

Pew Research Center. "Canada's Changing Religious Landscape." *Pew Research Center Religion Public Life Project RSS*, June 27, 2013. http://www.pewforum.org/2013/06/27/canadas-changing-religious-landscape/.

Rawls, John. *A Theory of Justice*. Cambridge: Harvard University Press, 1971.

Roof, Wade Clark. *Spiritual Marketplace*. Princeton: Princeton University Press, 1999.

Sandel, Michael. *Liberalism and the Limits of Justice*. 2nd ed. Cambridge: Cambridge University Press, 1998.

Schmidt, Leigh Eric. *Restless Souls: The Making of American Spirituality*. 2nd ed. Berkeley: University of California Press, 2012.

Sointu, Eeva, and Linda Woodhead. "Spirituality, Gender, and Expressive Selfhood." *Journal for the Scientific Study of Religion* 47 (2008) 259–76.

Starkey, Mike. *God, Sex and Generation X*. London: Triangle, 1997.

Tacey, David J. *The Spirituality Revolution: The Emergence of Contemporary Spirituality*. New York: Brunner-Routledge, 2004.

Taylor, Charles. *The Ethics of Authenticity*. Cambridge: Harvard University Press, 1991.

———. *A Secular Age*. Cambridge: Belknap Press of Harvard University Press, 2007.

———. *Sources of the Self: The Making of the Modern Identity*. Cambridge: Harvard University Press, 1989.

―――. *Varieties of Religion Today.* Cambridge: Harvard University Press, 2002.

Thomas, Owen C. "Spiritual but Not Religious: The Influence of the Current Romantic Movement." *Anglican Theological Review* 88 (2006) 397–415.

Watts, Galen. "Missing the Forest for the Trees: 'Spiritual' Religion in a Secular Age." *Toronto Journal of Theology* 43 (2018) 243–56.

―――. "On the Politics of Self-Spirituality: A Canadian Case Study." *Studies in Religion* 47 (2018) 345–72.

―――. "Recovering Enchantment: Addiction, Spirituality, and Charles Taylor's Malaise of Modernity." *Journal of Contemporary Religion* 34 (2019) 39–56.

Webster, David. *Dispirited: How Contemporary Spirituality Makes Us Stupid, Selfish and Unhappy.* Alresford, UK: Zero, 2012.

Winograd, Morley, and Michael D. Hais. *Millennial Momentum: How a New Generation Is Remaking America.* New Brunswick, NJ: Rutgers University Press, 2011.

Wuthnow, Robert. *After the Baby Boomers: How Twenty- and Thirty-Somethings Are Shaping the Future of American Religion.* Princeton: Princeton University Press, 2007.

―――. *The Consciousness Reformation.* Berkeley: University of California Press, 1976.

PART 3

Curating and Enduring into the Future

7

Young Adults and the Church

Incarnation, Theosis, and a Non-binary Future for the Body of Christ

ANNE KYLE

Abstract

In *Gathering Those Driven Away*, Wendy Farley writes, "The wound in so much of Christianity [is that] it cannot perceive in its own members the beauty of Christ's body."[1] In a time of changing spirituality for millennials, a growing number of nones, and a felt division between the institutional church and church "dropouts," Farley's writings on incarnation become especially relevant. For Farley, Christ's transparency to divinity demonstrates humanity's full potential for theosis. I extend Farley's analysis to the case of the millennial exodus. Farley's nonbinary theology offers a perspective which validates the spirituality of young adults outside the institutional church. Envisioning the future, I offer an ecclesiology which commits itself to recognizing the Divinity of the outsider and which breaks down the secular/sacred divide: a Body of Christ which risks orthodoxy for the sake of loving humanity into its fullest self.

---

1. Farley, *Gathering*, 2.

Introduction

Compared to decades previous, young adult church attendance is in decline, and the institutional church has very little idea of how to approach this phenomenon.[2] It is an exodus for which the institutional church is unprepared, and one which poses some difficult questions for those of us, myself included (as both a seminarian and young adult), who align with the institutional church: How do these young adults who have left their church communities fit in our theologies? Do we have a responsibility to reverse the trend? In light of an exit of the pews, what kind of relationship can we build towards? What will the future hold? These are pressing questions, yet, for those of us still inside the metaphorical church walls, I see our biggest obstacle to imagining a positive future as fear: fear of change and, ultimately, of institutional death.

I am interested in theologies that nurture a communicative and life-giving relationship between young adults and the institutional church: a charitable relationship. While, certainly, relationships require participation on at least two ends, this chapter addresses what the institutional church can do to display charity toward young adults. I use the word "charity" to mean a love of and goodwill toward humankind.[3] Charity is love which always trusts, always hopes, and always perseveres.[4] Charity does not boast and is not proud, but charity is kind.[5] Charity is honest. Charity looks for and believes in the good of the other. Charity values others not for what they offer but for who they are, in and of themselves.

To shed light on the church's relationship with young adults leaving the pews, I look to the church's current relationship with other "church outcasts." In the aim of a charitable future, I turn to Wendy Farley's theology of incarnation, as outlined in her book *Gathering Those Driven Away*. Farley, professor of Christian Spirituality at San Francisco Theological Seminary, brings queer theory into a theological space as she considers what the non-binary nature of incarnation means for church outcasts. Farley's theology provides a wariness of idolatry and a vision of Divinity which challenges institutional exclusivity. While fear surrounding the exodus—fear of change and of institutional death—facilitates idolatry,

---

2. Pew Research Center, "Millennials."

3. *Merriam-Webster.com Dictionary*, "Charity," line 12.

4. 1 Cor 13:6 NRSV.

5. 1 Cor 13:4 NRSV.

practices of humility on the part of the church pave the way for a charitable relationship between young adults and the institution.

Farley's theological insights are relevant for addressing the situation of young adults and the church. I begin this exploration with an overview of Farley's theology of incarnation. Secondly, I argue that fear surrounding young adults' absence from Sunday morning services engenders idolatry, as Farley defines idolatry. In the third section, I outline practices of humility that will facilitate a charitable relationship between the church and young adults going forward.

Though I believe the concept of *ekklesia* (the Greek word translated as "church") encompasses more than organizational structures, for the purposes of this chapter, "church" refers to the institutional aspect of Christianity in the United States. I will use the term "the Body of Christ," by contrast, to refer to the spiritual component of Christian community, across the entire world. The Body of Christ is larger than its various institutions, and its edges and boundaries are only truly seen from God's perspective. Young adults refer to people in the United States ages eighteen to twenty-nine, unless otherwise specified. Millennials, according to Pew Research Center, are people born between 1981 and 1996.[6] This means that, in 2019, those who were ages twenty-three to twenty-nine are both millennials and young adults.

At this point in time, research about one group reflects on the other. I am a young adult and a millennial invested in the institutional church; I use the first-person plural for the institutional church. While it is vital for people of faith to take seriously overarching trends and correlations available through research regarding young adults and religious participation, it is equally vital for us to recognize that in every institution and generation, there is far more variety and individuality than could possibly be represented, in any one presentation of research or in this chapter. It is my hope that, in acknowledging statistics about young adults and religious engagement, we may better honor people: groups as well as individuals.

Wendy Farley's Theology of Incarnation

Theologically, I would like to start with the Incarnation. What is known as the Kenotic (self-emptying) passage in Philippians says of Jesus Christ:

6. Dimock, "Defining Generations," para. 5.

"though he was in the form of God, [he] did not regard equality with God as something to be exploited but emptied himself . . . And being found in human form, he humbled himself and became obedient to the point of death—even death on a cross."[7] Incarnation was this self-emptying. If Jesus modeled what it looks like to approach humanity, then we, the church, might learn from incarnation in how to approach each other. Let us dive into Farley's theology of incarnation.

Central to Farley's theology of incarnation is her discussion of idolatry and domination. Farley argues that a commitment to our own ideas of God over a commitment to God not only leads to violence against others' but also constitutes a violation of the first commandment: thou shalt have no other gods before me. Farley argues that binary thinking in traditional theology has caused harm and is an example of idolatry. She writes, "The desire for pure or total truth seems laudable, but the cruelty of movements committed to this fantasy suggests that it is dangerous to imagine that we possess a correct belief. We do not so easily evade the human condition."[8] She names, as examples, the torture of the Inquisition, the burnings of witch hunts, and the excommunications of Catholic anathemas. This is what Farley calls Christianity's "logic of domination."[9] The logic of domination is an abuse of power stemming from a commitment to "ideas about God [which] displace the desire for the Good beyond even our best thoughts."[10] It is an act of holding high one idea at the expense of others. It is the pattern of suppression which stems from the prideful belief that "[o]ur tribe has a special relation to God."[11]

For Farley, idolatry is the refusal to hold the ultimate deity in nonduality. She argues that monotheism has less to do with the exclusivity of God and more to do with putting down definitions which might confine God. To conflate anything else with God—to replace God with our own "fears and desires"—is idolatry.[12] To avoid idolatry, one must cleave the concept of God from any image. Farley wants to ensure that Christians do not become too attached to any one image, no matter how seemingly

---

7. Phil 2:6–8 NRSV.
8. Farley, *Gathering*, 43.
9. Farley, *Gathering*, 15.
10. Farley, *Gathering*, 11.
11. Farley, *Gathering*, 42.
12. Farley, *Gathering*, 53.

harmless or benevolent. She sees faith as bigger than orthodoxy: faith is able to tolerate a God not entirely within our intellectual grasp.

Binary theology denies the multiplicity of the Divine. The incarnation, by contrast, affirms Divinity's nonduality: Jesus Christ is not only God nor only human but, as the Creed of Chalcedon affirms, is both, indivisibly and inseparably. How do humanity and Divinity make themselves singularly and wholly present in the person of Jesus Christ? As Farley colorfully says, "It is nonsensical to think that a human body can manifest Beyond Being. It is like imagining the inexhaustible brilliance of the sun as a cave-dwelling fish."[13] However, it is nonsense on which the creed insists. It is not logical: it is theological, and who Jesus is (and, therefore, our salvation) depends on it.

The marriage of humanity and Divinity in Jesus rests, for Farley, in her understanding of the nondual nature of God: God is not just God in the abstract, God is also enfleshed in humanity. To approach the nonsense of this seeming contradiction, Farley uses the language of transparency. Jesus Christ shows us a human being "maximally transparent" to Divinity.[14] Her "transparency" language is her attempt to describe the nonduality of the incarnation: that Divinity is not separate nor the same as humanity, but, instead, shows the full potential of humanity. In this metaphor, Divinity illuminates humanity. The second person of the Trinity, whom she calls Wisdom, is the agent of this illumination.

Other human beings, then, besides Jesus, embody Wisdom. She describes the human form as particularly suited for Divinity.[15] She writes, "The incarnation is possible because humanity, created in the divine image, shares nonduality with its divine source."[16] Farley locates humanity's problem not as sin but as estrangement from God.[17] We have fallen out of touch with our true selves: as Farley puts it, "Divinity lies dormant in us."[18] All of humanity bears the image of God and is meant for a return to that Divinity. Farley is clear, however, that not everyone reaches this point in their lifetimes here on earth: she writes, "Few of us extend to

---

13. Farley, *Gathering*, 116.
14. Farley, *Gathering*, 148.
15. Farley, *Gathering*, 134.
16. Farley, *Gathering*, 90.
17. Farley, *Gathering*, 142.
18. Farley.

the utmost our full reach as God-bearers."[19] Still, we are created with the *imago dei*, the image of God, and, for Farley, this means we are not completely one way (human): we possess nonduality.

As she demonstrates, what these voices show us is that Divinity can be found in even the most unlikely of people and places. Drunkards and prostitutes display God. Women and slaves are Christ to others. She pays special attention, for example, to liberationist, feminist, and womanist theologians who see the Gospel only in the liberation of the poor and suffering. She points to Odetta Holmes' songwriting which places Christ as the abused and lynched Black person.[20] She describes an impromptu ritual for a miscarriage, and the Mother Christ who ministered there.[21] In a particularly poignant example, she writes, "Marcella Althaus-Reid describes a similar parallel between the murder of an Argentinian transvestite and the crucifixion of Christ."[22] In this example, Farley shows how Christ can be seen in the suffering and dignity of those who counter gender norms: "those driven away" from the church. For all of these—and for us—salvation is the process of *theosis*: a healing into our true identity. Healing comes from looking to Christ figures and recognizing ourselves.

The Way of Fear

The coming of age of the millennial generation has sparked a countless number of studies, blog posts, podcast episodes, and newspaper articles. The Christian community has not been exempt from this fascination. Particularly, the church has noticed a decline in church attendance in correlation with this generation's coming of age. Researchers confirm that the church in America has been experiencing a decrease in numbers. Accompanying these reports is a great amount of fear from churches: members of the institution fear the institution's demise and stress about the moral and spiritual lives of young adults. However, the way forward for institutional engagement with young adults is not to focus on the possibility of institutional death. Fear regarding young adults and the church not only prevents the church from adopting an attitude of humility which

19. Farley.
20. Farley, *Gathering*, 139.
21. Farley, *Gathering*, 136–37.
22. Farley, *Gathering*, 139.

might facilitate relationship, it also paves the pathway to the dangerous idolatry which Farley describes.

Judgment of Young Adults and Fear of Dissolution

While the institutional church is far from falling off the face of the earth, data supports a general decline in those who identify as Christian in America. Faced with this rejection, judgment and fear—not humility— have been the overwhelming response. In conversations surrounding statistical decline of the church, it is not difficult to spot judgment of young adults. As prime examples, we turn to evangelical and post-evangelical voices. David Kinnaman is president of Barna Group, a leading research company, and author of several books on precisely this topic of young adults leaving the church, and Christian Smith, Professor of Sociology at the University of Notre Dame, writes on modern American religion. In their perspective, young adults who have left the church are lost sheep, whose souls are in peril. In *You Lost Me*, Kinnaman writes, "Why should we concern ourselves with the faith journeys of young adults? Why does all this matter? First, it's a matter of heart. The spiritual lives of millions of young people are at stake."[23] Even those who are not antagonistic to religion get a dose of criticism in *You Lost Me*. Kinnaman writes, "A nomad who self-describes as a Christian is not necessarily in a better state of faith than a non-believer. In fact the Bible serves up special criticism for those who are 'lukewarm,' neither in nor out (see Rev. 3:16)."[24] Kinnaman objects to the perceived lack of orthodoxy, "meaningful accountability," or "faith vitality" in those who have left the church.[25] Continuing in his critique, Kinnaman writes, "To follow Jesus, young adults in the next generation—just like the generations before them—will have to learn humility."[26] His book suggests, however, that there is only one path to this humility. He writes, "If younger generations are to avoid the mistakes of the past, young leaders desperately need a sense of what has gone before—and you can only get that sense from soul-shaping friendships with older Christians."[27] Others indicate that young adults are morally

23. Kinnaman and Hawkins, *You Lost Me*, 31.

24. Kinnaman and Hawkins, *You Lost Me*, 70.

25. Kinnaman and Hawkins, *You Lost Me*, 70.

26. Kinnaman and Hawkins, *You Lost Me*, 118.

27. Kinnaman and Hawkins, *You Lost Me*, 204.

adrift. Christian Smith, author of *Lost in Transition: The Dark Side of Emerging Adulthood*, comments on the lack of connection that eighteen to twenty-three-year-old have with other age-groups, saying, "In short, the structural position of many emerging adults results in the relatively immature socializing the relatively immature, the morally blind leading the morally blind, and so on."[28] He also writes, "The problem is more that many of them [young adults] are simply lost. They do not adequately know the moral landscape of the real world that they inhabit. And they do not adequately understand where they themselves stand."[29]

Ultimately, there is a fear that the church, as an institution, might die out. Churches trip over themselves, wondering "why nobody wants to be around Christians anymore."[30] Catholic scholar Brett Hoover writes, "I fear that if church does not leave the building, we may soon find that there is nobody there but us old folks."[31] Forbes writer Chris Ladd adds an interesting commentary saying, "Growth in evangelical congregations has not arrested the overall slide . . . Those venture-churches seem to act as the exit foyer of Christianity, swelling momentarily as people leave the faith community entirely."[32] Religion News Service writer Tobin Grant states bluntly, "in a few years the largest 'religion' in the U.S. may be no religion at all."[33]

This fear and judgment feed off each other. Churches fear dying out and, in frustration, blame the social, intellectual, or spiritual characteristics of young adults—especially young adults who have left them. These churches are caught up in the number of young adults who count in the Christian column, so to speak, and the number of young adults attending worship services.[34] However, the numbers themselves are not the place for churches to turn their focus. A lack of people in pews points to the reality that whatever patterns fed church attendance in the past, those patterns have broken down. A focus on numbers distracts from questions about connection to God or connection with each other. Metrics such as numbers of conversations with a spiritual mentor, time spent in

28. Smith et al., *Lost in Transition*, 235.
29. Smith et al., *Lost in Transition*, 69.
30. McSwain, "Why Nobody Wants to Be Around Christians Anymore," para. 1.
31. Plekon, *The Church Has Left*, location 777.
32. Ladd, "Organized Religion Is Being Replaced," para. 5.
33. Grant, "Americans Lost Their Religion," para. 6.
34. Kinnaman and Hawkins, *You Lost Me*, 70.

meditative practices, number of pages journaled, or spiritually-themed podcast episodes in one's feed might more closely describe whether or not a young adult is spiritually connected or not. Ushering young adults into church seats may not address any kind of spiritual question: neither does an attitude of dismissal reflect a genuine interest in well-being. Finding various metrics and asking young adults genuine questions require gentleness and the humility of recognizing that the institutional church might not already know the answers. Judgment and fear, by contrast, trigger defensive postures.

Fear and Idolatry

According to Farley's paradigm, when the church refuses to see Christ outside of itself, it succumbs to idolatry. When the church limits God's ability to show up and transform lives outside of its own community, it holds itself too highly and denies the expansive nature of God. If becoming like Christ means becoming like the people in one particular church, then God is not fecund, God is not expansive, and God only manifests in certain situations.

The assumption that the institution holds the keys to best spiritual practices and the belief that God is only found in the institutional church and not "out there" (the world) quarantine God to activities of the institutionalized church. Another problem with this view is that the church's actions are equated with God's actions. Therefore, when priests abuse children or when senior pastors embezzle money, they are protected. Their actions are "God's" actions, and the church cannot be wrong.

The institutional church continually makes the mistake of equating distance from the institution as distance from God. This is the idolatry which Farley speaks of—the idolatry which so easily turns into exclusive language and dismissal of young adult experience. We see here a golden calf scenario: the people of God want to name where God is instead of waiting for God to reveal Godself, and they are anxious about the unknown. They note that Moses has gone up to the mountain, and they worry, saying, "we do not know what has become of him."[35] Young adults have gone up to the mountain to hear from God, and we, the institutional church, do not know what has become of them. They have left the group, and God is speaking to them in God's own, mysterious, way. We have not

35. Exodus 32:1, NRSV.

heard from them in some time. Consequently, we have become fearful. Exodus 32 leads readers through a story in which an anxiety and desire to keep God in one known and controllable place leads to the most famous idolatry in the Hebrew Bible. Also notice what happens to the Ten Commandments: Moses breaks them in anger. The communication from God, the lessons learned from the mountaintop, all shatter in the disruption of the golden calf. If God is speaking to young adults away from the institutional community, then the church, by making an idol of itself, misses out on their insights and misses out on God's own revelation.

Non-binary Theology and Humility

Farley's theology renounces any one exclusive understanding of God, in effect combatting the fear which insists on exclusivity. It can be comforting to know that God is outside institutions, and that God's people, the Body of Christ, are outside the institution of church. As Dr. Emily Peck-McClain, of Wesley Theological Seminary, insists, "The church cannot die."[36] Christ is alive and well outside any institution. The Body of Christ is bigger than the institutional church, and the Body of Christ will outlast the institutional church.

Farley does not place any stake in the continuation of the institution of the church. The implication of her theology is that the church may die. She confirms one of the institutions deepest fears: that it is not needed. Christ will continue to save whether or not the institution lives. Farley's description of personal *theosis*, healing into our identity, renders the institution as incidental. As scary as this conclusion may seem for the church, young adults do not absolutely need the church, especially when the church is concerned only with self-preservation and not God's revelation. *Gathering Those Driven Away*, however, sees this statement as a liberating message, not one of terror. Some churches compare themselves to Noah's ark, on their way to salvation in a drowning world. If young adults believed they missed the ark of the church, they can rest their fears: Noah's flood is not the operative metaphor for the Body of Christ. One can be Christlike without fitting into the confines of ancient creeds or without pleasing an oppressive institution.

Ironically, if the institution is to have any relationship with young adults, the institution needs to let its own death be a real possibility. In

36. Peck-McClain, "Generations Together."

light of declining numbers, an attitude of humility is the way forward
for the institution. If the church is to serve others, to be a blessing to
the nations, it cannot concern itself primarily with self-preservation. I
have demonstrated how an overly anxious concern about numbers does
not lead to relationship. In prioritizing our own institution, we slip into
judgment of others, and we limit the God we serve. When the institution
stops holding its own survival as its primary concern, it has the energy to
instead commit itself to outsiders. This has always been the paradoxical
situation of the church: a group committed to those outside itself. From
the very first book of the Bible, we see God's people as charged with being
a blessing to the nations.

Historically, the church has not always practiced this outward orientation, and this does not go unnoticed. There is a huge difference of intent
and attitude, for example, between churches which reach young adults
for the sake of the institution and those which reach young adults for the
sake of learning, appreciation, and community. It is time for the church
to ask itself if it is willing to sacrifice itself for the sake of those outside
of itself. If the answer is no, we have already lost future generations. One
must not pursue institutions over the presence of God. If we want even a
chance at fostering a charitable relationship with young adults, we cannot place institutional preservation as our highest value, even in a time
of decline in religious affiliation and church attendance. Instead, a value
on recognizing Divinity in each other will lead to charity. The way to this
value is through the virtue of humility.

The Way of Humility

Once we accept the reality of a dying institution and agree that fixation
and judgment are likely to lead to idolatry and unlikely to lead to relationship with young adults, we, the church, find ourselves at ground zero.
While we have not taken steps away from young adults, we have not taken
steps towards them. Imagining how the church might look in the future
requires imagining what charity looks like in this situation: how can we
be honest with young adults, trust young adults, hope for young adults,
and see the good in young adults? Some young adults are already on the
mountaintop like Moses, pursuing God. How do we let them teach us?

Research shows that young adults are suspicious of institutions and
display various kinds of spirituality and religious practices outside the

church. A church taking up Farley's theological lens will acknowledge institutional proclivity to domination, actively breakdown any dichotomy between the sacred and secular, view young adults as having Divine potential, and value young adult participation in the Body of Christ over institutional preservation. These practices of humility communicate charity and develop relationship.

Young Adults as Suspicious of Institutions: Acknowledging our Limitations

Barna Research Institute summarizes that young adults do not place trust in traditional authorities or social institutions.[37] Although decline in church attendance is one example of a willingness to challenge tradition, there are others. Young adults have had, for over a decade now, a reputation for delaying traditional markers of adulthood, such as living on one's own, completing school, getting married, or having children.[38]

No longer is the church the only place one can receive religious education or spiritual connection: technology has opened up many avenues for these pursuits. Perhaps this access to information has reinforced or fed a generation who finds itself motivated by questions.[39] The internet makes challenging local authorities with outside voices extremely easy. One may ask as many questions as one would like: the internet, a vast resource, points to many authorities.

In this mix of voices, young adults certainly listen to the perspective of those outside the traditional church. Why would a young adult go to one institution for all spiritual guidance when they can listen to an episode of a spirituality podcast on a morning commute or experience a connection with body, mind, and spirit through a session of Afro-yoga?[40] Most obviously, perhaps, young adults may value an outside perspective because they themselves are often considered outsiders. They support others who are outsiders as well. They largely support, for instance, communities that the institutional church has traditionally ostracized: LGBTQI groups, for

---

37. Kinnaman and Hawkins, *You Lost Me*, 47.
38. Arnett, "Emerging Adulthood," 469–80.
39. Pew Research Center, "Millennials," 25.
40. Martinbrough, "Going with the Flow," para. 6.

example.[41] Instead of adhering only to institutions, millennials are ready to accept many voices as authoritative.

Similarly, Farley is also willing to be suspicious of authority and listen to the outsider. She names domination and idolatry as a temptation of institutionalism. Because young adults are suspicious of authority, the path to a charitable relationship with young adults is through the institution's confession of its own proclivity to idolatry. The church needs to openly acknowledge its history of domination. Young adults are conscious of this bad track record and highly suspicious of institutional authorities. Young adults know that institutions can make gods of themselves and sacrifice much for their own survival. Farley shares with young adults a distrust of institutions—or, at least, an awareness of their limitations. In recognition of ecclesial brokenness, she writes, "the church is everything that we are: kind, compassionate, confused, cruel, mundane, redemptive, murderous, wise, ignorant."[42] Although she writes as an academic, and consequently supported by institutionalism, she also recognizes institutional capacity to use the logic of domination. The nature of an organization compels it to look out for its own survival. The fear of our own dissolution leads us to hold onto our idols tightly.

As demonstrated, unquestioned loyalty to these organizations raises red flags for young adults. By contrast, a self-critical institution will be able to affirm the discontinuities which some young adults already identify. The church needs to acknowledge hypocrisy, its failures in social justice movements, its privilege, and its willful ignorance. Theologian Jennifer McBride demonstrates what the church could do to be self-critical in her call for repentance. McBride believes the church should be an institution marked by recognition of failure:

> What younger generations are turned off by, it seems to me, is an attitude of moral superiority or judgmentalism that accompanies many attempts at public engagement. Through an alternative mode of confession and repentance, Christians present themselves before others not as models of righteousness but as people in need of constant conversion. This disposition takes seriously Jesus' command in the Sermon on the Mount, "Do not judge [others]," even as it allows Christians to make certain ethical judgments about injustice in society.[43]

41. Pew Research Center, "Millennials," 102.

42. Farley, *Gathering*, 17.

43. Heim, "The Witness of Sinners," 32–34.

McBride believes the church's claims to have special truth and special morality have led it astray. McBride calls this idolatry the church's triumphalism: a claim of access to special knowledge.

> Christians communicate to others that we are specially favored when we position ourselves as judges over society and standardbearers of morality . . . This presumption . . . contradicts Jesus, who did not present himself as a model of moral righteousness but belonged wholly to the world by taking the form of a sinner in public life.[44]

In a time in which leadership scandals (for instance, charges of sexual assault associated with #metoo) regularly make headlines, it is appropriate for the institution, to show our repentance.

Unfortunately, not all of our institutions practice this repentance. Instead, many see the institution as the standard. As just one example, of someone whose work focuses on young adults, Kinnaman is skeptical of attributing any true spirituality to those outside the church:

> They [nomads] can appear to be quite spiritual. But ask any pastor or church leader and he or she will tell you that, while nomads may show up every once in a while, they are missing from the faith community in ways that matter most and are not actively pursuing a deeper relationship with Christ.[45]

Kinnaman's mistake is asking those who are most invested in the survival of the church to assess these young adults' spirituality. He also locates God as inside the church: young adults who have gone up the mountain like Moses say otherwise. His book entwines fear for young adult's spiritual destinies, fear for the continuation of the church, and judgment on young adults' spiritual paths. He states, "I am concerned that too many [millennial] Christians are so interested in pursuing the good, the true, and the beautiful that they forget to acknowledge and draw near to the source of those pursuits—Jesus."[46] In this, he does what Farley warns against: he divorces Christ from what is, more largely, good and true and beautiful and places the church as the institution with best or only access to truth.

Acknowledging our limitations is certainly a practice of humility: it is also a practice of charity. Charity honors the truth, and the truth is

44. Heim, "The Witness of Sinners," 33.
45. Kinnaman and Hawkins, *You Lost Me*, 64.
46. Kinnaman and Hawkins, *You Lost Me,* 204.

that we, as a church, have limitations and failings. Young adults are very aware of these: the church builds a common ground of understanding by acknowledging truth of our failings as an institution. Both young adults and the church can attest to the same realities. This honesty builds trust with young adults and provides a foundation of charity.

Young Adults, Spiritual and Religious: Breaking the Divide between Sacred and Secular

To characterize religiously unaffiliated young adults as people without investment in religion or spirituality is to utilize an inadequate taxonomy. Many nones actually have spiritual and religious interests and beliefs. Turning to studies of millennials, one sees evidence of spirituality. According to a 2016 Gallup report, while only 27 percent of millennials go to church every week, over half (55 percent) of millennials consider religion important to them.

The mentioned studies reveal a complicated mix of practices, beliefs, and affiliation among young adults today. Because of the tension between both valuing spirituality and resisting institutions, today's young adults have created new spiritual categories. Dissatisfied with simply dividing the US population into "religiously affiliated" and "religiously unaffiliated," Pew Research Center used 2017 data to create seven religious profiles.[47] According to their report, 14 percent of eighteen to twenty-nine year-olds are "Religious traditionalists actively involved with their faith and engaged in their congregations." Pew calls this group "Sunday Stalwarts." While less involved with local religious groups, Pew describes 13 percent of eighteen to twenty-nine year-olds as "God and Country Believers" and as "[s]ocially and politically conservative, most likely to view immigrants as hurting American culture." These two are the smallest of the young adult population. Pew categorizes 17 percent of young adults as "Diversely Devout" who are religious in traditional ways but also believe in "psychics, reincarnation and that spiritual energy can be located in physical objects." Pew describes 21 percent of young adults as "Relaxed Religious." While this group sees religion as important to them, personally, they do not engage in many traditional practices, nor do they see belief in God as a prerequisite for someone to be "a moral person." They classify 24 percent as "Spiritually Awake" who indicate New Age beliefs

47. Pew Research Center, "A Portrait of Generation Next."'

and, for the most part, do not engage in traditional religious practices. The categories "Religion Resisters" and "Solidly Secular" hit the highest percentages for young adults with almost a third of those who are ages eighteen to twenty-nine falling into these categories. While the "Solidly Secular" camp does not ascribe to any religious or New Age beliefs, "Religion Resisters" see religion as having a negative net impact on society.[48]

These profiles are extremely helpful for today's modern context, in which we find Christians as diverse as politician Mike Pence and Lady Gaga, who openly critiqued the politician and his wife for their involvement in a Christian school that discriminates against LGBTQ students, making "What kind of Christian are you?" a necessary question.[49] Lady Gaga, in her mid-thirties, is not quite a young adult anymore, but is an older millennial. To add further complexity, Catholic professor Brett Hoover underscores that many of his spiritually-inclined young adult students find their spirituality outside the church:

> They . . . think of faith (or spirituality, as they often prefer) in individualistic terms, as a personal journey . . . they are resolutely seekers, not dwellers. Many do not even think of church as a reasonable place to go to seek the sacred or the transcendent. They look for God in nature or in the heartfelt conversation between friends. They may even expect to find the holy in meditation or prayer, but not in church. When I speak about church with my students, the first thing that comes to mind for many is boredom.[50]

Religiously unaffiliated people often look for community outside of church structures. Pew Research Forum describes millennials as "connected."[51] That connection comes digitally but also through secular spaces of community. *New York Times* writer Mark Oppenheimer wrote an article on the religiosity of CrossFit gyms. He interviewed a young adult, 27, who said, "There is something raw and vulnerable that happens to you when you go into the CrossFit gym . . . A workout can bring you to your knees, so to speak." He documents that she sees her gym as "intimate" and "supportive," and he links the culture to "effects more often

---

48. Pew Research Center, "A Portrait of Generation Next.'"

49. Graves-Fitzsimmons, "Christianity's Future," para. 1–23.

50. Plekon, *The Church Has Left*, location 770.

51. Pew Research Center, "A Portrait of Generational Next," 19.

associated with church."[52] In a report called *How We Gather,* Harvard Divinity School graduates presented their research about where millennials seek and find community—and, maybe, even religion—in secular spaces.[53] *How We Gather* gives ten case studies of organizations that provide, for young adults, some combination of six identified themes: personal transformation, social transformation, purpose finding, creativity, and accountability. These organizations, such as Soul Cycle, CTZNWELL, millennial Trains Project, and Camp Grounded bring community and meaning and impact for millennials. *How We Gather* says, "Overwhelmingly, these organizations use secular language while mirroring many of the functions fulfilled by religious community. Examples include fellowship, personal reflection, pilgrimage, aesthetic discipline, liturgy, confession, and worship."[54] They have the effects of personal relationship, community for the neighborhood, and social good for the larger society.

These practices do not prove that young adults are not interested in God: instead, they point to a millennial's readiness to see religiosity in traditionally "secular" spaces. Reporter Sigal Samuel describes a Ritual Design Lab, which provides religious rituals for modern life—the death of a computer, for instance. It is the brainchild of Stanford Institute of Design professors Kursat Ozenc and Margaret Hagan who teach a course on ritual design. They report that many of their students are secular. Samuel quotes Ozenc saying,

> The new generation, they want bite-size spirituality instead of a whole menu of courses. Design thinking can offer this, because the whole premise of design is human-centeredness. It can help people shape their spirituality based on their needs. Institutionalized religions somehow forget this—that at the center of any religion should be the person.[55]

This Lab is also creating spaces for "pop-up prayer," for prayer in everyday spaces, and have intentionally geared their kits for an interfaith audience. These kind of classes and innovations serve the varied kinds of spiritual young people in the United States today.

All of this research shows how important it is for the church to realize that young adults are finding connection to the Holy outside of the

52. Oppenheimer, "Others Go to CrossFit," para. 22.
53. Thurston and ter Kuile, "How We Gather," 4.
54. Thurston and ter Kuile, "How We Gather," 7.
55. Samuel, "A Design Lab Is Making Rituals for Secular People," para. 4.

institution of the church. This reality shows how much of a theological resource Wendy Farley offers the church as it seeks to respond. On the path to a charitable relationship with young adults, the institution of the church needs to realize that the divide between the sacred and the secular is one of the church's own making (built, admittedly, with the help of other cultural and political forces) and does not reflect reality. There is no divide. Farley's emphasis on the outsider's experience, which results in an erasure of insider/outsider divides, in this case, has the effect of breaking down a perceived sacred/secular divide. As research shows, young adults often find Divinity in places outside the church.

Farley lays out, "Since the practice of incarnation is everything we do, there is not a separate set of practices that are 'religious.'"[56] Without the necessity of throwing one's energy into protecting the institution of the church as it is, one can put energy towards other pursuits. Two young adult pastors, Teri Petersen and Amy Fetterman, wrote a book in an effort to make the everyday sacred: they offer examples of spirituality outside the church in their practical book on spirituality entitled, *Who's Got Time? Spirituality for a Busy Generation*. They suggest spiritual practices which are (or could become) part of daily experience: eating a meal, yoga, listening to music, and taking a daydreaming break.[57] By looking for the sacred moments—or sacred reality—of traditionally "secular" spaces, the church starts to speak a language in which we find young adults already fluent. From studies, we see that young adults are willing (and actually do) see their lives and relationships and practices as full of spiritual and religious meaning. If churches are not able to speak of everyday, secular spaces as having the potential to channel the Divine, then they will not speak the same language as young adults. Without this communication, there is less of a chance of relationship. Additionally, refusal to see the sacred nature of the everyday is a direct dismissal of many young adults' values, and a lack of effort to see why they value spirituality outside the church translates as the church's low investment in the relationship. Young adults can teach the church the language of spirituality, religiosity, and community outside the institution.

56. Farley, *Gathering*, 206.
57. Fetterman, *Time*, locations 502, 596, 709, 878.

A New Lens: Young Adults' Potential for Divinity

Trusting the spiritual narratives of young adults outside the institution is a way of affirming the sacred nature of a secular young adult. Farley's theology aligns with this perspective. She sees everyone as having the potential for *theosis*. According to her, those outside the church can become more like Jesus than those inside the church. On the path to a charitable relationship with young adults, the institution of the church should value the Divine in young adults. Young adults can be part of the body of Christ even if they are not part of the institutional church. Though young adults may be estranged from church, they are, like the rest of humanity, made in the image of God, and made to be Divine. Young adults are good, capable of goodness, and capable of growing to be more like Jesus without the help of any institution.

For Farley, the problem of the human condition is distance from God. She writes, "While creation is good, we humans suffer an estrangement from our Divine source. It is part of the great beauty of the Christian faith that it envisions our Beloved as being unable to tolerate this estrangement."[58] In this perspective, we see that young adult sin is not their transgression of moralisms but Christ saves young adults from separation from Divinity. The church can help mend that estrangement by bringing to light the Divine in young adults. Seeing young adults as having the potential for *theosis* is an empowering vision, and, in this way, it lends itself to fostering a charitable relationship. Charity always hopes—and hopes what is good—for the other. Charity looks for and believes that good.[59]

This means that the church must be willing to recognize Divinity in those who do not look like the church and are not participating in church. While Farley is careful to say that ethical considerations need not be cast aside, she wants to prioritize a particular lens for viewing people whom the church labels as sinners or heretics: a lens which sees everyone as having the face of God, even those who do not make loving choices. It is not difficult to find examples of young adults actively participating in activities and lifestyles which the moralisms of the US church have condemned: drugs, alcohol, living with partners, casual sexual relationships, gambling, etc. Farley's theology of incarnation emphasizes that all people

58. Farley, *Gathering,* 142.
59. 1 Cor 13:6, NRSV.

have the same *imago dei*, and, therefore, these people also have valuable contributions for the community of God.

Farley's theology is not without its weaknesses when applied to this topic. While Farley recognizes the dangers of institutionalism, one important point she misses is the institution's usefulness in the work of bringing people together to identify God in one another and in the world. Churches can help people see through this lens. Churches have the theological resources to view all people as valuable for the Body of Christ. Placing young adults in positions of leadership, acknowledging the failings of the institutional church, and being open to structural change will help the church integrate this lens. Then, in community, we can encourage each other as we see each other in light of Christ in us. Being accountable to other people's perspectives and other people's sacred nature facilitates the attitude of humility for which her theology advocates. As the Body of Christ, we can call out and illuminate in each other our true humanity, which is Divinity. Her theology does, however, provide a helpful place to begin.

A Nonbinary Future

Karl Rahner, writing in the mid-1900s, predicted that "in the future Christians would be mystics or they would be nothing."[60] In that young adults are committed to personal experiences with God over institutional mandates, they may be following this path. If so, they are mystics who are also unattached to the institution, something studies are showing us now. Hoover writes, "leaving the church building may simply be the price we must pay if we religious people wish to speak with the younger generation about spiritual things."[61] If the institution does not start to take an interest in young adults themselves, and not for the purpose of institutional preservation, we will continue to alienate future generations.

What this requires of the church is to refrain from using orthodoxy as a weapon, to lay down pride, and to open our hands in recognition that the incarnation is a mystery greater than us. This shift in perspective will build a body of Christ less committed to the orthodoxy of councils and more committed to the experience of God. While this method may threaten the survival of the institutional church as it is today, the Body

60. Knitter, *Without Buddha*, 15.
61. Plekton, *The Church Has Left*, location 774.

of Christ will not die. Instead, the institution will stop existing for itself and, instead, exist for those outside of itself. With new spiritual practices which bless secular spaces and honor outsiders, the church can move forward with humility.

Conclusion

Farley's book is not an ecclesiology, and her theology gives the institution only a marginal role in the process of personal *theosis*. However, I find her perspective helpful for the church. How does the church reach young adults who leave the institution? How does it particularly treat those who leave because they have not found the church to be hospitable to them or the church has kicked them out, explicitly or implicitly? It is not by insisting on our position as the only ones who know God.

Farley writes, "Lovers, besotted with their beloved, are not less but infinitely more acutely attuned to the way their beloved remains mysterious, evanescent, sun glittering on waves."[62] We can start to gather these folks by acknowledging that God is too big to be known. If nothing else, Farley wants to warn against the pride of saying too definitively, *this* is God, and *this* is not. As an institution, we must allow for space for knowing and not knowing, loosening our grip on proclaiming truth. In humility, the church can build toward a more charitable relationship with young adults by acknowledging our failings, valuing what young adults value, communicating in their language, and empowering them. Ultimately, the institution needs to show young adults that their incorporation in the Body of Christ is more important than institutional survival.

Given the church's current situation, many call for changes to our spiritual practices. In a time of disconnect with young adults, church folk, naturally, look for avenues of communication. Like others, Kinnaman calls for changes in practical programs and outward expressions of our churches. In recognizing a disconnect between church and faith-filled Christians, he writes,

> We need new architects to design interconnected approaches to faith transference. We need new ecosystems of spiritual and vocational apprenticeship that can support deeper relationships and more vibrant faith formation . . . We need to renew our catechisms and confirmations—not because we need new

62. Farley, *Gathering,* 64.

theology, but because their current forms too rarely produce young people of deep, abiding faith.[63]

However, a new theology—Farley's theology of incarnation—may actually help. The values she emphasizes in her theology align with young adults' values and prompt the church to an inward shift which may prove more effective than new programs. The church needs to let go of fear.

At the Transfiguration, Peter wants to set up dwellings, tents, for Jesus, Moses, and Elijah, as was their tradition. Meanwhile, God speaks directly from the clouds, saying, "This is my Son, the Beloved; with him I am well pleased."[64] Instead of affirming structures of religion, God confronts them with the identity of the man in front of them and God's love for this human: Son of God, whom God loves and in whom God is pleased. Jesus comforts the disciples, who are floored by this experience, telling them, "Get up and do not be afraid."[65] Neither does the church need to fear the identity of young adults as the beloved of God or fear the ways that God chooses to speak with young adults. They stand before God without any mitigating structure.

Bibliography

Arnett, Jeffrey Jensen. "Emerging Adulthood: A Theory of Development from the Late Teens Through the Twenties." *American Psychologist* 55 (2000) 469–80.

Dimock, Michael. "Defining Generations: Where Millennials End and Generation Z Begins." Pew Research Center. http://www.pewresearch.org/fact-tank/2019/01/17/where-millennials-end-and-generation-z-begins/.

Farley, Wendy. *Gathering Those Driven Away: A Theology of Incarnation.* Louisville: Westminster John Knox, 2011.

Fetterman, Amy, and Teri Peterson. *Who's Got Time?: Spirituality for a Busy Generation.* St. Louis: Chalice, 2013. Kindle Edition.

Grant, Tobin. "ANALYSIS: 7.5 million Americans lost their religion since 2012." Religion News Service, Mar. 12, 2015. https://religionnews.com/2015/03/12/analysis-7-5-million-americans-lost-religion-since-2012/.

Graves-Fitzsimmons, Guthrie. "Christianity's Future Looks More Like Lady Gaga than Mike Pence." CNN, Jan. 24, 2019. https://www.cnn.com/2019/01/24/opinions/christianitys-future-looks-more-like-lady-gaga-than-mike-pence-graves-fitzsimmons/index.html.

Heim, David. "The Witness of Sinners." *Christian Century* 130 (2013) 32–34.

63. Kinnaman and Hawkins, *You Lost Me*, 13.

64. Matthew 17:5, NRSV.

65. Matthew 17:7, NRSV.

Kinnaman, David, and Aly Hawkins. *You Lost Me: Why Young Christians Are Leaving Church and Rethinking Faith.* Reprint ed. Grand Rapids: Baker, 2016.

Knitter, Paul F. *Without Buddha I Could not Be a Christian.* Oxford: Oneworld, 2013.

Ladd, Chris. "Organized Religion Is Being Replaced By Disorganized Religion." *Forbes,* Mar. 30, 2017. https://www.forbes.com/sites/chrisladd/2017/03/30/organized-religion-is-being-replaced-by-disorganized-religion/.

Merriam-Webster.com Dictionary. s.v. "charity." https://www.merriamwebster.com/dictionary/charity.

Martinbrough, Tiffany. "Going with the Flow (and the Drumbeat, Too)." *The New York Times,* Mar. 29, 2018. https://www.nytimes.com/2018/03/29/nyregion/afro-flow-yoga.html.

McSwain, Steve. "Why Nobody Wants to Be Around Christians Anymore." *HuffPost,* Sept. 4, 2014. https://www.huffingtonpost.com/steve-mcswain/why-nobody-wants-to-bear_b_5759918.html.

The New Revised Standard Version Bible. Oxford University Press, 1998.

Oppenheimer, Mark. "When Some Turn to Church, Others Go to CrossFit." *The New York Times,* Nov. 28, 2015. https://www.nytimes.com/2015/11/28/us/some-turn-to-church-others-to-crossfit.html.

Peck-McClain, Emily. "Generations Together." Class lecture, CF150 Ministry with Young Adults I from Wesley Theological Seminary, Washington, D.C., December 8, 2018.

Pew Research Center. "Millennials: Confident. Connected. Open to Change." 24 February 2010. http://www.pewsocialtrends.org/2010/02/24/millennials-confident-connected-open-to-change/.

———. "A Portrait of 'Generation Next.'" 9 January, 2007.

Plekon, Michael. *The Church Has Left the Building: Faith, Parish, and Ministry in the Twenty-First Century.* Eugene, OR: Cascade Books, 2016. Kindle.

Samuel, Sigal. "A Design Lab Is Making Rituals for Secular People." *The Atlantic,* May 7, 2018. https://www.theatlantic.com/technology/archive/2018/05/ritual-design-lab-secular-atheist/559535/.

Smith, Christian, Kari Christoffersen, Hilary Davidson, and Patricia Snell Herzog. *Lost in Transition: The Dark Side of Emerging Adulthood.* 1st ed. New York: Oxford University Press, 2011.

Thurston, Angie, and Casper ter Kuile. *How We Gather.* April 11, 2017. https://static1.squarespace.com/static/5a32a872ace8649fe18ae512/t/5a6f3b9bec212de83ac8 1b77/1517239214228/How_We_Gather_Digital_4.11.17.pdf.

8

Network-Based Christianity in the Pacific Northwest

Evolution of the Emerging Church or New Organizational Form?

DUSTIN D. BENAC

Abstract

In response to speculation about the future and significance of the Emerging Church, this chapter presents findings from primary research in the Pacific Northwest. The first part introduces the history and current work of the Parish Collective, which is a network of neighborhood-based parish expressions that seeks to connect isolated, neighborhood-based 'parish' leaders. Part II considers the organizational context that characterizes this movement to describe this network-based form in relation to a broader field of organized religious activity. Part III develops a constructive account of "ecclesial ecology" in order to consider the Parish Collective as a case that may point to the emergence of a new organizational form. This chapter concludes by suggesting how attention to network-based forms of religion may impact future research within and beyond the region.

Introduction[1]

Douglas Gay introduces his exploration of emerging ecclesiology, *Remixing The Church*, by questioning whether "emerging" adequately describes the loosely related ecclesial expressions that have historically gone by this term. Gay writes: "It may be that we are very close to the end of 'emerging' as a useful term for the Church."[2] The rapid expansion of the movement and the attendant constellation of practices yield a situation in which, according to Gay, "The qualifier is in danger of eclipsing the main term."[3] Nevertheless, as Gerardo Martí and Gladys Ganiel suggest in their transatlantic study, *The Deconstructed Church*, this movement remains "one of the most important reframings of religion within Western Christianity in the last two decades."[4] The apparent contrast between the significance of this movement and questions about what the term emergent/ing describes invites renewed reflection about the evolution of Christian thought and practice and the forms of scholarship that may attend to its historical and current manifestations.

In order to address this need, however, it is necessary to consider the characteristics of new forms of organizing Christian thought and practice and the relationship between these expressions and a broader ecology of ecclesial life. To this end, this chapter employs primary research on the Parish Collective (PC), which is a network of local, neighborhood-based ecclesial expressions that has emerged out of the Pacific Northwest, as a case to consider the evolution of Christian thought and practice within (and beyond) the region. Daniel Gay, Gerardo Martí, and Gladys Ganiel's work introduces an interpretive question on which this chapter's analysis hinges: Does the PC represent the evolution of the Emerging Church or point to the emergence of a new organizational form? As argued here, while the PC may have a genealogical connection to Emerging Christianity, their organizing work and animating theological commitments are distinct in kind. Emerging from the Pacific Northwest's distinct religious climate, which includes a history of religious entrepreneurship and a marginal social position for religious organizations, the PC provides a

---

1. The research for this project was completed through research and training grants from The M. J. Murdock Charitable Trust, Duke Interdisciplinary Studies, and St. Louis University's Lived Religion in a Digital Age initiative.

2. Gay, *Remixing The Church*, xi.

3. Gay, *Remixing The Church*, xiii.

4. Martí and Ganiel, *The Deconstructed Church*, 5.

case to consider the conditions and conceptual frameworks that support ecclesial innovation. Further, attention to the broader ecclesial ecology suggests that that the densely networked, multi-denominational, and localized characteristics of the PC may represent a new organizational form. Three parts develop this argument: Part I introduces the history and current work of the Parish Collective. Part II considers the broader organizational context that surrounds this movement. Part III develops a constructive account of "ecclesial ecology" in order to consider whether the PC's work represents a novel organizational form.[5]

Parish Collective: Context, History, and Current Work

Less than a mile from Pike Place Market and in neighborhoods across the Pacific Northwest, a "movement" is taking place. Individuals are (re)turning to neighborhoods across the region, in Seattle, Portland, Tacoma, Vancouver, British Columbia, and Spokane, drawn by an ecclesial vision and a commitment to faithful presence. Individuals and organizations from beyond the region, in Cincinnati, Ohio, Ottawa, Ontario, Chattanooga, Tennessee, the United Kingdom, and Australia, are also linking with partners and practitioners to support and pursue a more interconnected common life. Centrally located within this movement, the Parish Collective connects and resources local leaders and communities who are working to reground the life of faith in relation to neighborhoods.

Exiting the ferry and passing Pike Place, I walk a mile and a half to the Seattle School of Theology and Psychology, where the PC is hosting its annual Inhabit conference. Individuals from across and beyond the region have gathered for a two-day event that "is designed to facilitate

---

5. The material that appears here is based on original qualitative research in the Pacific Northwest. This research included semi-structured interviews and participant observation based in the Pacific Northwest, with a primary focus on the adaptive work that organizes two collaborative hubs within the region: The Office of Church Engagement (OCE) and the Parish Collective (PC). Research interviews generated over 44 hours of data. Participant observation was restricted to attending the annual conferences each organization hosts. This included three days at the Parish Collective's Inhabit conference and three days at the Office of Church Engagement's Ministry Summit. Finally, I reviewed approximately 25 documents that emerged from or in connection to one of these hubs. 'Documents' includes: books, program books, websites, news releases, promotional materials, videos, and internal documents. All individuals identified in this essay have provided written consent.

conversation, collaboration, and connection."[6] The air on this April morning is crisp and cloudless. Turning a corner and walking uphill, I approach a three-story red brick building. About 250 pastors, teachers, nonprofit professionals, organizers, church planters, restless creatives, and everyday people of faith mill about before the day's events. Many greet one another with hugs instead of handshakes; I later come to realize how this is like a gathering of close friends. The Olympics rise across the Puget Sound to preside, like silent witnesses, over the gathering.

The next forty-eight hours are brisk without feeling breathless. Each day follows a rhythm that is organized around gathering, workshops, meals, singing, stories from neighborhoods, and a keynote. The margins for each day and session include time for prayer, connection, and conversation. Session topics include: "Churches, Denominations and our Task to Shape Culture" (facilitated by Leroy Barber), "Life in the Zone of Social Abandonment" (facilitated by Lisa Etter Carlson & Ericka Frodsham), "Church Forsaken" (facilitated by Jonathan Brooks), "Soul Things Versus Material Things" (facilitated by Shalom Agtarap), and "Making Disciples in the Neighborhood" (facilitated by James Helms). Conversations continue between sessions and plenaries, frequently migrate to local eateries, and carry on into the evening. With a cadence that reflects a liturgical rhythm, the time together dually binds parish practitioners together and invites them to consider God's ongoing activity in their neighborhoods. The result, according to a key organizer and convener, Christiana Rice, is a reorientation of the individual and collective imagination that situates the work of God and the work of a community of faith within a particular place. She observes: "We're not telling church stories anymore; we're not telling self-glorifying stories anymore; we truly are telling the stories of God's renewal and restoration of a place in view of everyday stories of real people."[7]

Context: Adaptive Ethos of the Pacific Northwest

The PC's organizing and collaborative work is imprinted by the adaptive ethos of Cascadia and the broader Pacific Northwest. To return to the

---

6. Parish Collective, "Inhabit Pamphlet."

7. Lauren Goldbloom, who serves as an area connector in Spokane, WA, offers a corroborating perspective, when she describes her work as "not in any sense a 'church' space," placing 'church' in scare quotes as she speaks.

image of the Olympics in the opening vignette, the striking features of the region cast a long shadow over their organizing and convening work. Further, reflecting the broader national loosening of connections to denominational bodies,[8] Patricia Killen observes how individuals who enter Cascadia typically "experience a loosening of connection to social institutions."[9] As she notes:

> Each person who enters the region must choose whether, if, and how to reconnect. That choice is part of a larger question of community in the Pacific Northwest, a question about how an individual can be fully free, in nature, and part of society. People seek community, often through churches, and yet feel ambivalent about the constraints that community entails. This ambivalence leads some out of churches and drives others toward intense commitment and ownership.[10]

The dynamic Killen identifies represents a historic and ongoing challenge within the region. Lest this description of the social landscape of Cascadia mischaracterize the PC's work within and beyond the region, the region's characteristic entrepreneurial spirit also creates the possibility for experiments in new forms of community to emerge. For religious communities, the region's open religious environment creates a context that fosters a tradition of religious entrepreneurship that finds fertile cultural soil (and souls) in the region.[11] As the organizing vision of the PC suggests, individuals within the region desire connection and belonging, one only needs to listen to the needs within a given place and reimagine how to gather.

8. Chaves, *American Religion*.

9. Killen, "Memory, Novelty and Possibility in this Place," 66.

10. Killen, "Introduction—Patterns of the Past, Prospects for the Future," 13.

11. For example, James Wellman's comparative study of evangelical and liberal congregations within the Pacific Northwest leads him to conclude: "[E]ntrepreneurial evangelicals have carved out a foothold in the region" See, Wellman, *Evangelical vs. Liberal*, 271. Similarly, even though the region has been designated as the "none zone" that is "home to the least institutionally religious people in North America." See Todd, *Cascadia: The Elusive Utopia*, 11. Christopher James identified 105 new churches in Seattle that were "started, rebirthed, and/or relocated" between January 1, 2001 and June 1, 2014. See James, *Church Planting in Post-Christian Soil*, 31. Of the 105 churches, approximately twenty-five percent reflect what he identifies as the Neighborhood Incarnation model, which draws heavily on the PC's work.

This region is also regarded as a "model of the future"[12] that provides a context for models of environmental and urban sustainability in a global, technological age.[13] As a result, religious organizations in Cascadia may adopt the future-oriented sensibility that marks the broader region. Meanwhile, for the broader study of religious and cultural change, Mark Silk suggests that the distinguishing features of Cascadia make it a "regional laboratory of demography indicating where North America north of the Mexico border is headed when it comes to religion."[14] Indeed, as Killen observes, the tensions, possibilities, and challenges that are inherent to Cascadia provide an opportunity to consider a way of life that may emerge within this context. In the Pacific Northwest—where shifting geographical, social, and cultural landscapes meet shifting conventions for religious organization and practice—there is the possibility to discern the forms of practice and practical wisdom that are required for this "new age."[15]

For the PC, the influence of these dimensions is evidenced both in the history of their founding and the particular neighborhood expressions that have gathered around their work. For example, Soerens was a co-founding advisor for Impact Hub-Seattle; the PC's collaborative work was catalyzed both by the experience of isolation and the realization that other experiments within the region desired connection and community; it has drawn inspiration from a startup culture through its lean and decentralized organizational approach; and the frequent description of the PC's work as a "movement" reflects the region's broader future-oriented sensibility. Organizers and participants share this future-oriented sensibility across this network. As one participant reflects: "This is that in-between stage . . . We're on maybe a one hundred or a two hundred year curve, and we may never see what may evolve out of this, but we are in the place of figuring it out."

Nevertheless, the work of the PC also emerges from the particular neighborhoods where neighborhood expressions take place. For organizers and participants alike, they frequently cannot tell the story of their involvement with the PC without also telling the story the story of their neighborhoods. For example, as James Helms, who lives in the Rocky Butte community of Portland, OR, observes:

12. Wexler, "Conjectures on Workplace Spirituality in Cascadia," 218–19.

13. Killen, "Memory, Novelty and Possibility in this Place," 83.

14. Silk, "The Pacific Northwest is the American Religious Future."

15. Benac, "Theological Education for a New Age."

My life is lived as a series of overlays; I don't have much distinction between work, home life, community life. It's one life that I
live, so that takes me to connect with the people around me in
my direct neighborhood . . . If we would continue to tell stories,
it would include my neighbors and it would also include people
in my hub . . . For me, 'hub' is about relationship . . . The deeper
relationships, institutionally, are [interpersonal] relationships.

For Helms, the priority of friendships within the neighborhood re-
locates the collective activity that can transform individuals and community away from the organization to the specific locale where it takes
place.[16] Simultaneously, in discussing these relationships, Helms begins
to tell the stories of the people and friendships that surround him in the
neighborhood; it is as if he cannot talk about the forms of partnership
without sharing something of the story of the lives that surround this
work. While the particularities of his neighborhood reflect the broader
regional trends—e.g., income inequality, transience, a rapid pace of life—
attention to the neighborhood also suggests that the regional trends are
refracted through the social and cultural prism of a common life that
takes place in a given neighborhood. In this sense, even as the organizing
work of the PC may emerge from an adaptive and entrepreneurial ethos,
its particular form and expression is disciplined by connection to and
embeddedness within the neighborhood.

Mission

The mission of the Parish Collective is to "grow roots and weave links"
among followers of Jesus who seek to grow "expression[s] of love and care
in the[ir] neighborhood."[17] For the organizers, three animating commit-

16. As Rachel Schneider demonstrates, an abiding commitment to friendship
distinguishes one prominent expression of the ECM's new monasticism Schneider,
"'A Web of Subversive Friends'" However, the importance of friendship within estab-
lished and alternative forms of Christian community extends beyond both the PC
and new monasticism. For example, friendship networks contributed to the spread of
Christianity in the first few centuries of its existence See Stark, *The Rise of Christianity*
According to Robert Wilken, friendship organized one of the early experiments in
Christian education and training in Alexandria. Wilken, "Alexandria: A School for
Training in Virtue," *Schools of Thought in the Christian Tradition*. Finally, Paul Wadell
identifies friendship as a central component of a moral life. See Wadell, *Friendship and
the Moral Life*.

17. Parish Collective, "Learn How It Works." This summary of the PC mission

ments guide their organizing and collaborative work. First, the neighbor-hood, or the parish, is the principal contextual center for a transformative ecclesial life. As explained in a collaborative work, *The New Parish: How Neighborhood Churches are Transforming Mission, Discipleship and Community*, 'parish' "refers to all the relationships (including the land) where the local church lives out its faith together." This reoriented ecclesial life, as a "life together in a definable place," provides a "geography large enough to live life together (live, work, play, etc.) and small enough to be known as a character within it."[18] As Tim Soerens, who serves as a Co-Founding Director for the Parish Collective, explains: "Part of what we found [and] that we're still finding is that . . . when you have the neighborhood or the parish as the primary context of engagement, then—for better or worse, and it's always both—neighborhood pushes back."[19] Expressing more than a social enterprise or a commitment to the common good, this de-scription of the neighborhood reflects a vision to see and encounter God through a placed-based understanding of ecclesial life. As Paul Sparks, who also serves a Co-Founding Director, notes: "The work is guided by a theological understanding of the neighborhood as the place where fol-lowers of Jesus may pursue a form of being together that seeks God's shalom. This is the telos." As a result, the parish becomes the contextual center out of which connections, mission, and partnerships emerge from the "particulars of ordinary life,"[20] redounding to direct and discipline the ecclesial parish-based expressions that take place as Jesus followers link within and across neighborhoods.

Second, the PC's mission is based on an animating commitment that parish-based expressions are already happening, but the individuals pursuing this work are frequently isolated and do not know one another. As Sparks and Soerens reflect on the genesis of their work, isolation was both one of the primary challenges that catalyzed their early orga-nizing of the Parish Collective and remains a challenge for those they

---

reflects a composite of different ways their work is framed for different contexts.

18. Sparks et al., *The New Parish*, 23.

19. As described elsewhere by Soerens and other PC organizers, the "for worse" does not offer a critique of neighborhoods or of the need for faithful presence. Rather, his description reflects an acute understanding of the complex and slow process neigh-borhood work requires. And, in doing so, the life of a particular neighborhood may disrupt and redirect individual's expectations about the form of faithful presence that may serve their neighbors.

20. Sparks et al., *The New Parish*, 68.

serve. For example, around 2008, as they were both experimenting with neighborhood-based church expressions, they also began meeting with other parish expressions across the region. Across these conversations— and sometimes from individuals who lived just a few streets away—they encountered a gap between individuals' animating desires and current experiences: many individuals desired to reimagine church in the neighborhood, but these practitioners were frequently isolated. As they reflect:

> [W]e were talking to people all over and the common sense was we saw small teams are doing this neighborhood work, we feel like it's really profound and beautiful, gritty and resilient, and we feel alone. We don't know if what we're doing really matters that much. Our denominations, or our networks, or whatever church planting network oftentimes give us permission to do what we are doing—to be kind of thinking publicly about a neighborhood, or parish—but it's also kind of seen as on the side. It's not the big thing as like growing a church or starting a church. And the truth is, while we still like what we're doing, is it what we're supposed to be doing? We also don't know necessarily how much longer we'll be able to keep at it because we just feel alone.

As expressed here, the fluid 'we' reflects the dually collective and personal need that catalyzed this work. In these encounters and conversations, the isolation and loneliness of others resonated with their own experience and their sense for the new possibilities that were emerging, leading them to consider the need for new forms to organize and support this kind of parish-based work.[21]

Following insights from John McKnight and Peter Block, the PC's work is also organized by a sense that this type of work is already happening.[22] This organizing commitment is frequently expressed in terms of abundance. "[W]e see the abundance we have—individually, as neighbors and in this place of ours," writes Sparks, Soerens, and Friesen.[23] Anecdotes from multiple interviewees corroborate this sentiment. For example, Rich Jones, who served as a pastor and community organizer before beginning to engage more actively within the PC, reflects:

21. As a video introducing the Parish Collective's work explains: "Living local; it's a global movement taking place right in your own neighborhood and it's catching on like wildfire." Parish Collective, "About."

22. According to one pastor and parish leader, John McKnight, Peter Block, and Walter Brueggemann are the "unofficial elders of the Parish Collective."

23. Sparks et al., *The New Parish*, 99.

A few years back, I start finding out that other people were doing this community-based thing, and I realized that there were
other kindred spirits out there. I read *The New Parish* and I met
with Tim Soerens several years ago, actually at a neighborhood
economics deal. And then from there it's just been magical . . .
It's been great. And then [I met] Paul Sparks, and Dwight, and
Christiana, and other folks in the orbit of Parish Collective. And
then a few years ago we decide we wanted to do a gathering in
Cincinnati.[24]

As a result, in the face of the challenges that confront individuals and
communities, the PC seeks to organize and connect individuals and communities around the assumption, as Sparks and Soerens observe, "that we
will find the resources for our complex problem, among us."

Nevertheless, the vitality of neighborhoods and parish expressions
requires relational connections in order for individuals and communities to be able to reimagine the structure of their common life. With the
neighborhood as the "ecclesial center,"[25] new possibilities may emerge for
a "way of life" in which the "local church learns to rely on the Spirit's movement in every situation as a way of being faithfully present to the relationships in your context."[26] Accordingly, a third animating commitment is
the need for an arena to provide the resources and relational connections
that are required to start, support, and sustain neighborhood-based parish expressions. As Sparks describes it, they understand the work of the
PC as both "a network and a platform." Sparks explains: "The network
represents the relational connectivity, the platform represents the 'grease'
that you apply to those links to make good connections happen." As
expanded below, these twin dimensions reflect their animating vision.
As a result, their work is not solely connecting isolated ministry leaders
who are experimenting with new forms of Christian organization and
community. Nor is it solely an effort to revitalize ecclesial expression by
enriching ordinary life within one's neighborhood. Rather, these two

24. The community Jones describes here is located in Cincinnati, OH. While this
is not based in the Pacific Northwest, a distinctive component of the PC's work is the
network of partnerships and parish-based expressions that extend beyond the region.

25. Sparks et al., *The New Parish*, 74. The identification of the neighborhood as the
ecclesial center neither denigrates nor denies the importance of congregations and
related forms of Christian organization. As they observed: "This is not to downplay
church gatherings or religious structures. It is to call attention to just how far they
have become disconnected from the particulars of ordinary life" Sparks et al., *The New
Parish*, 68.

26. Sparks et al., 85.

dimensions of their work—connecting parish-based expressions and enriching the ordinary life of the neighborhood—direct and reinforce the other. To borrow language from Peter Block—whom the organizers identify as a friend and key conversation partner—this combined work represents an attempt to "discover and create the means . . . that bring a new possibility into being."[27] As a result, the collaborative, connective, and ecclesial nature of the PC's work over a decade seeks to create the conditions where new possibilities may emerge through encounters within the neighborhood and across parish-based experiments. As one practitioner observes, the encounters with neighbors in the neighborhood invite transformation.

> [I]t's my neighbors that are saving me, because it's just like the harvest; it feeds us. We don't grow this stuff; we just nurture it. God does the work . . . [I]t's the neighbors that are giving me life. I think there's a mutual transformation that's happening. Hopefully they're seeing the Christ in me. And I know I see that my neighbors are made in the image of God. When I'm engaging with them, I'm engaging with God.[28]

Notably, the "mutual transformation" that is envisioned here represents an understanding of salvation that is found in the neighborhood and through encounter with one's neighbors. This point is succinctly expressed by another participant, who notes, "I do not go to neighborhood to seek converts; I go into the neighborhood for my own conversion."

Finally, the combination of these three animating commitments represents what the organizers and practitioners alike describe as a 'movement.' Soerens and Christiana Rice, who is both an early partner and has recently moved into a key organizing role, express this when they write: "Beyond our church growth charts and measurement sticks there is a movement bursting up from the ground, a counter narrative to the anxious grip of the past. A movement is growing to reclaim the ancient idea of the parish for the 21st century."[29] Similarly, when Sparks and Soerens reflect on the history of the PC, they note: "[W]e felt like maybe there's a movement because people who feel like they are alone, actually aren't. And so, the nucleus of a lot of our work began [with the idea that] if we can identify and connect those people, it feels like there's a

27. Block, *Community*, 79.
28. 'Harvest' here is a reference to Jesus's words in Matt 9:37-38.
29. Soerens and Rice, "Five Hopeful Signs."

movement already. It feels like it just needs to be uncovered; it needs to be connected." Although there is some variation among organizers and participants about whether they are *starting* a movement or identifying and connecting an *existing* movement, the ubiquity of this language invokes a sense in which the Spirit is on the move even as they seek to nurture the conditions that can enliven a parish-based renewal.

Programmatic Structure

The PC's programmatic structure organizes their work in a way that both reflects the region's adaptive ethos and responds to the challenge local, parish-based leaders face. The PC organizes its work as a "flywheel" that includes three components: organizing, training, and events. When taken together, these three components "work together in mutually reinforcing ways to grow connection and belonging across a particular city-region."[30]

A brief explanation of each element provides an orientation to how the PC's mission and history of adaptation informs their specific programs. The first component of the PC's flywheel approach, organizing, reflects its commitment to support and connect local, neighborhood-based parish expressions. The primary objective is to "foster relational connectivity" through online and on-the-ground organizing.[31] Reflecting the connective and collaborative approach that marked the early phases of the PC's organizing work, this organizing work attempts to create what the organizers describe as a "tertiary network" that does not replace existing forms of religious networks (e.g., denominations), but enriches and strengthens them. Sparks describes the importance of this relational connectivity:

> [P]art of our early journey as friends was the recognition that, while the local neighborhood form was critical, the only way you could sustain or grow, or discover from your blind spots about your current reality in the neighborhood was through networks. You need to be connecting with other parties who are experiencing it from their particulars and who, who could see from the outside what was going on in your place.

With this intention in view, individuals can digitally link with other parish-based expressions and discover other practitioners within and

---

30. Parish Collective, "6-Series Document."
31. Parish Collective, "6-Series Document."

beyond their region through a free, online portal. As of May 2019, 2,587 have joined the PC's platform and identified themselves as involved or interested in some kind of parish-related work.[32]

The PC also supports on-the-ground organizing by identifying and resourcing local organizers that they identify as "area connectors" who support and connect parish-expressions within their area. Area connectors typically have a history of engagement within their local context as well as some engagement with the PC. Area connectors are contextually embedded relational resources who connect individuals, communities, and projects seeking to support the flourishing of their context. The PC's paradigm for the organizing that takes place at the area level draws heavily on John McKnight's approach to asset based community development.[33] For example, when asked what else he needs to continue his work, area connector, Rich Jones, replied: "Need? I don't know about need. Again, we have everything we need. [We only] need more awareness of the abundance that's already there, the gifts that are already there . . . I don't know if I need anything other than to stay curious and listen."

Trainings are the second component to the PC's flywheel programmatic structure. Their training "helps individuals and congregations live into a new way of being the church together in the everyday life of the neighborhood."[34] The Leadership in the New Parish Certificate provided an initial platform to develop a pedagogy and methodology to support, train, and resource new parish leaders throughout the Pacific Northwest. Co-taught by Sparks, Soerens, and Friesen through The Seattle School of Theology and Psychology, the program combines contextual experience in neighborhoods, narrative work around personal trauma, sharing and listening to what has been learned from being deeply rooted in the neighborhood, and identifying and cultivating "rooting" and "linking" practices that sustain neighborhood work. To date, sixty-seven individuals have completed the Leadership in the New Parish Certificate over five cohorts. However, the program was discontinued by The Seattle School of Theology and Psychology in 2019.

---

32. Of these, more than forty-five percent (1,178) are located in the Pacific Northwest and eighty-eight percent (2,283) are locate in North America. Of the remaining twelve percent, there are high concentrations in the United Kingdom, Australia, and New Zealand.

33. For example, see Sparks et al., *The New Parish*, 99. See also McKnight and Block, *The Abundant Community*.

34. Parish Collective, "6-Series Document."

The PC has recently translated this contextual approach to training into a Learning Communities model in order to provide regional forums for training and contextual reflection. Launched in 2019 in the Pacific Northwest through a partnership with the Pacific Northwest Conference of the United Methodist Church, this pilot program seeks to "spark [the] collective imagination"[35] through a combination of regional, intensive training programs, "guided practice," and curated fieldwork through parish immersions.[36] In partnership with parachurch organizations, such as the Navigators (a national parachurch organization),[37] they have also employed a similar approach to train and resource local ministry leaders.

The third element of the PC's flywheel, events, offers curated gatherings that provide opportunities for parish leaders to connect and "celebrate the stories, ideas, and practices" that are "re-founding the church in the neighborhood."[38] Modeled after the template of PC's flagship conference, Inhabit, these regional gatherings combine worship, stories from local neighborhoods,[39] plenary conversations, breakout training sessions, neighborhood tours, and ample time on the margins for mingling and conversation between friends and practitioners. With events in San Diego, CA, Cincinnati, OH, Birmingham, UK, and Hamilton, ON, Canada, this convening work is intended both to enliven the "imagination" that directs the engagement within neighborhoods and across cities and to counteract the all-to-common loneliness that many organizers and practitioners identify as a central challenge for their work.

Christiana Rice, who transitioned into a key organizing role in PC in 2019, works to curate these spaces in ways that attend to how individuals "come together around an experience that is going to shape our imagination about who God is and what God's up to." Both a practitioner—she lives in a neighborhood church community that she helped found ten years ago—and a curator of environments, she combines a relational, placed-based sensitivity with attention to the collective experience that occurs when people gather. When asked to reflect on how she understands her work curating events in relation the PC's broader work, Rice

35. Parish Collective, "New Parish Learning Communities."

36. Parish Collective, "6-Series Document."

37. Navigators is a parachurch organization with ministries for college students and military families.

38. Parish Collective, "6-Series Document."

39. Called 'Parish Portraits,' these are delivered in a Pecha Kucha format that combines twenty images with a seven-minute description of a particular neighborhood.

begins by noting that "Christ is our unifier" before noting how she works to curate an environment that is "nourishing to the soul," includes "attention to place," "deep learning," and "inspiration from stories." Because the PC's events typically include a myriad of practitioners, stories, musicians, plenary speakers, and training sessions,[40] her approach is highly relational, but it also attends to the particular details that invite people to consider "what is God doing to transform lives, and how does that impact the culture of a neighborhood?" She also closely attends to how gathering may invite people to "think about how to be together in the room in the way they want to be together in the neighborhood." Thus, through these three interlocking and mutually-reinforcing dimensions, the PC's "flywheel effect" seeks to enliven neighborhood-work by connecting various experiments within a city and across a region, cultivating a new imagination for the kind of leadership that is required to be in a neighborhood in this way, and contributing to the transformation of neighborhoods and cities.[41]

Emerging-Missional Traditions

Finally, the PC's work emerges in the wake of the Emerging Church tradition and in conversation with the missional theology movement.[42] Although organizers are reticent to make a direct genealogical link to either tradition/movement—they prefer to note the relational connections and the practice of responding to what is already emerging[43]—these twin influences contribute to the PC's work in direct and indirect manners. The analysis of the combination of observations from PC organizers with research on the Emerging Church and missional theology demonstrates the connection between the PC and these loosely configured traditions of thought and practice.

---

40. For example, the two-day Inhabit conference lists more than seventy individuals as plenary speakers, musicians, or workshop facilitators.

41. The PC identifies the telos of their work as "help[ing] parishioners develop the right web of relationships for their holistic growth and neighborhood transformation." See Parish Collective, "6-Series Document."

42. Although the internal logic of Emerging Church may resist the concept of a fixed "tradition," Phyllis Tickle notes how emergence Christians have "shared sensibilities, values, and positions." Tickle, *Emergence Christianity*, 115.

43. As Rice observes, the mission of the PC is "connection oriented."

First, the Emerging Church tradition represents a transnational reframing of Christianity that is characterized by an emphasis on community, hyper-local congregations, flat leadership structures, a network-based approach, missional theology, and an ant-institutional bias.[44] As Michael Clawson observes: "The desire for more authentic and organic forms of organization rather than the top-down businesslike models of the new paradigm, has also led those in the ECM to move, however imperfectly, toward smaller, less institutionalized, and more collaborative forms of religious community with more horizontal and open-source models of shared leadership."[45] As described by practitioners and students of this "movement,"[46] the attempt to reframe Christian thought, organization, and practice[47] reflects the "adaptive ethos"[48] that is driven by the "religious institutional entrepreneurs"[49] of the Emerging Church. Although the coherence of the Emerging Church as a single and clearly identifiable movement has lessened in recent years, the movement remains, according to Gerardo Martí and Gladys Ganiel, "one of the most important reframings of religion within Western Christianity in the last two decades,"[50] whose influence has bled across the theological and organizational distinctions that once provided the occasion for its work.[51]

With this in view, the Emerging Church tradition represents both an early incubator for the work of the PC and a foil as their work and organizing evolved. As an early incubator, the growth of Emerging Christianity in the early part of the twenty-first century provided an alternative to mainline thought and practice. For example, one of the early organizers for the PC notes the influence of iconic Emerging Church pastor, Rob Bell, on his early interest and formation in ministry. Attending seminary

44. This description combines insights from Martí and Ganiel, *The Deconstructed Church*; McKnight et al., *Church in the Present Tense*; Packard, *The Emerging Church*; Clawson and Stace, *Crossing Boundaries, Redefining Faith*.

45. Clawson, "A Brief History of the Emerging Church," 22–23.

46. Clawson and Stace, *Crossing Boundaries, Redefining Faith*, 7.

47. As Martí observes, "[T]he ECM involves an earnest attempt to fundamentally redefine contemporary Christianity." Martí, "Emerging Christianity through a Social Science Lens," 62.

48. Clawson, "A Brief History of the Emerging Church," 27.

49. Martí and Ganiel, *Deconstructed Church*, 25.

50. Martí and Ganiel, *Deconstructed Church*, 5.

51. For example, Elaine Heath describes how the missional/emergent church movement is impacting mainline thought and practice. Heath, "A New Days Rising in the Church," 26–35.

in Grand Rapids at the time, Bell's work and ministry presented a sharp contrast to his current educational setting. "I was really compelled by him and I loved what he was doing," he reflects. While other influences also contributed to the trajectory and work of the PC, the work of Bell and others provided avenues to consider the forms of Christian thought and practice beyond the confines of conventional Christianity.[52]

At the same time, prominent Emerging Church voices within the Pacific Northwest during the PC's early stages provided a foil for the local, neighborhood-based vision that organized their work. As one interviewee observed, the controversy surrounding Mark Driscoll contributed to a "Mark Driscoll phenomenon" in which his acerbic form of mega-church Christianity starkly contrasted with the PC's vision for neighborhood-based ecclesial expressions. According to Dwight Friesen, who co-authored *The New Parish* with Sparks and Soerens,

> [I]n terms of the Christian world and Seattle, which is a small world [and] Seattle is a predominantly secular environment . . . people assume [Driscoll's] was the loudest voice of Christianity in the Seattle area. So, to all of a sudden be championing these small faithful expressions that weren't about a big show and absurd 'theology' or 'biblical preaching', but actually a lived expression of Jesus in the ordinary stuff was, I think, a breath of fresh air."

Much as Sparks and others noted the limits of the attractional model and the need to deconstruct pastor-centric approaches to church leadership, the Emerging Church also provides a point of contrast for the practice and early experiments with localized neighborhood expressions. If the Emerging Church provided space for early organizers to consider the possibilities of Christianity beyond received templates, the period of its popularity also demonstrated the internal limitations of this strain of Christian thought and practice.

At the same time, the PC's history, structure, and animating vision were refracted through engagement with missional theology. For example, the relational connection with Michael Frost and Alan Hirsch both catalyzed some of the earliest work of the PC around a missional understanding of the church in the neighborhood and remains an ongoing

---

52. Similarly, Friesen was a member of the Emergent Village network at an early stage in his vocational journey. See Friesen, *Thy Kingdom Connected*, 72. Lloyd Chia identifies Friesen as an "emergent thinker and author." Chia, "From Boundaries to Borderlands," 155.

point of connection. As evidenced by Christiana Rice's co-authored work with Michael Frost, *To Alter Your World: Partnering with God to Rebirth Our Communities*, this relational connection and attendant missional paradigm have continued within the PC's organizing work. Alan Roxburgh, who lives and works in Vancouver, BC, also remains an ongoing influence across this network. Accordingly, while the PC employs a collaborative and decentralized-leadership approach to support a network of neighborhood-based parish expressions, it is calibrated by engagement within the neighborhood. Further, while their history of local and institutional engagement may reflect and refine some of the "shared sensibilities"[53] that organized Emerging Christianity and missional theology, their work and engagement seek generative ways to reach beyond a single silo or tradition. Drawing upon more than a decade of learnings, their collective work prioritizes placed, local expression of faith communities *and* identifies the need for meaningful institutional partnerships. Without privileging one over the other, their organizing, events, and collaborative work supports the conditions where local and institutional forms of organizing a religious life may enrich and support the other. Accordingly, demonstrating a point of decisive departure from Emerging Christianity, the PC has identified the need to "dance well with institutions" and clearly states that they are not "anti-institutional." While participants still identify a tension between institutionalized and grassroots, neighborhood-based religious expressions, at the organizational level, the PC's organizing work frequently includes partnering with and coming alongside established institutions (e.g., seminaries, denominations, parachurch) to equip and resource students, ministers, and local leaders.

And it is at this point that the genealogical connection with the Emerging Church tradition begins to lessen and fray. In comparison to attempts by Emerging Church thinkers to identify the boundaries and defend the legitimacy of their movement, PC organizers are less interested in doing so. The work of the neighborhood invites a collaborative, ecumenical, and missional way of connecting and linking for followers of Jesus. The practice of neighborliness requires a posture to receive and be received across traditional boundaries. Accordingly, as much as the Emerging-missional traditions provides an incubator and foil for the PC's early work, their collaborative work remains a "convergence space,"[54] one

53. Tickle, *Emergence Christianity*, 115.

54. Lloyd Chia attributes this to Tony Jones, but the referenced blog post does not include this phrase. See Chia, "From Boundaries to Borderlands," 147.

that now reaches beyond a single tradition or denomination by weaving the fabric of love and connection within and across neighborhoods. Hence, through their engagement with an eclectic array of religious organizations, they pursue a bridge-building and boundary-cross form of work that seeks to (re)ground ecclesial life, including a range of institutional expressions, in proximity to the neighborhood.

Organizational Context

The PC's organizational context provides a second avenue to explore the distinctive features of their collaborative and adaptive work. Although their connecting work may indeed reflect what Brad Christerson and Richard Flory identify as the "rise of network Christianity,"[55] a finer analysis of the organizational context provides insight into the distinguishing feature of the PC's work and particular form of organization.[56] Specifically, complementary insights from network analysis and field-level analysis direct attention to the relationship between a dense network and the broader organizational field that enables and directs this collaborative activity.

Network Analysis

First, network analysis provides an analytical category to understand and critically engage the PC's work. In response to the experience of isolation, the PC is marked by a highly connective and collaborative approach, leading to a dense network of relationships and partnerships.[57] As described by the PC, their attempt to "weave links" represents an attempt to connect and resource networks of leaders and the communities

---

55. Christerson and Flory, *The Rise of Network Christianity*.

56. As one practitioner reflected on his six years of engagement with the PC, he identified a dialectic between organized activity and local expressions as a tension for the PC's organized work. As he queried, "How do you build an organization that," and then takes a long pause before concluding, "is not an organization?" That is to say, how do you organize a network that seeks to connect and support local parish expressions, but do so in a manner that always allows the needs and concerns of the neighborhood to talk back?

57. Following Richard Scott and Gerald Davis, a network is "a system of relationships among parts." Scott and Davis, *Organizations and Organizing*, 280.

they serve. Further, as noted above, organizers of the PC describe this as "tertiary network" and as a "network and platform."[58]

A network perspective offers resources to consider the enabling conditions, forms of connection, network structure, and the relationship between networks and the emergence of new organizations.[59] First, the PC is built upon decades of accrued trust—both within the region and between friends. At every level of the PC, trust functions like ligaments within a body, connecting disparate parts, spanning gaps, and enabling individuals and organizations to work together. Once formed, these networks both permit nimble and adaptive responses and serve as sites for new connections to form. To borrow language from Soerens, they try to be the "connecting tissues." The result is a network of interconnected faith leaders, communities, and organizations that are rooted in their context and may respond nimbly when challenges or opportunities arise.

Furthermore, network theory also offers resources to consider the different forms of connection that comprise the networks that have formed around their work.[60] Across the PC, there is a proliferation of both strong and weak ties. The relational capital, which is to say strong ties, that predated the PC created the conditions for it to form and expand. Moreover, the various programmatic dimensions seek to strengthen ties by providing additional points of connection across members within this network. At the same time, weak ties play a critical role within their work by connecting disparate networks and facilitating the transmission of information, ideas, and practices. When considered together, these individuals become the bridges for information, ideas, and connections to move between separated and siloed sectors of the region. As a result, individuals and ideas begin to connect and flow between Vancouver, BC, Seattle, Tacoma, and Portland or a national parachurch ministry begins to resource its leaders to attend to the needs of particular neighborhoods. Although individuals may still note the importance of friendship for the connections between these disparate parts, this level of connection lacks the relational redundancy that characterizes strong ties and may have the fragility that comes from distance or less-frequent interactions. In

58. Published during the early phase of the PC's organization, Dwight Friesen's *Thy Kingdom Connected* draws insight from network theory to develop a "networked paradigm" that reflects a "richly interconnective vision of interpersonal relations [that] requires a deep understanding of the self-in-relationship, which makes possible the offering of our individuated self to the other." Friesen, *Thy Kingdom Connected*, 26.

59. Powell, "Neither Market nor Hierarchy."

60. Burt, *Structural Holes*.

many cases, the organizers of the PC stand at the nexus of multiple, non-redundant networks that engage large numbers of individuals and communities, but nevertheless remain siloed from the others. For the PC, their work has produced a dense network of regional partners and has begun to reproduce similar clusters in other domestic and international regions that share a similar cultural climate.

The structure of this network comes into sharper focus when this macro view is considered alongside a qualitative assessment of the partnerships that surround this site. Through semi-structured interviews, I asked: Who are they key individuals or organizations that you consider partners for your work? Figure 8.1 provides additional insight into the relational structure that organizes the PC.

FIGURE 8.1

Relational Structure of Parish Collective

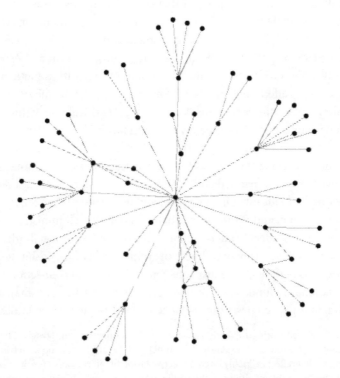

The network(s) visualized here represent the relational forms of partnership that organizes this collective work within the region. In some cases, individuals' responses do represent some form of formal partnership at the organizational level (e.g., Navigators), but the identification of an organizational partner was frequently followed by mentioning specific individuals within that organization that are the primary source of connection. Hence, the kinds of connections presented here are relationally inflected points of contact, each of which frequently has its own history and context. Notably, as demonstrated above, this network includes a central point (the PC) surrounded by multiple loosely configured networks. While select individuals may occupy a central position within this network, the localized, neighborhood-based dimension of this work leads to a geographically determined form of partnership. At the same time, the partners visualized above extend well beyond the Pacific Northwest, including partners from as far away as San Diego, Ottawa, and the UK.

Field-Level Analysis

The diversity of the PC's individual and organizational partners directs attention beyond the confines of network analysis. Although the PC emerges from partnerships among individuals within these networks, it also exists within and emerges from a broader organized pattern of activity and social relations. Accordingly, a "field-level" perspective clarifies the organizational setting(s) in which this adaptive work takes place. An organizational field is defined as: "Those organizations that, in the aggregate, constitute a recognized area of institutional life."[61] Further, organizational fields represent an organized domain of social life that includes a commingling of shared values and processes of social exchange that constitute a shared field of organized meaning.[62] As Paul DiMaggio and Walter Powell suggest: "The virtue of this unit of analysis is that it directs our attention not simply to competing firms . . . or to networks of organizations that actually interact . . . but to the totality of relevant actors."[63] This level of analysis requires attending to the composite of organizations that collectively constitute and sustain an organizational field.

As applied to the PC, this form of analysis directs attention to the constellation of organizations that supports and surrounds this particular organizational and ecclesial adaptation. Specifically, it includes

61. DiMaggio and Powell, "The Iron Cage Revisited," 148.

62. Scott, *Institutions and Organizations*.

63. DiMaggio and Powell, "The Iron Cage Revisited," 148.

cross-pollinating forms of partnership between theological schools, philanthropy, nonprofit organizations, congregations, publishers, denominations, and parish-based expressions. Partners include existing organizations, national nonprofits, community-based coalitions, neighborhood-based parish leaders. In nearly every case, a relational connection provides the primary means for partnership. Nevertheless, this collaborative and organizing work also occurs against the backdrop of a porous and fluctuating organizational field that provides opportunities to explore new forms of gathering, leadership, education, and organization within the region. As Powell observes, "[W]hen the boundaries of established fields are rearranged," it introduces the potential for a "quite dramatic form of institutional change."[64] Accordingly, the work of the PC seeks to identify 'place' as a unifying concern, connecting and organizing individuals across discrete sectors in response to the particular gifts and challenges of their place.

When combined in this way, network theory and a field-level approach direct attention to a final feature of this organizing work: it creates the contexts for entrepreneurial activity and the emergence of new organizational forms. Due to the structure of networks—which includes both strong and weak ties—individuals and actors within a network have access to resources, relationships, and information that they otherwise would not possess. Further, through participation within a broader organizational field, these trust-filled relationships may be(come) value-infused and supported through organizational holding environments. Indeed, the PC has the capacity to facilitate the transfer of existing ideas, resources, relationships, and information. At the same time, it may also provide generative contexts that incubate new ideas and new meaning systems.

Further, the network of formal and informal partnerships and interpersonal relationships that organizes the PC creates a social and organizational boundary space where new organizational practices and new forms of religious organizations may emerge. As Martin Ruef notes, new organizations are often "hatched within existing organizational arrangements."[65] While this kind of religious and organizational entrepreneurship may occur within any network, the emergence of this organizational and ecclesial adaptation reflects the distinct entrepreneurial

64. Powell, "Expanding the Scope," 200. Powell's description of "institutional change" in this sentence applies equally to the study of the PC.

65. Ruef, "The Emergence of Organizational Forms," 670.

ethos that marks religion in the Pacific Northwest. Nevertheless, it is not just the presence of networks alone that may incubate new ideas and organizational forms. As Niall Ferguson notes, "[T]he point of contact between diverse networks may be the place to look for novelty."[66] Indeed, this densely networked collaborative activity, out of and alongside existing organizations, creates the conditions for new organizational forms to emerge.

Ecclesial Ecology and the Emergence of Organizational Forms

Accordingly, this final section develops a constructive account of an 'ecclesial ecology' in order to consider the Parish Collective as a case that may point to the emergence of new organizational form. As used here, 'ecclesial ecology' is defined as the constellation of various established and emerging forms of organized, ecclesial life that constitute the organizational and ecclesial context where individuals and communities engage in the forms of individual and collective change that may orient an integrated life through worship and community.[67] This section will briefly introduce this concept and apply it to the PC to argue that this organizing and collaborative work may point to the emergence of a new organizational form.

First, attention to the ecclesial ecology directs attention to the interaction between organizations and the broader network of relations—or organizational ecology—that supports and sustains changes within and beyond the PC. Much as Michael Hannan and John Freeman note in their description of organizational ecology as a form of organizational analysis, change within organizational environments occurs *both* through the formation of new organizations and the disbanding of existing organizations. Hannan and Freeman write: "[E]cological analysis is appropriate when organizations are subject to strong inertial pressures and face

66. Ferguson, *The Square and the Tower*, 42.

67. My use and definition of 'ecclesial ecology' is not identical to Christopher James's use of the term in *Church Planting in Post-Christian Soil*. While this phrase organizes his description of the variation in church expression across the landscape of congregations in Seattle, his use of the term under explores both the broader ecclesial context and surrounding organizational ecology. For my earliest use of this term. See Benac "Theological Education for a New Age," *The Presbyterian Outlook*.

changeable, uncertain environments."[68] By attending to the constellation of changes that take place in a surrounding organizational environment, their approach seeks to consider "conditions under which transformation occurs."[69]

Further, the work of organizational ecologists provides resources to consider the conditions that can lead to the formation of new organizational forms. Although existing organizations rarely change rapidly enough to respond to their changing environment, two factors can introduce change within specific organizations as well as the broader field: the introduction of new organizations or organizational forms or the death of older organizations and existing organizational forms.[70] According to this perspective, change in the organizational environment invites (and requires) adaptation by the organizations that occupy a given field. These changes can involve changes in the number or types of organizations that occupy a common field, the expansion or contraction of key organizations, variation in the availability of resources, or changes in the social legitimacy that organizations have in a given organizational field. At either extreme of this lifecycle for organizations, the birth of new organizations or the death of existing organizations requires adaptation for the other actors within this field.[71] In addition to these dynamics that occur within organizations, two external factors contribute to the establishment of new organizational forms. First, legitimization from other powerful actors within populations of organizations contributes to the formation and identification of discrete organizational forms. Second, new organizational forms may emerge when they become taken-for-granted in the minds of actors within an organizational field. As considered in relation to the PC, early grants from the M. J. Murdock Charitable Trust and partnership with the Seattle School of Theology and Psychology gave legitimacy to their early organizing work. Moreover, a history of successful action and the development of a shared repertoire of expertise may

68. Hannan and Freeman, *Organizational Ecology*, 13.

69. Aldrich and Ruef, *Organizations Evolving*, 37.

70. Hannan and Freeman, *Organizational Ecology*, 12.

71. An implicit premise of this ecological approach is that the organizational environment contains finite resources that are distributed within an organizational ecosystem. The work and witness of this site partially confirms this premise, but it also does not entirely validate it. The PC is experimenting with ways to reach beyond the zero-sum calculus that views an organizational ecosystem according to a predetermine assessment of the finite resources.

contribute to this form being taken-for-granted in by members of this broader organizational field.

Nevertheless, the organizing and collaborative work that takes place in and through the PC is organized by an ecclesial vision. More specifically, the "nimble adaptability"[72] that organizes the PC emerges from an "ecclesial understanding" in which the forms of partnership and presence are constitutive of the church and a way of life for followers of Jesus. As Sparks, Soerens, and Friesen observe: "The life of worship is more than what you do together at your Sunday gathering; it encompasses the whole of your collective lives together . . . The local church learns to rely on the Spirit's movement in every situation as a way of being faithfully present to the relationships in your context."[73] Even as this collaborative work seeks to engage across lines of difference that are determined by organizations, denominations, and even faith, organizers note the priority of retaining an ecclesial understanding of this work. As Rice observes: "We can't lose sight of the ecclesial vision of the church as a people who are coming around this vision that I think is what Jesus came to show us."

Accordingly, the organizing, connecting, and collaborative work that emerges around the PC is dually oriented in relation to the challenges that contemporary communities face and according to an ecclesial vision of the conditions that may organize a common life. As one participant observes: busyness, isolation, and fragmentation discourage people from viewing church as "an organizing principle of life." However, he also notes: "There has to be some way for people who are willing to give them a form to live into . . . If we can create the forms that allow people to live into something that is meaningful and beautiful, there are people that want that and are willing to make sacrifices." Indeed, across the PC, the collective effort that is manifest in this local and connective work seeks to give people and faith leaders forms that "allow people to live into something that is meaningful and beautiful."

In response to this assessment and the description of the PC's work, it is now possible to consider the question that introduced this analysis: Does their work represent the evolution of the Emerging Church or point to the emergence of a new organizational form? Indeed, the self-assessment by organizers and participants across the PC make a sharp distinction between their work and the Emerging Church tradition. Although

72. Rice and Frost, *To Alter Your World*, 97.

73. Sparks et al., *The New Parish*, 85.

there may exist *a degree* of genealogical connection and some common organizing principles, their organizing work and animating theological commitments are distinct in kind. Furthermore, the expansion of their work to include and intersect with a range of individuals from across the denominational spectrum and an eclectic array of religious organizations represents a bridge-building and boundary-cross form of work. Admittedly, the networked, multi-organizational, and collaborative character that marks the PC may promote some confusion and ambiguity. Is it a parachurch organization? Is it a subsidiary of a host educational institution? Is it simply networks of churches? Rather than pressing them into existing organizational forms, however, it is better to consider the possibility that they represent a novel form of organizing Christian communities in response to the adaptive challenges they face.

Further, attending to the broader ecclesial ecology provides an impetus to consider whether similar forms of adaptation are taking place beyond this discrete case. If the kind of connecting and convening work that organizes the PC points to the emergence of a novel organizational form, it is likely that similar organizing work is taking place both within and beyond the region. Future research may consider similar organizational forms that are emerging within and beyond the Pacific Northwest.[74]

Conclusion

The history of innovation and adaptation that characterizes religious organization in the Pacific Northwest creates a fertile context for organizational and ecclesial adaptation. Beyond the Pacific Northwest, religious organizations have "long served as foundries of organizational forms and issues,"[75] and, as N. J. Demerath and Terry Schmitt conclude: "There is immense potential for research payoff in attending to them."[76] Accordingly, this chapter has used primary research on the Parish Collective as a case to consider the conditions that may promote the emergence of new organizational forms. While the Emerging Church tradition provided an early incubator and foil for this organizing and connecting work, the history and evolution of the PC extends well beyond this "reframing of

---

74. This question is picked up and explored in Benac, "Adaptive Church."

75. Demerath and Schmitt, "Transcending Sacred and Secular," 396.

76. Demerath and Schmitt, "Transcending Sacred and Secular," 396.

religion."[77] Further, organizational theory provides conceptual resources to explore the organizational context that surrounds this adaptive expression. When considered in relation to a broader ecclesial ecology, the characteristics of the PC's work may point to the emergence of a novel organizational form.

Further research is required in order to substantiate this final claim. Although complementary research has identified a kindred ecclesial adaptation in the region,[78] similar networked forms of Christianity may already exist or may begin popping up within and beyond the region. Indeed, this conclusion is consistent with the PC's assessment of their position within a broader landscape, as Sparks observes: "[W]e would look at ourselves as one network among, hopefully, many that either are arising or will arise."[79] Accordingly, future research may replicate and constructively extend these methods in order to identify, describe, and consider the possibilities of organizing an ecclesial life dually in relation to a local context and the institutional structures that support religious life. This line of research may also fruitfully engage theological studies in order to understand and constructively consider the relationship between religious thought and practice and this form of individual and collective action. Finally, this future work invites interdisciplinary perspectives that may include contributions from scholars of American religion, sociology, organizational theory, practical theology, leadership studies, congregational studies, philanthropy, and practitioners. Through conversation with the practitioners who are embedded in this work, scholarship might organize its own ecological approach to education and research, drawing wisdom from these communities and practitioners. Ultimately, imitating the practical wisdom that the Parish Collective exemplifies, the pursuit of this research requires a richly connective, collaborative, contextual, and imaginative form of engagement.

Bibliography

Aldrich, Howard, and Martin Ruef. *Organizations Evolving*. 2nd ed. London: Sage, 2006.

77. Martí and Ganiel, *The Deconstructed Church*, 5.

78. Benac, "Adaptive Church."

79. This observation comes in the context of his discussion of the diversity of partners that are required to support and sustain this work.

Benac, Dustin. "Adaptive Church: A Practical Theology of Adaptive Work in the Pacific Northwest." ThD diss., Duke University, 2020.

———. "Theological Education for a New Age." *The Presbyterian Outlook*, September 25, 2018.

Block, Peter. *Community: The Structure of Belonging*. San Francisco: Berrett-Koehler, 2008.

Burt, Ronald. *Structural Holes: The Social Structure of Competition*. Cambridge: Harvard University Press, 1992.

Chaves, Mark. *American Religion: Contemporary Trends*. Princeton: Princeton University Press, 2011.

Chia, Lloyd. "From Boundaries to Borderlands: The Emerging Church's Imaginative Work of Fostering Relationship across Difference." In *Crossing Boundaries, Redefining Faith*, edited by Michael Clawson and April Stace. Eugene, OR: Pickwick Publications, 2016.

Christerson, Brad, and Richard Flory. *The Rise of Network Christianity: How Independent Leaders Are Changing the Religious Landscape*. Oxford: Oxford University Press, 2017.

Clawson, Michael. "A Brief History of the Emerging Church Movement in the United States." In *Crossing Boundaries, Redefining Faith: Interdisciplinary Perspectives on the Emerging Church Movement*, edited by Michael Clawson and April Stace. Eugene, OR: Pickwick Publications, 2016.

Clawson, Michael, and April Stace, eds. *Crossing Boundaries, Redefining Faith: Interdisciplinary Perspectives on the Emerging Church Movement*. Eugene, OR: Pickwick Publications, 2016.

Demerath, Nicholas Jay, and Terry Schmitt. "Transcending Sacred and Secular: Mutual Benefits in Analyzing Religious and Nonreligious Organizations." In *Sacred Companies: Organizational Aspects of Religion and Religious Aspects of Organizations*, edited by Nicholas Jay Demerath, Peter Hall, Terry Schmitt, and Rhys Williams. Oxford: Oxford University Press, 1998.

DiMaggio, Paul, and Walter Powell. "The Iron Cage Revisited: Institutional Isomorphism and Collective Rationality in Organizational Fields." *American Sociological Review* 48, no. 2 (1983) 147–60.

Gay, Douglas. *Remixing The Church: Toward an Emerging Ecclesiology*. London: SCM, 2011.

Heath, Elaine. "A New Days Rising in the Church." In *The Hyphenateds: How Emergence Christianity Is Re-Traditioning Mainline Practice*. Edited by Phil Snider. Danvers, MA: Chalice, 2011.

Friesen, Dwight. *Thy Kingdom Connected: What the Church Can Learn from Facebook, the Internet and Other Networks*. Grand Rapids: Baker, 2009.

———. *What the Church Can Learn from Facebook, the Internet and Other Networks*. Grand Rapids: Baker, 2009.

Ferguson, Niall. *The Square and the Tower: Networks and Power, from the Freemasons to Facebook*. New York: Penguin, 2017.

Hannan, Michael, and John Freeman. *Organizational Ecology*. Cambridge: Harvard University Press, 1989.

James, Christopher. *Church Planting in Post-Christian Soil: Theology and Practice*. New York: Oxford University Press, 2018.

Killen, Patricia. "Introduction—Patterns of the Past, Prospects for the Future: Religion in the None Zone." In *Religion & Public Life in the Pacific Northwest: The None Zone,* edited by Patricia Killen and Mark Silk, 9-20. Walnut Creek, CA: AltaMira, 2004.

———. "Memory, Novelty and Possibility in This Place." In *Cascadia: The Elusive Utopia: Exploring the Spirit of the Pacific Northwest,* edited by Douglas Todd. Vancouver: Ronsdale, 2008.

Martí, Gerardo. "Emerging Christianity through a Social Science Lens: The ECM as a Case of Religious Institutional Entrepreneurship." In *Crossing Boundaries, Redefining Faith,* edited by Michael Clawson and April Stace. Eugene, OR: Pickwick Publications, 2016.

Martí, Gerardo, and Gladys Ganiel. *The Deconstructed Church: Understanding Emerging Christianity.* Oxford: Oxford University Press, 2014.

McKnight, John, and Peter Block. *The Abundant Community: Awakening the Power of Families and Neighborhoods.* Oakland, CA: Berrett-Koehler, 2012.

McKnight, Scot et al. *Church in the Present Tense: A Candid Look at What's Emerging.* Grand Rapids: Brazos, 2011.

Packard, Josh. *The Emerging Church: Religion on the Margins.* Boulder, CO: First Forum, 2012.

Parish Collective. "6-Series Document." 2019.

———. "Inhabit Pamphlet." 2019.

———. "Learn How It Works." https://parishcollective.org/learn-how-it-works/.

———. "New Parish Learning Communities." 2019.

Powell, Walter. "Expanding the Scope of Institutional Analysis." In *The New Institutionalism in Organizational Analysis,* edited by Walter Powell and Paul DiMaggio. Chicago: University of Chicago Press, 1991.

———. "Neither Market nor Hierarchy: Network Forms of Organization." *Research in Organizational Behavior* 12 (1990) 295–336.

Rice, Christiana, and Michael Frost. *To Alter Your World: Partnering with God to Rebirth our Communities.* Downers Grove, IL: InterVarsity, 2017.

Ruef, Martin. "The Emergence of Organizational Forms: A Community Ecology Approach." *American Journal of Sociology* 106 (2000) 658–714.

Silk, Mark. "The Pacific Northwest Is the American Religious Future." *Religious News Service.* June 4, 2019.

Scott, W. Richard. *Institutions and Organizations: Ideas, Interests, and Identities.* 4th ed. London: Sage, 2014.

Scott, W. Richard, and Gerald F. Davis. *Organizations and Organizing: Rational, Natural, and Open Systems Perspectives.* Upper Saddle River, NJ: Pearson, 2007.

Schneider, Rachel C. "'A Web of Subversive Friends': New Monasticism in the United States and South Africa." *Religions* 9.6 (2018) 184.

Soerens, Tim, and Christiana Rice. "Five Hopeful Signs That Dare Us to Be the Church." https://medium.com/parish-collective/five-hopeful-signs-that-dare-us-to-be-the-church-641b75239e2c.

Stark, Rodney. *The Rise of Christianity: How the Obscure, Marginal Jesus Movement Became the Dominant Religious Force in the Western World in a Few Centuries.* Princeton: Princeton University Press, 1996.

Sparks, Paul et al. *The New Parish: How the Neighborhood Is Transforming Mission, Discipleship and Community.* Downers Grove, IL: InterVarsity, 2014.

Todd, Douglas. "Introduction." In *Cascadia: The Elusive Utopia: Exploring the Spirit of the Pacific Northwest*, edited by Douglas Todd, 1–32. Vancouver: Ronsdale, 2008.

Tickle, Phyllis. *Emergence Christianity: What It Is, Where It Is Going, and Why It Matters*. Grand Rapids: Baker, 2012.

Wadell, Paul. *Friendship and the Moral Life*. Notre Dame: University of Notre Dame Press, 1989.

Wellman, James. *Evangelical vs. Liberal: The Clash of Christian Cultures in the Pacific Northwest*. New York: Oxford, 2008.

Wexler, Mark. "Conjectures on Workplace Spirituality in Cascadia." In *Cascadia: The Elusive Utopia: Exploring the Spirit of the Pacific Northwest*, edited by Douglas Todd, 215–40. Vancouver: Ronsdale, 2008.

Wilken, Robert. "Alexandria: A School for Training in Virtue." In *Schools of Thought in the Christian Tradition*, edited by Patrick Henry, 15–18. Philadelphia: Fortress, 1984.

9

The Emerging Church Movement
Possible Futures and Trajectories

RACHEL C. SCHNEIDER, TERRY SHOEMAKER,
AND XOCHITL ALVIZO

Abstract

This chapter offers four near-future directions for the Emerging Church Movement. The trajectories we develop focus on the future of the movement as it relates to the intersection of two emphases in form—institutional or post-institutional and individual or collective. These elements are at the core of many religious expressions in the Western world today. As a forecasting team, our research covers various aspects of the ECM such as its forms (institutional, parachurch, non-traditional, and innovative), geographical locations (spanning the United States and South Africa), disciplinary approaches (sociological, theological, and anthropological), and incorporates qualitative and quantitative data collections. The objective of this project is not to predict or even suggest trajectories for the future of the ECM, but rather to provide a framework for future research trajectories.

Introduction

Over the last half century, scholars of religion have resisted the temptation to forecast or predict what religion, broadly speaking, will look like in the future. This resistance regarding prediction is probably connected with the failed secularization theory that posited the demise of religion.[1] Because the number of social variables that inform and influence religion across the globe was misunderstood, many did not anticipate the re-emergence of religion. This previous misstep of scholarship need not preclude scholarship, however, from offering future possibilities of specific religious movements based on collected data and knowledge of changing social environments.[2] Using a forecasting technique, this chapter explicates and provides reasoning for the most probable near-future strands of development that the Emerging Church Movement (ECM) will take. The trajectories we develop focus on the future of the movement as it relates to the intersection of two emphases in form—institutional or post-institutional and individual or collective. These elements are at the core of many religious expressions in the Western world today. Thus, while the objective of this chapter is to offer forecasting courses for the future of the ECM, we also hope to supply a motivation for scholars of religion to experience anew the role of forecasting within the field.

Forecasting is a technique utilized in multiple academic disciplines as well as regularly adopted by various industries. Sociological use of forecasting methods is found throughout the twentieth century.[3] Throughout its usage, sociologists have debated its benefits, adequacy as a technique, and appropriateness. Many of the academic critiques of forecasting in general are grounded on an assumption that academic forecasting is a determinative or prescriptive technique, either attempting to offer *exactly* what *will* happen or what *should* happen.[4] We recognize the intent of these critiques. But instead of offering exact predictions of what the ECM will look like in five to ten years or suggesting to ECM leaders strategies for their future, our goal, rather, is to imagine and map out, based on data

---

1. See for example Stark, "Secularization, R.I.P."; Casanova, *Public Religions*.

2. For scholarly examples of predicting the futures of Christianity, see Cox, *The Future of Faith*; Cupitt, *After God*; Davie et al., *Predicting Religion*.

3. Hensel, "Sociology and Social Forecasting."

4. For a history of sociological forecasting techniques, see Hensel, "Sociology and Social Forecasting."

collected over the last decade, four most possible trajectories of the ECM while also noting current trends that may impact the movement's future.

The Emerging Church movement or what is known in scholarship more broadly as Emerging Christianities (EC) has received some scholarly attention over the last decade.[5] Much of this scholarship shows how the movement has been forming in relation to that from which it emerged, namely conservative forms of Protestantism. For instance, Martí and Ganiel argue that the movement is constituted by the ability to provide individuals the opportunity to deconstruct subjective spiritual and religious commitments that were formed in previous religious communities. Significantly, then, much of the initial energy in the ECM was directed towards a *reorienting away* from Protestant host traditions. That is, Emerging Christian communities supply communal places for this individual work of "placing into question the beliefs and practices that have held sway among conventional Christians."[6] At the same time, there remains ambiguity in exactly what the ECM is reorienting toward. For example, James Bielo's research defines the ECM as consisting of missionality, ancient-future orientations, and church planting. His conclusions define success of the movement in relation to what extent it will be able to influence the host traditions from which it has emerged.[7]

How the movement navigates the relationship with its host traditions is central in studies of the ECM, and we agree that this reformative work has been key within most Emerging Christian communities. Yet, if we consider new religious movements as developing life forms, we might metaphorically understand EC initially as breaking away from the parental host. The formative years of the tradition then have been about constructing its own identity, both collectively and individually, while also learning how to make the movement financially sustainable. As the ECM now embarks toward subsequent phases of its development, new forms of expression will begin to materialize.

Based on our collective data and analysis, we want to offer possibilities regarding these future phases of ECM's development. In other words, we focus our attention on that which is being constructed, rather than deconstructed. As a forecasting team, our research covers various aspects of the ECM such as its forms (institutional, parachurch, non-traditional,

5. See for example Bielo, *Emerging Evangelicals*; Martí and Ganiel, *The Deconstructed Church*; Reed and Zbaraschuk, *The Emerging Church, Millennials, and Religion*.

6. Martí and Ganiel, *The Deconstructed Church*, 26.

7. Bielo, *Emerging Evangelicals*, 203.

and innovative), geographical locations (spanning the United States and South Africa), disciplinary approaches (sociological, theological, and anthropological), and incorporates qualitative and quantitative data collections. This collaborative approach grounds our abilities to forecast future shapes and forms of the ECM.

Method

In exploring possible future trajectories of the ECM, we began with our own ethnographic data and current research observations. We then considered this data in light of two aspects of the movement that have characterized the ECM's development since its formation and will likely continue to drive much of its immediate direction.

The first forecasting element relates to a question of institutional form. The ECM inherited traditional modes of institutions that included particular leadership structures, buildings, and worship forms. While EC communities experimented with various elements of the institution, for the most part, institutional organization remains the typical form of these religious communities. However, the tension between traditional and less-traditional institutional forms, especially as it relates to maintaining emerging commitments, becomes then a key factor to consider in exploring future possibilities of the ECM.

The second aspect regards the question of individual freedoms in relation to a communal or collective structure. The ECM pronounced itself as a place that valued individual expression and placed less emphasis on things like tithing, membership, or public accountability.[8] Thus, individuals can typically participate in the movement with less social pressures than other forms of conservative Protestant churches. Martí and Ganiel capture this in what they call *cooperative egoism*, which involves "the management and assertion of one's individuated self," even while simultaneously involving, "connection, empathy, and love for others."[9] The flexibility of participants' relationship to the institution vis-à-vis collective expectations and commitments creates the opportunity for multiple variations in how the ECM could take shape in the future. Likewise, within the ECM, institutional affiliations often reflect individual

8. Martí and Ganiel, *The Deconstructed Church*, 27–28. Packard, "Resisting Institutionalization."

9. Martí and Ganiel, *The Deconstructed Church*, 166.

commitments. Many EC churches are autonomous with self-ascribed connections and networks with other churches and parachurch organizations. The fluidity in these relationships creates an atmosphere that is flexible to change at various levels.

While these two elements play into the ambiguity often described within the movement, we utilize these elements to create a conceptual grid that allows us to classify and map four possible trajectories based on their intersection.[10] On the horizontal axis, we map out possible trajectories based on traditional and non-traditional institutional forms. On the vertical axis, we consider trajectories that emphasize the individual versus those that emphasize the collective.

FIGURE 9.1

FOUR TRAJECTORIES OF EMERGING CHURCH MOVEMENT

The first two trajectories are obviously closely associated. Trajectory Three and Four differ from Trajectory One and Two in that they extend beyond the traditional religious institution. On the left side of the grid, then, we focus on expressions that extend beyond traditional

10. Douglas, "Grid and Group," *Natural Symbols*, 57–71.

Christianity. Unlike the other trajectories, Trajectory Three assumes that a portion of those participating in the ECM will deprioritize Christianity, and possibly traditional religion altogether, to focus attention on progressive political concerns like justice and equality. Although some might initially be motivated by religiosity to participate in social change movements, others might find that this work is and was what they were seeking all along. Trajectory Four indicates a future of experimenting with mystical experiences outside of the church institution. This direction echoes current trends of Spiritual But Not Religious (SBNR) but is distinctive in that it includes collective forms to discuss spiritual experiences and experiments, even if it remains focused on individual experience. Of course, none of these trajectories are completely partitioned from others. It is easy to imagine that Emerging Christians could easily operate within multiple forecasting trajectories simultaneously.

Before turning to forecasted trajectories, we want to briefly recognize that some have pronounced the death of the ECM.[11] We maintain that these pronouncements are premature and typically proclaimed by those who are antagonistic to the movement. As stated previously, we alternatively argue herein that the movement is entering new phases rather than a demise. Or, drawing from Martí and Ganiel, "rather than declaring its death, we see the ECM as moving beyond specific groups, congregations, and collectives that explicitly take on the moniker of 'emerging' . . . to an investigation of a broader movement that manifest in various religious arenas."[12]

In forecasting what Emerging Christianities could look like in future forms, we propose that both the types and rates of change—whether change of institutional form and practice; change of social and moral norms; or change in politics or personal spiritual practice—should be considered. Because EC communities are contextually situated, and often attempt to explicitly recognize and reflect on their situatedness,

11. Many of the critiques of the ECM, both externally and internally, questioned the viability of a movement not demanding more concrete forms of commitment like membership and financial investment. Works like Dean Kelley's *Why Conservative Churches are Growing* (1972) argue that when serious demands are made upon adherents, commitments are made stronger. Thus, the argument is that ECM would not be sustainable. See also: Anderson, "The Emerging Church Is Dead(?)"; "The Death of the Emerging Church"; James, "What Happened to the 'Emergent Church'?"; Nash, "Voices"; Patton, "What Do You Think Happened to the Emerging Church?"; Scaramang, "R.I.P. Emerging Church."

12. Martí and Ganiel, *The Deconstructed Church*, 175.

modifications and change are often relatively dependent on what degrees and types of modifications are permitted within their social milieu. This is not to say that these church communities are absolutely bound by their contexts. In fact, many of the EC communities work to stretch normative social conditions—for example acceptance and affirmation of LGBTQ+ members and leaders; yet some communities are bound more than others by restrictive social norms. Thus, we could imagine that in the near future, say ten or fifteen years, some EC communities might show little recognizable changes in their formal modes of operation, even though there may occur major shifts in the social norms they hold. Specifically, the forms of worship and ritual gatherings could remain relatively constant in relation to current forms. Alternatively, the social milieu of other EC communities might foster shifts in ecclesial structures and institutional forms, and some Emerging Christians may cultivate identities and practices outside of traditional religious institutions.

Traditional Religious Institutional Trajectories

Trajectory One: Religious Rehabilitation

The first trajectory we see is a future of the movement where EC communities remain within a traditional institutional form even while creating space for individuals to reshape their social and moral norms in relation to a harmful religious past. Take for instance, the example of EC communities within the Bible Belt region of the United States. The Bible Belt region tends to be more conservative than other regions within the United States and claims more religiosity.[13] Various forms of conservative Protestantism dominate the area including high numbers of Baptist, Methodist, and Pentecostal churches. In addition, a conglomeration of Christian symbols and organizations are also publicly perceptible. The ways that these organizations create a socially conservative and restrictive moral context leads Bernadette Barton to refer to the conditions as a "Bible Belt panopticon" that regulates religious and political values and morals.[14] Yet, scholarship contends that the conservative Protestantism of the region also tends to encourage religious innovation with forms of

13. Pew Research Center, "Religion by Political Ideology"; Norman, "The Religious Regions of the U.S."

14. Barton, "1Cross + 3Nails = 4GVN."

practice.[15] These innovations tend to be less about reshaping the tradition's positions on political and social issues but more focused on worship practices and how to increase membership numbers and participation.

Conclusions drawn from current literature, then, might lead to expecting that EC communities within the Bible Belt region will progress at a slower rate of modification than other regions as it pertains to social and moral norms, but actually innovate more quickly than other regions in how they construct worship gatherings. In other words, forecasters might assume that EC communities in this region of the United States will operate within social parameters more constrained than EC communities in the New England or West Coast region regarding morals and social norms. And, because they do not rely on standardized liturgical norms, EC communities in the Bible Belt might have more leeway in re-stylizing how the religious communities model their gatherings and worship.

Ethnographic research conducted by Shoemaker in the Upper South region of the Bible Belt suggests the opposite, however. What has been discovered is that many EC communities in the area tend to vary less in worship form as compared to other conservative Protestant communities in the region, yet, at the same time, focus more on individual and collective moral formations that directly challenge the conservative, social conditions of the Bible Belt. Many of the EC communities within the Bible Belt tend to, on the surface, operate similarly to other conservative Protestant communities. This includes a host of shared rituals like communal singing of newer and non-traditional hymns (sometimes referred to as praise songs typically with a live band), a sermon as a central part of the service (packaged as highly relevant to the cultural tastes of the community and not based on a yearly liturgical schedule), and preserving a familiar order of worship while allowing small modifications with the forms on a given Sunday (for instance, mixing up the order of worship or modifications in how the communion ritual is performed).

The relatively little modifications in the forms of worship and gatherings of EC communities in the Bible Belt are less important to these EC communities than objectives of moral reconstitution. A majority of religious communities in the Bible Belt are composed of participants who were acculturated in the morally restrictive region that Barton describes. In the region, sexual, racial, and gender normativity are highly valued,

---

15. Lee and Sinitiere, *Holy Mavericks.*

and measures are implemented to maintain those norms. Religion and religious institutions are often utilized as the primary instruments to maintain normativity through a constructed social hierarchy. "Members of each group are expected to submit to those above them, and to exert dominion over those below. Those in authority are automatically 'right' in their ideas about the social world, because they are closer to God," argues Barton.[16] Thus, any modifications to social norms still remain heavily regulated by religious institutions as in the case of EC communities in the Bible Belt.[17] In other words, in order to socially reorient collective understandings of sexuality and other social issues in a context of the Bible Belt, a strategic place to begin is within a Christian community that utilizes a bible-based language to construct the argument for acceptance and affirmation and maintains a familiar order of worship.

The objective of reorienting social norms from within religious communities of the Bible Belt also sheds light on the importance of maintaining specific forms of the religious gathering. For many within Bible Belt EC communities, the acculturation of social norms was developed through the physical practices of church. Shared songs, repeated rituals, and sermons all conveyed the expectations of the milieu. These familiar practices are utilized now to reform and affirm the new moral orientation of members. For instance, a biblical text can be re-sermonized as an argument for gender or racial equality. The form stays the same, but the central message is modified. This is a process of individual and collective rehabilitating through reorienting the common and shared practices and rituals. The shared habits within the religious community construct a continuous reaffirmation of values, both religious and political, that reinforces new ways of being Christian in the South. This legitimizes currently held positions while also delegitimizing previously inherited individual positions and social norms. In sum, the objectives of religious rehabilitation are fueled by the habituating of shared (but relatively recognizable) religious forms.

Thus, we conclude that the variable of institutional change within EC communities of the Bible Belt depends upon the speed of rehabilitation. Unfortunately, the speed of rehabilitation may differ significantly between communities in different regions and settings. Within EC communities of the Bible Belt, there may be various individual levels of moral

16. Barton, "1Cross + 3Nails = 4GVN," 74.

17. Obviously there are other places besides the institutional church in which moral orientation work is developed and cultivated.

rehabilitation. However, what Bible Belt EC communities reveal is that the variable of institutional change within these communities often depends upon how quickly or slowly members are rehabilitated into newer religious and moral orientations. And this rate of institutional change often depends upon the forms of conditioning that the members have previously experienced in their youth and adult life. Therefore, the future institutional shape of EC communities within conservative and restrictive contexts closely corresponds to the rate of change of moral rehabilitation.

In the short term, the forecast of some EC communities in these contexts is little to no significant modifications in religious forms and practices. This is due to the required need for many participants to work out previous religious inheritance and conditioning. However, should a collective rehabilitation be achieved, then the forms of practices might reflect that achievement. Or stated otherwise, should the forms of EC communities drastically modify, much would be revealed about the moral reorientations of the religious community and possibly the region.

Another possible variable would be a shift in the types of participants within these communities. An issue that some Bible Belt EC communities, as well as other in other regions, are facing currently is the integration of participants who experienced very little of the shared conditionings of the original members. These new participants could force the communities toward adopting modifications quicker, both in form and objective. We foresee that the continued need for moral reorientation within EC communities could stagnate alteration in the form and objective in the coming years. However, the long term reveals that much of this rehabilitation work will be accomplished eventually and that this will produce changes in the forms internally and externally.

Trajectory Two: Reorientation of Church Polity

The second trajectory in which the future of the movement may remain within a traditional institutional form, while still *emerging* in the ways it seeks to, is focused on congregational polity and its relationship to the larger denominational institution. Currently, there exists a mix within EC communities in how they relate or do not relate to larger denominational bodies and the creative ways in which they organize their governance and leadership structures as a result. Qualitative research conducted by Alvizo with EC communities revealed that most congregations maintain a traditional structure of single-person pastoral leadership (sometimes a two-person team), and in the case of an existing denominational affiliation, a typical governance and decision-making process that aligns with the polity of the denomination.[18]

The broad view of the ECM's pattern regarding polity and denominational structure presents as if there is little change in this aspect of the movement; yet there is a minority of communities within the movement that are reorienting in ways that construct new forms of polity and structure. It is this small group of congregations that hold promise in forecasting a trajectory of church that may help provide the substructure for emerging forms that go beyond changing worship and may support the moral reorientation of Trajectory One.

In the research Alvizo conducted, which included the top twelve EC communities most mentioned in the literature (at the time of her study), five of these had mainline denominational affiliations—not quite the majority, but even without denominational affiliation, nine of the twelve had the traditional leadership structure of having one or two persons function as the pastoral and de facto decision-makers of the community in ways typical of how congregations function generally. A majority of these have an advisory board or committee to which the leader was accountable. The leadership of these communities made intentional effort to bring in varying levels of community input and participation, but in the day to day functioning of the church, this kind of leadership structure meant that decision making was ultimately in the hands of a few.

That notwithstanding, in a small number of EC communities, the movement's stated priority to have a participatory mode of leadership and decision-making took deeper root and shaped its leadership structure in less traditional ways. In a few cases, the community's polity, or stance toward their polity, reflected a form of governance that was more creative, inclusive, and participatory than is typical in more mainstream forms of church. From these few communities, three trajectories come to view that reflect EC communities' possibility to emerge at the level of their polity: loose denominational affiliation (as in liberally held and/or minimalist in approach), leadership of facilitation (that makes possible the leadership of the collective), and entrepreneurial organizational structure.

18. Alvizo, "A Feminist Theological Analysis."

Liberal Approach to Denominational Affiliation

Forecasting the future forms of emerging Christianity, one obvious consideration is the movement's ties to larger denominational structures. There exists a spectrum of how ECM communities that are reorienting their polity hold their denominational identity and their relationship to the larger institution. Of the twelve congregations in Alvizo's study, more than half of the communities were independent and had no denominational ties—three had never had denominational ties at all, four began with denominational ties and later disaffiliated, and of the five that were denominationally affiliated, two came to their affiliation a few years after forming the congregation. What stood out among some of the congregations, however, was the way they held or let go of their denominational ties.

One congregation that affiliated a few years after forming (name here withheld in sensitivity to their denominational relationship) exemplified a loose approach to its denominational affiliation even as they moved newly into the mainline denominational structure. In choosing to come under the larger structure of a denomination, two things were emphasized in their process: 1) "we will do this only if we all agree"; and 2) "this affiliation will not change how we do things on a day to day." On this latter point, one example of how this worked out was in their practice of the communion ritual. While the larger denomination requires that an ordained person lead communion, this congregation's practice was to have communion intentionally led by a lay person—not an ordained clergy person—in order to deconstruct the hierarchical model of church with which they had newly affiliated. They continued to practice lay-led communion, despite the (new to them) denominational rules. The congregation refused to allow its denominational affiliation to stop them from diffusing centralized leadership practices in both its decision-making and its ritualizing. So, while the congregation was becoming part of the larger denominational institution, it was holding that affiliation more liberally, loosely, even as they explicitly recognized that they should probably "not tell" their denominational leadership. The emphasis to move into the affiliation only by consensus, and to not lose their own way of doing things, prioritizes the participation and inclusion of the whole community, the collective, as its preferred mode of operating. The community sought to govern itself even as they entered the new relationship with the denomination.

A contrasting example is of an EC community that began as part of a larger denominational body but decided to become independent when they realized that their politics were moving in a more liberal direction than those of the denomination. The decision to make this move was set in motion during a community meeting in which one of their agenda items was to decide how to distribute their congregational tithe (10 percent of their income to support another ministry/nonprofit). One of their members raised concern that their denomination was no longer an institution they felt good about supporting because of its more conservative theology and politics (some related to LGBTQ people and to women in ordained leadership). That concern, raised from within the collective, initiated a series of other community meetings that eventually led the congregation to disaffiliate from their denomination. Again, the community's denominational tie was less important to them than the community's collective and participatory decision-making process. In both of these EC community examples, a loose approach to their denominational affiliation allowed the will of the collective to determine just how much the denomination would shape and govern them.

Leadership of the Collective

The ECM's emphasis on decentralizing leadership is one of its earliest expressed commitments.[19] Three of the twelve EC communities in Alvizo's study had a qualitatively different polity than the rest. What stood out about the polity of these three communities was the manner in which the pastor or leader carried out their role—more as a facilitator or animator of the community, as opposed to a shepherd or priest. Of these three communities, two of them began with a denominational affiliation but no longer had it at the time of the study and the third was never affiliated. The first, The Gathering in Salem, Massachusetts, began as an outreach to nontraditional communities, in this case, neopagans. It was initiated out of the International Church of the Foursquare Gospel but a short time after was disaffiliated when the denomination excommunicated its pastor Phil Wyman, "for being friends with the witches,"—as reported by one community member during their interview. The second, Journey Church in Dallas, Texas began as part of the Baptist General Convention of Texas

19. See Jones, *The Church is Flat*; Martí and Ganiel, *The Deconstructed Church*; Alvizo, "A Feminist Theological Analysis."

as a young adult worship service of an established church, but soon became its own congregation and unaffiliated themselves from the denomination as they developed in a theologically divergent direction. The third of these communities, IkonNYC, was a (purposefully) one-year church experiment that was formed by an ad hoc collective of post-evangelicals and was facilitated by Peter Rollins.

Each of these congregations embodied its decentralized leadership differently. In the case of The Gathering, an outsider could walk into the meeting space and struggle to identify "the leader" or a person "in charge." Though Phil Wyman was indeed the paid pastor—and continues with the church today—he performed his role more like the coordinator of the community. The environment resembled that of a community drop-in center, with people coming by throughout the day, whether for a scheduled program or simply because they happened to walk by. In interviews with community members, there was explicit statements made about how Phil served as the support person that encouraged the various projects and activities arising from within the community and was not the initiator of them; he was one among the many—swallowed up in a room buzzing with activity with many "hands on deck" and no one person standing out as more in charge than another. The liveliness of the environment itself reflected a non-centralized leadership mode of operating in which it was clear that a multiplicity of people shared a sense of ownership.

The decision-making and leadership structure of The Gathering was likewise community-oriented, and Phil facilitated, more than led, the community's activities and decisions. The church council, made up of community members who "prayed and discerned" about whether to serve in the leadership team before doing so (some of whom were explicitly invited to consider serving because of the specific skills they would bring), made larger decisions about funding and forecasting budget and not necessarily about the day-to-day workings of the community. One member explained, "There is leadership [council] but it just doesn't feel like you have to run things by the council before you [move forward with an idea]—it doesn't feel like that. It's like a group of people that help guide the church, in a way—kind of just have a conversation about where we're going and checking on things . . . " During an interview when asked about the leadership and decision-making process of the community, the focus group of twelve people simultaneously laughed, with multiple people making snarky remarks in response (indecipherable in the audio recording for a second), after which one member summarized:

> M: Let the record show that when the question on leadership was asked, Joyce snorted and laughed.
>
> F: I just laughed because I think people sort of said that there isn't leadership.

Amidst the light-heartedness, however, one person interjected: "I actually have a very different view. Everyone leads in their own way. Everyone has their own little job that they kind of fall into so it's, really, it's a group of leaders, which is strange."

"A group of leaders," is the apt description for the polity that stood out not only at the Gathering, but at Journey Church in Dallas, Texas. Journey Church had a well-developed structured leadership model that formed collectively in direct response to a "community revolt" that occurred when the former (and founding) pastor made the unilateral decision about the leadership structure the church was to implement upon his leaving—an incident they now refer to as "the great elder debate." Danielle Shroyer, the pastor in place during Alvizo's study, reported the story:

> When the former pastor was leaving, before he left he was trying to be strategic in putting a team in place so that it would be OK when he left. But he ended up just doing, was just going to the community and saying: "Hey, we're now gonna have a team of elders"—And Journey went ballistic!—"And that's who they're gonna be." And that's just not at all what we are all about. OH no! So there was like a huge uproar, I mean a massive huge uproar about, "Who decided this?" "Can't we talk about it?" "How did you decide who the elders are gonna be?" I mean, it was not good. So now, it's a very open process.

The uproar was due to the fact that the pastor altogether bypassed the community in the decision-making process. The presumption that one person, even if it was the pastor, could (and did) take it upon themselves to decide about the governance structure of the whole community without involvement of the community itself was considered unacceptable. The community orientation and involvement in decision-making was default to the expectations of who they were and how they do things.

The third example is Ikon NYC, which had an altogether different structure, though still overlapping in some elements with The Gathering and with Journey Church in terms of their orienting principles—governing as a collective and decentralizing leadership, or as Danielle Shroyer of Journey Church described, "giving power away in as many ways as I can figure out how to do." At Ikon NYC, the power was given away through an open call; a public invitation shared through social networks and social media calling for the participation of anyone interested to help form a one-year experimental church focused on performance art and liturgy. The self-selecting group gathered weekly to plan twelve monthly gatherings over the course of a year. They allowed themselves free creative range to plan a liturgically oriented performance art event designed to deconstruct the certainty that church often promotes. Peter Rollins, philosopher and theologian, served as the animator facilitating the collective project.

This flexibility and freedom to both lead the liturgical design of the church and to collectively govern all its processes was repeatedly referenced throughout the interviews with all three of these EC communities. Additionally, for Journey and IkonNYC, it was important to them that their polity was constructed communally from the start. That all three of these communities were denominationally unaffiliated and the degree to which that made a difference in shaping their particular polity is an open and worthwhile question; what is clear, however, is that these three communities represent a form of polity that by intentional design decentered the leader and centralized the collective. The "leader" instead became a facilitator to the participation and leadership of the many.

Entrepreneurial Organizational Structure

The last potential trajectory of the more radical reorientation of church polity within EC communities reaches forward to creative entrepreneurial endeavors (or back to "ancient future" forms) that place it on the boundary of traditional structures and, for some, outside the traditional funding sources of the church. Dinner church, coffee house church, and "common cause communities"[20] are models of organizing church in ways that integrate more seamlessly into the social fabric of the larger community. These enterprising models of church cut through the usual divide between those inside and those outside church. They go beyond the walls of their actual or metaphorical church building to organize in creatively

20. See "Community Development + Political Organizing" of Trajectory Three.

sustainable ways. EC communities that fall under the entrepreneurial organizing structure category are communities experimenting in ways that still keep them within the fold of a mainline denomination. Yet, it may be that the very fact of their unconventional form, their existence beyond the walls of a traditional building, and their practice of a participatory and creative model of church, may lead them to outcomes yet unforeseen as it relates to the polity of the denomination, especially as this impacts their financial sustainability.

In a study of specifically Wesleyan-rooted congregations in the United States, "Radical Economics and Wesleyan Congregations in the U.S.," Alvizo and Stone studied congregations identified by their denomination as practicing a more radical economics.[21] Among the twenty congregations in the study, two communities fell within the ECM and both reflected the entrepreneurial orientation of this trajectory—Simple Church (Grafton, MA) and Union Coffee (Dallas, TX). Both United Methodist by denominational affiliation, these two communities were intentional in modeling their church in a form that was more financially sustainable and more integrated into their surrounding community than a traditional church model. From the start they formed in ways that more organically integrated them into the social fabric of their broader context, Simple Church as a soup and bread dinner gathering that also runs a bread baking and catering trade, the funds from which go directly back to support the church; and Union Coffee formed around a coffee shop and food truck business—the funds shared back with the church itself as well as with other nonprofits in the community (ten percent of all its sales, not just its profits, are given away every four months to different nonprofits). As Simple Church's promotional video states, and applies to both of these examples, these churches "don't have a steeple" or a pew—but instead have a table or a coffee shop through which they extend their welcome and either a good cup of coffee or a simple soup and bread dinner.

Other similar efforts include St. Lydia's in Brooklyn, NY (one of the earliest contemporary models of dinner church), and the Dinner Church Collective (part of the U.S. version of the Church of England's Fresh Expressions), which, along with Simple Church and Union Coffee, reflect a larger movement within the ECM, spanning across the country, that incorporates a trade-oriented element to church and successfully so. Union Coffee in Dallas, with one "top-rated independent coffee shop" and three

21. Alvizo and Stone, "Radical Economics."

worshiping communities, is currently working to open another site, and Simple Church has a website-creating business (small steeple), a woodworking business, and an event catering business. Each of these dinner or coffee church communities are denominationally affiliated, though not as financially dependent as other creative new church starts. Additionally, while each has a board of directors (or advisory council) and is situated within their mainline Christian denomination, their solidly ECM model puts them at the boundary of their denominational institution. The longterm impact of the symbiotic relationship between the denomination and the entrepreneurial church, which sees itself as part of a movement and intentionally structures in ways that extend beyond traditional church polity, will be worth tracking, especially in this changing religious landscape. And the eventual impact of the congregations' more radical forms on the larger denominational institutions remains to be seen, but it has great potential for the financial viability of a church that can no longer depend on inherited practices of institutional loyalty, financial support, and participation.

In sum, while the initial ECM proposed radical maneuvers, the truth is that in many ways the early manifestation of its efforts was mainly in the area of play in its worship modality. However, going beyond the worship service is vital to the future long-term impact of the movement on larger church and denominational structures. Thus, the communities highlighted in Trajectory Two present a range of possible futures that point to a way of doing church focused on engaging the entire collective as a top priority. Not only is the vision and direction of the church, as much as possible, decided upon by the whole collective (as with the first two examples), but the sustainability-seeking models of these communities may lead these collectives to build new and creative governing structures that impact the future of the denominational structures themselves. Though the degree to which a radically participatory governance structure is institutionalized into the polity of the broader ECM varies, each of these few congregations, or collectives, make an explicit effort to structure participation and flexibility into their polity, and do so even when it comes at the cost of their denominational ties or their compliance with the denomination's overarching polity, putting them on the boundary of their denominational systems. The more radically organized collectives hold their denominational identity loosely or not at all.

As a whole, the communities of Trajectory Two represent a possible future direction of the ECM that continues to decenter the singular leader, prioritizes the community, and challenges the boundaries of their denominational ties within which they exist (when that is the case). For congregations within the ECM who enter newly into a denominational affiliation, contributing factors will likely be either financial sustainability or the pastor's decision for formal ordination within a denomination. But then there are also the more entrepreneurial forms: communities that may seek to figure out how to exist both within and outside of larger institutional structures by being radically different in form or finding ways to support themselves through a related trade.

Non-Traditional Religious Trajectories

Trajectory Three: The Political Move

Another future possibility we see is a diffusion of ECM ideals into social justice movements and political activism, in some instances pushing expressions of EC beyond traditional institutional forms. In this trajectory, not only are spiritual practices seen as a vital tool to further social change but social change *itself*—and the political struggle it entails—may become imbued with spiritual meaning. As a person once involved with the ECM reflected: "I now see that I've switched from pursuing spiritual, transcendent experiences to validate my relationship with God, to pursuing physical actions (especially through politics) to practice my faith." In this way, sociopolitical engagement—particularly around issues of race, class, gender, and sexuality—becomes seen as a spiritual good: vital to self-transformation and to opening up alternative social futures aligned with one's core values.

Importantly, the work of religious deconstruction has often been bound up with a vision of broader social change, and this may increasingly involve what we term sacred micropolitics. Sacred micropolitics refers to efforts to challenge conservative political norms of dominant religious groups. While at times linked to macro-political goals of governmental or institutional change, the term micropolitics indexes efforts to create concrete social change through diffuse interactions "among individuals, collectives, movement networks, and wider society.[22] Within the ECM, we can see the roots of sacred micropolitics in the tendency of Emerging Christians to identify as "post-creedal" and to understand

22. Yates, "Rethinking Prefiguration," 2. For more on the micropolitics of the ECM, see Martí and Ganiel, *The Deconstructed Church,* 26–7, 163.

authentic religion/spirituality as defined by everyday practices in the "real world."[23] We can also see it in the tendency of some in the ECM to understand individual and group practices as "inherently political": offering a lived critique of oppressive structures through the creation of alternate spiritual communities.[24]

While the ECM has always had a political dimension, it has primarily understood itself to be a religious movement formed in reaction to conservative Protestantism. What may shift in the future, however, is that for some a focus on the political becomes primary. We predict that this will happen in several ways. The first is through the creation of non-church organizations that seek to push religious institutions and individuals towards increased engagement with social justice issues while also contributing to wider social change. The second is through the formation of collectives in which a commitment to progressive politics itself drives the creation of new spiritual practices beyond, or outside of, institutionalized religion.

Community Development + Political Organizing

Currently, there is a trend of those with links to the ECM experimenting with different modes of social and political engagement. The first is through the creation of non-profit organizations whose primary focus is to engage with social justice issues. These organizations, which tend to be independent of specific churches or denominations, often seek to create ecumenical and inclusive spaces where a variety of Christian(ish) individuals can converge around shared ethical and political concerns, such as racial justice or economic inequality. One example of this is the School for Conversion, founded by Jonathan Wilson Hartgrove in Durham, North Carolina. The school is involved in a number of projects intended to address the "neighborhood to prison pipeline," while also providing regular opportunities for "community education" designed to encourage local congregations to "seek community and relationships beyond traditional church spaces." Ultimately, its goal is to bring people "across lines of division" such as race, class, religion, or incarceration, so that

---

23. Martí and Ganiel, *The Deconstructed Church*, 134.

24. Martí and Ganiel, *The Deconstructed Church*, 135. This understanding is perhaps most pronounced in the new monasticism stream of the ECM.

they can "unlearn habits of social division."[25] Another example, drawn from South Africa, is The Warehouse, a non-profit that sees itself working with churches to effectively address "poverty, injustice, and division" through equipping them with theology and tools to engage with systemic inequality. Similar to the School for Conversion, the Warehouse seeks to facilitate "transformative encounters" that equip (largely white liberal) Christians with the "skills and postures to deal with the challenges of our contemporary, complex world," including sustained focus on issues of power and racial privilege as well as public campaigns on issues like water access and sanitation.[26] A final example is Oasis Global, a non-profit network founded by Steve Chalke, a leader in the UK who has often been linked to the ECM. Oasis predominantly focuses on community development projects in countries like Uganda, the UK, India, and Belgium that aim to address issues of human trafficking, health, and unemployment through embedding a "team of activists, volunteers, and professionals" in local communities to work alongside community members for change.[27] Oasis is also linked to the Open Church Network which seeks to push churches to become "more actively engaged in serving their communities" particularly around LGBTQ+ inclusion.[28]

Schneider has argued, drawing on ethnographic research in South Africa, that these kinds of efforts can be seen as an outgrowth of the new monastic stream of the ECM, which often pairs intentional living and spiritual practices with local/contextual engagement.[29] At the same time, it is important to recognize that, in the examples above, the scope of focus extends beyond cultivating a distinctive or shared way of life among a small, committed group. In fact, increasingly the emphasis is on creating social change by educating and mobilizing a broad network of others, including those located in traditional church institutions. Thus, these kinds of non-profits can be seen as connected to Trajectory One in that they are seeking to support rehabituation or revitalization of churches while engaging with larger issues of social concern. However, because these groups are strategically positioned outside of institutions, there is freedom to respond directly to pressing social issues beyond what might

25. School for Coversion. https://www.schoolforconversion.org/

26. The Warehouse. https://warehouse.org.za/

27. Oasis Global. https://www.oasisglobal.org

28. Open Church Network. https://openchurch.network/

29. Schneider, "A Web of Subversive Friends."

be supported by religious institutions who may be perceived as slow, apathetic, or constraining.

Because the ECM has often defined itself against conservative Protestant Christianity, a related mode of social engagement could seek to publicly engage conservative religion and politics along the lines of ECM leader Doug Pagitt's non-profit organization Greater Things. Similar to the examples above, the Greater Things Foundation sees itself as a catalyst to organize and push Christian leaders and churches to challenge narratives that reinforce "exclusion, violence, greed, sexism, exploitation, and racism rooted in white supremacy."[30] But this work has extended from the micro to the macro-political through the "Vote Common Good" campaign.[31] Co-directed by Pagitt, the campaign explicitly sought to organize pastors and churches to "bring an end to the Trump administration." Again, a non-profit structure offers Emerging Christians an opportunity to be much more explicit and targeted in their political engagement than would be allowed by existing churches and denominations, even as they rely on religious institutions for support. Additionally, to the extent these groups strive to address systemic racism and white supremacy, this can also be seen as an internalization of critiques that the ECM has a whiteness problem due to its evangelical origins and reflect a desire to deconstruct this inheritance as part of the work of social change.[32]

Political Spiritualities

Yet another possible form that the political move in the ECM could take in the future is the creation of communities whereby a commitment to a progressive politics itself fuels new spiritual practices and discourses. The last several years have seen a notable emergence of flexible and experimental networks that seek to both deconstruct and reconstruct notions of religious community, symbols, and spaces in light of social

30. https://www.greaterthingsfoundation.org/

31. https://www.votecommongood.com/

32. These critiques have been most strongly articulated by Rah Soong-Chan, Jason Mach, Brian McLaren, Debbie Blue, and Julie Clawson in a 2010 *Sojourners* article, "Is the Emerging Church for Whites Only?" with a 2012 response by Tony Jones in *Patheos*, "How White Is the Emerging Church?" For scholarly attention to the role of race in the Emerging Church Movement, see Bielo, *Emerging Evangelicals,* 133–37; and Schneider, "Race and the Emerging Church," 212–35.

justice concerns. While participants may be connected to religious communities, they just as likely may not be, as a result of their progressive political orientations. At times ephemeral, these experimental networks have paid specific attention to the sociopolitical concerns of people of color, women, and members of the LGBTQ+ community and intentionally sought to be boundary-spanning. For example, the W/Collective sees itself as providing a space especially for "faith leaders who do not have a denominational tie and are seeking community."[33] Participants often come from an evangelical heritage and have experienced exclusion due to progressive politics, theologies, or identities. Thus, the W/Collective is set up to provide a collective space of belonging and networking for individuals who might otherwise be isolated. Other examples of this are the Why Christian[34] and She is Called[35] projects that sought similarly to link "pastors, practitioners, artists, dreamers, and doubters" around a post-creedal Christian vision that took seriously the leadership and contributions of women, people of color, and members of the LGBTQ+ community.

Those affiliated with these networks seem to be trying to create generative spaces for those who seek spiritual community and belonging outside of existing institutions due to their progressive politics, even as they derive meaning from a sense of collective struggle against exclusionary frameworks. In many ways, they can be seen as a constructive response to critiques of ECM leadership as primarily white, cisgender, heterosexual, and male dominated. Thus, it may be the case, in light of Trajectory Two, that these networks have the potential to support transformation of church polity in the future, though it is unclear how these networks might do so without sizable financial resources to support leaders who exist outside of institutional affiliations.

An alternate possibility could be that leaders shift their energy towards participation in social movements that are completely detached from any religious institution yet where a commitment to a progressive politics continues to fuel spiritual experimentation. We see a future where some ECM participants increasingly seek to forge networks and communities that push beyond church and/or Christian frameworks to give birth to new or hybrid forms of spirituality that are understood as

33. https://withcollective.org/about/
34. https://whychristian.net/
35. https://www.sheiscalled.com/

inherently political in light of the cultural dominance of Christianity. This could look like something akin to the Mystic Soul project: a network formed specifically to center people of color (POC) at the "intersection of spirituality, activism, and healing." Recognizing that "the POC community has a unique lineage of embodying action and contemplation as a way of life," Mystic Soul sees their network as a collective working to decolonize religion, specifically Christianity, in ways that link activism and mysticism together in a radical way. Mystic Soul focuses specifically on developing practices and a "rule of life" that support the holistic well-being of people of color, specifically queer and trans people of color, in a hostile world, and it frames this work as an intervention into colonizing religion.[36] Alternately, ECM participants might find themselves drawn to activist communities that in turn spur spiritual reconfiguration. Southerners on New Ground (SONG)—an activist organization that works on issues of race, class, gender, and sexuality in the southern United States—offers a glimpse of what this trajectory could look like. SONG sees its core work as creating collective liberation for oppressed peoples, but their activism is undergirded with core "spiritual" values that include "joy, creativity, compassion, connectedness to earth, and a commitment to something greater than our individual selves as integral to spiritual survival."[37] This is a distinctly post-Christian and immanent spirituality that, nonetheless, sees human collectivity and shared struggle as crucial to long-term social change. Though SONG and Mystic Soul are not connected to the ECM, they offer a sacred micropolitics shorn of Christianity that some Emerging Christians may find increasingly attractive.

Trajectory Four: The Mystic Move

Much of the early articulations of the ECM focused on creating confidence within the community that legitimated the freedoms to move away from the typical Protestant host tradition or, minimally, to transform the host tradition. This is reflected in the institutional approaches of both Trajectories One and Two. A move away from an inherited religious tradition creates numerous questions about reality, world construction, meaning, religiosity, and spirituality. In attempting to create some

36. https://www.mysticsoulproject.com/
37. https://southernersonnewground.org/

certainty, there was an emphasis on experimentation and experience.[38] Much of the experimentation centered on worship forms that would evoke a religious or spiritual experience. Likewise, the ECM's emphasis on political action and social reforms, which are more fully explicated in the forecasting Trajectory Three, informed a drive for spiritual grounding through collective experience and shared struggle. These elements converge in Trajectory Four where participants move outside of the religious institution to achieve a religious experience through experimenting with Christian and non-Christian forms of mysticism.

As the ECM matures, we envision that some participants will eventually abandon the traditional institution altogether. Although the church institution supplied a means by which participants worked through their religious heritage (See Trajectory One), we could envision larger numbers of ECM participants moving outside of the religious institution because they see institutional structures as tainted beyond correction. Such critiques are that the inherited, church structures are inherently patriarchal, paternal, and colonial. Coupled with this understanding is the idea that these characteristics inhibit an individual's ability to experiment and achieve authentic spiritual experience. In other words, the institutional form is constraining to the types of religious and spiritual experiences that some EC participants are seeking. Furthermore, recurring in Shoemaker's qualitative interviews were several accounts of fatigue in trying to "fix the church," or "make the church work." In other words, a kind of exhaustion could be manifesting for some in trying to reform the church and navigate the post-evangelical world. Likewise, the heavy emphasis on social justice work and political action might equally create disillusionment with American politics. Due to this, we forecast that a move toward mysticism (Trajectory Four), or individual spiritualism, will attract some participants of the ECM.

Of the forecasting trajectories, the mystic move is the blurriest for prediction. Mysticism tends to be fluid, moving in directions as guided by the experience, which can often be described as ineffable. What we are certain of is that the move toward mysticism is not necessarily an orientation towards new monasticism like that of Shane Claiborne and the Simple Way. The new monastic movements tend toward more social and political objectives based on a small community of people sharing life together committed to bettering the world. Instead, the mystic move is an

38. See Kimball, *The Emerging Church*; Jones, *The New Christians*.

attempt to connect with the divine that ultimately finds the divine in one's Self and in fellow humans. As one project consultant explains, "[Christian mysticism] is an internalizing of the divine voice. It is my voice that is the divine voice. I call it my inner-divinity . . . It's both internal and external, but this moves faith away from a purely intellectual form." In their research, Martí and Ganiel capture a parallel emphasis in their findings: "The activity of God is seen as involving the work of the people; that is, God works through people. The individual is continually validated as the source and repository of sacred principles and is the locus of action for achieving goals."[39] The mystic move, then, is the trajectory that moves furthest away from religious institutions and, in many ways, community as well. Because it is much more about the individual journey, while a community or person may aid in the mystic experience, attachment to these are fluid and may be short-lived.

There are three noteworthy aspects in which Trajectory Four is taking shape within and outside of Emerging Christian communities. This includes a reliance on the spirit, the development of "guru" type figures, and annual gatherings that incorporate mystical elements for some participants. Each aspect indicates that the path moving forward for some EC participants might be the embracing of an organic and fluid type of spirituality complementary to but distinct from the ECM.

Within some American EC communities, Shoemaker's observations have noted a significant reliance and concentration on the spirit of the godhead. Whereas Evangelical and Fundamentalist churches tend to focus more on the Father-God and Jesus-Son elements of the Trinity, some EC communities are redirecting their attention to the Spirit. God-Father and Jesus-Son are paradigms for understanding the divine that are based in masculine notions.[40] Within the mystical move, the Spirit theologically is more malleable and less deterministic. The Spirit also permits more gender fluidity in understanding the divine. Thus, the Spirit is understood as not constrained by religious institutions or categories. These communities embrace Christian mystic resources such as Julian of Norwich, who constructed a notion of Jesus as a caring mother. What many within the ECM seek are expressions that recognize

39. Martí and Ganiel, *The Deconstructed Church,* 186.

40. See Bacon, *What's Right with the Trinity?* for a feminist critique of the trinitarian concepts.

the inherent equality and value of all humans, as well as recognizing the harm in masculine constructs within Christianity.[41]

Alternatively, we anticipate another trajectory of the mystic move advancing around "modern gurus," such as Rob Bell, former lead pastor at Mars Hill Church in Grand Rapids, Michigan. Bell now tours internationally giving talks and offering advice and direction to followers, as well as hosts more intimate moments in small groups.[42] Like some parts of American Evangelicalism that are based on a cult of personality, especially in televangelism and megachurches, this can lead to many followers committed more to the individual religious leader than to the community.[43] What is emerging then is something akin to modern, charismatic leaders disassociated with any institutional church revolving around the leadership, wisdom, and personality of individuals. While attending a Rob Bell tour, Shoemaker was informed by some of the participants that they considered Bell their "guru," describing how they follow him on his tour and private, spiritual training sessions. We could easily imagine other EC leaders, following Bell's lead, untethering themselves from the church institution and building a following disassociated from organized religiosity.[44]

The move toward mysticism does reflect current trends of Spiritual But Not Religious (SBNR) in which individuals seek unique paths of spirituality due to recognizing the inability of religious institutions to meet their needs. Like SBNR, EC mystics will appropriate whatever religious resources are available to facilitate their spiritual experiences. Although there is a rich tradition of mysticism in Christianity, we forecast that resources from other traditions will be increasingly integrated. Styles of currently forming religious hybridity are quickly becoming more the norm than the exception. These trends reflect an Ottoian move toward the religious and/or spiritual experience over the institutional formalization of religion. It is well known that Otto argued that religious institutions emerge in trying to recapture a previously occurring and primary individual religious experience.[45] In this way, the religious institution,

---

41. See Alvizo and Martí, "Emerging Out of Patriarchy?"

42. https://robbell.com/.

43. Kyle, *Evangelicalism*.

44. Peter Rollins is another successful example that preceded Rob Bell, https://peterrollins.com/, and some may argue that Nadia Bolz-Weber is following a similar trajectory, https://nadiabolzweber.com/.

45. Otto, *The Idea of the Holy*.

although it might have good intentions, simply cannot supply the experience that is demanded. For example, the Wild Goose Festival, an annual festival of progressive Christians, many of which were associated with the EC, offers sessions outside of traditional Christianity like yoga, meditation, and mystical wisdom.

The move toward mysticism, however, is not completely divorced from social conditions. Many within the ECM were acculturated religiously in an intense time of the American culture wars. The culture wars create distinctive categories of insider/outsider dynamics. These social conditions develop a need to find value in human worth beyond the bifurcation of a culture war society. Where some might find the need to work toward ameliorating the conditions of the culture war more explicitly through the political (see Trajectory Three), Trajectory Four looks for answers in a spiritual format incumbent upon the individual in finding the divine, which is imagined to concomitantly result in discovering spiritually the value of fellow humans. Or stated differently, Trajectory Four represents a kind of holistic healing and reconciliation through discovering the value of one's self, others, and nature.

Conclusion

The Emerging Church movement should be understood as a movement that has yet to take any determinative form because it tends to innovate to the needs of its participants. At the same time, as Martí and Ganiel confirm, Emerging Christianity has certain distinctive characteristics that support its continuing future, including its *collective institutional entrepreneurship*, its *pluralist congregational* practices, and its commitment to "exercising individual religious autonomy while participating in a collective congregational life."[46] Its deconstructive nature and the flux of participant demands pushes EC institutions to continuously (re)consider its shapes, forms, and structures.

On the one hand, for some ECM participants, the institutional church provides a place to continue to work out religious needs, desires, and commitments and this function will likely persist in the future (Trajectories One and Two). The familiarity of the church institution provides a place to continue working out their religious rehabilitation, although this could change in the future with a radical overhaul of those

46. Martí and Ganiel, *The Deconstructed Church*, 164.

structures. On the other hand, some EC participants might find any over-haul of church too little, too late (Trajectories Three and Four). In order to find the religious or spiritual experience they seek, some may gravitate towards mystical paths while others will move toward political participation and other kinds of collectivities that meet their spiritual needs.

Each of the paths presented within this project indicate that there are numerous courses and offshoots of those trajectories that could continue to manifest as EC participants mature. There are obvious overlaps in the four trajectories proposed. It would be easy to imagine an ECM participant engaging in two or more paths simultaneously. For instance, a participant could straddle Trajectories One and Four. The rehabilitation process could be occurring within the institution while forms of mysticism are practiced outside of the institution. There are several combinations easily constructed and lived in these courses.

In this exercise, we focused our attention on the institutional or non-institutional trajectories that could develop and whether the individual or collective experience will be prioritized. This lays the foundation for future research regarding Emerging Christianities and how religious trajectories are navigated in the contemporary world. We admit and have discovered within our research a portion of EC participants who take the course of completely divorcing themselves of religion altogether (atheist and agnostic categories). For some, the ECM was a liminal space to disavow themselves of their religious heritage. In other words, the ECM supplied a place to be both in religion and outside, and eventually, some discovered they were more comfortable outside of religion altogether.

The ECM provides a fascinating case study into religious developments in the contemporary, Western world today. This movement reflects various aspects of religious transformation, deconversion, reformation, shifts, and change. Many of the participants disavow the need to articulate any singular or defined religiosity or spirituality, withdraw from many of the dominant culture war issues, and live more comfortably than their religious predecessors in a secularizing society. Secularism, contemporary politics, and religious marketplace all influence and inform participant and collective decision-making and will continue to do so. Familial ties and social networks also apply pressure for certain religious moves. These social contexts and forces cannot be ignored. Thus, the examination of these movements cannot be extracted from their social environments.

The forecasting of religious movements provides a method of predicting most probable future trajectories based from current data collection while considering social trends. Taken together this technique of developing trajectories is intended to supply only possibilities, not determine exact futures, and to invite critical reflection of those within the movements. And for those of us conducting the research, these trajectories are useful in pointing our research in new directions possibly unanticipated—for research is not constrained in the past or present but can be future oriented as well.

Bibliography

Alvizo, Xochitl. "A Feminist Theological Analysis of the Leadership Structures of the Emerging Church." In *Crossing Boundaries, Redefining Faith: Interdisciplinary Perspectives on the Emerging Church Movement*, edited by Michael Clawson and April Stace, 92–119. Eugene, OR: Pickwick Publications, 2016.

Alvizo, Xochitl, and Gerardo Martí, "Emerging Out of Patriarchy?" In *The Emerging Church, Millennials, and Religion*. Volume 1: *Prospects and Problems*, edited by Randall Reed and Michael Zbaraschuk, 236–59. Eugene, OR: Cascade Books, 2018.

Alvizo, Xochitl, and Bryan Stone, "Radical Economics and Wesleyan Congregations in the U.S." *The Oxford Institute of Methodist Theological Studies*, working group papers, 2018. https://oxford-institute.org/working-group-papers-at-2018-institute?.

Anderson, Matthew Lee. "The Emerging Church Is Dead(?)." *Mere Orthodoxy | Christianity, Politics, and Culture*, February 8, 2010. https://mereorthodoxy.com/the-emerging-church-is-dead/.

Bacon, Hannah. *What's Right with the Trinity? Conversations in Feminist Theology.* Ashgate New Critical Thinking in Religion, Theology and Biblical Studies. Burlington, VT: Ashgate, 2009.

Barton, Bernadette. "1Cross + 3Nails = 4GVN: Compulsory Christianity and Homosexuality in the Bible Belt Panopticon." *Feminist Formations* 23 (2011) 70–93.

Bielo, James. *Emerging Evangelicals: Faith, Modernity, and the Desire for Authenticity.* New York: New York University Press, 2011.

Casanova, Jose. *Public Religions in the Modern World.* Chicago: University of Chicago Press, 1994.

Cox, Harvey. *The Future of Faith.* New York: HarperOne, 2009.

Cupitt, Don. *After God: The Future of Religion.* London: Weidenfeld & Nicolson, 1997.

Davie, Grace, et al. *Predicting Religion: Christian, Secular and Alternative Futures.* Burlington, VT: Ashgate, 2003.

"The Death of the Emerging Church." *Pastor Scott's Thoughts.* April 10, 2010. https://drtscott.typepad.com/pastor_scotts_thoughts/2010/08/the-death-of-the-emerging-church.html.

Douglas, Mary. *Natural Symbols: Explorations in Cosmology.* 2nd ed. New York: Routledge, 1996.

Hensel, Richard L. "Sociology and Social Forecasting," *Annual Review of Sociology* 8 (1982) 57–79.

James, Samuel D. "What Happened to the 'Emergent Church'?" *Letter & Liturgy* (blog), April 20, 2015. https://letterandliturgy.wordpress.com/2015/04/20/what-happened-to-the-emergent-church/.

Jones, Tony. *The Church Is Flat: The Relational Ecclesiology of the Emerging Church Movement.* Minneapolis: The JoPa Group, 2011.

———. "How White Is the Emerging Church?" *Patheos.* https://www.patheos.com/blogs/tonyjones/2012/05/08/how-white-is-the-emerging-church/.

———. *The New Christians: Dispatches from the Emergent Frontier.* San Francisco, CA: Jossey-Bass, 2008.

Kelley, Dean. *Why Conservative Churches Are Growing.* New York: Harper & Row, 1972.

Kimball, Dan. *The Emerging Church: Vintage Christianity for New Generations.* Grand Rapids, MI: Zondervan, 2003.

Kyle, Richard. *Evangelicalism: An Americanized Christianity.* New York: Taylor & Francis, 2006.

Lee, Shayne, and Luke Phillip Sinitiere. *Holy Mavericks: Evangelical Innovators and the Spiritual Marketplace.* New York: New York University Press, 2009.

Martí, Gerardo, and Gladys Ganiel. *The Deconstructed Church: Understanding Emerging Christianity.* Oxford: Oxford University Press, 2014.

Nash, Craig. "Voices: Whatever Happened to the Emerging Church?" *Baptist Standard,* Jan. 10, 2018. https://www.baptiststandard.com/opinion/voices/voices-whatever-happened-emerging-church/.

Norman, Jim. "The Religious Regions of the U.S." *Gallup,* April 6, 2018. https://news.gallup.com/poll/232223/religious-regions.aspx.

Otto, Rudolph. *The Idea of the Holy.* Translated by John W. Harvey. 2nd ed. London: Oxford University Press, 1958.

Packard, Josh. "Resisting Institutionalization: Religious Professionals in the Emerging Church," *Sociological Inquiry* 81 (2011) 3–33.

Patton, C. Michael. "What Do You Think Happened to the Emerging Church?" *Credo House Ministries* (blog), July 9, 2015. https://credohouse.org/blog/what-happened-to-the-emerging-church.

Pew Research Center. "Religion by Political Ideology." https://www.pewforum.org/religious-landscape-study/compare/region/by/political-ideology/.

Reed, Randall, and G. Michael Zbaraschuk, eds. *The Emerging Church, Millennials, and Religion.* Volume 1: *Prospects and Problems.* Eugene, OR: Cascade Books, 2018.

Scaramang, Url. "R.I.P. Emerging Church." *Christianity Today.* September 19, 2008. https://www.christianitytoday.com/pastors/2008/september-online-only/rip-emerging-church.html.

Schneider, Rachel C. "Race and the Emerging Church: A View from South Africa." In *The Emerging Church, Millennials, and Religion.* Volume 1: *Prospects and Problems,* edited by Randall Reed and G. Michael Zbaraschuk, 212–35. Eugene, OR: Cascade Books, 2018.

———. "'A Web of Subversive Friends': New Monasticism in the United States and South Africa." *Religions* 9.6 (2018) 184.

Soong-Chan, Rah, Jason Mach, Brian McLaren, Debbie Blue, and Julie Clawson. "Is the Emerging Church for Whites Only?" *Sojourners,* May 2010. https://sojo.net/magazine/may-2010/emerging-church-whites-only.

Stark, Rodney. "Secularization, R.I.P." *Sociology of Religion* 60 (1999) 249–73.

Yates, Luke. "Rethinking Prefiguration: Alternatives, Micropolitics, and Goals in Social Movements." *Social Movement Studies* 14 (2015) 1–21.

Index